RHETORICAL LISTENING IN ACTION

STUDIES IN RHETORICS AND FEMINISMS
Series Editors: Cheryl Glenn and Shirley Wilson Logan

The series promotes and amplifies the interdisciplinarity of rhetorics and feminisms, connecting rhetorical inquiry with contemporary academic, sociopolitical, and economic concerns. Books in the series explore such enduring questions of rhetoric's rich and complex histories (globally and locally) as well as rhetoric's relevance to current public exigencies of social justice, power, opportunity, inclusion, equity, and diversity. This attention to interdisciplinarity has already transformed the rhetorical tradition as we have known it (upper-class, public, powerful, mostly political, antagonistic, and delivered by men) into regendered, inclusionary rhetorics (democratic, deliberative, diverse, collaborative, private, intersectional, and delivered by all people). Our cultural, political, and intellectual advancements will be enriched by exploring the varied ways rhetorics and feminisms intersect and animate one another (and take us in new political, cultural, scientific, communicative, and pedagogical directions).

BOOKS IN THE SERIES

A Rhetoric of Becoming: USAmerican Women in Qatar by Nancy Small (2022)
Rhetorical Listening in Action: A Concept-Tactic Approach by Krista Ratcliffe
   and Kyle Jensen (2022)

RHETORICAL LISTENING IN ACTION

A Concept-Tactic Approach

Krista Ratcliffe and Kyle Jensen

Parlor Press
Anderson, South Carolina
www.parlorpress.com

Parlor Press LLC, Anderson, South Carolina, USA
© 2022 by Krista Ratcliffe and Kyle Jensen.
All rights reserved.
Printed in the United States of America on acid-free paper.

S A N: 2 5 4 - 8 8 7 9

Library of Congress Cataloging-in-Publication Data on File

1 2 3 4 5

978-1-64317-323-8 (paperback)
978-1-64317-324-5 (hardcover)
978-1-64317-325-2 (PDF)
978-1-64317-326-9 (EPUB)

Cover design by Kyle Jensen.
Cover image by Orfeas Green on Unsplash. Used by permission.

Parlor Press, LLC is an independent publisher of scholarly and trade titles
in print and multimedia formats. This book is available in paper and ebook
formats from Parlor Press on the World Wide Web at www.parlorpress.com
or through online and brick-and-mortar bookstores. For submission information or to find out about Parlor Press publications, write to Parlor Press,
3015 Brackenberry Drive, Anderson, South Carolina, 29621, or email edi-
tor@parlorpress.com.

Contents

To our daughters …

Zadie, Lia, Gwendolyn Jensen and Olivia Ratcliffe Brown

Acknowledgments

We would like to thank all the people who helped us write this book: the students in our classes who tested and honed the concepts and tactics, the administrators who invited us to give professional development talks, the teachers who expressed interest in teaching rhetorical listening, the organizers and members of the 2019 RSA Summer Institute at the University of Maryland who attended our "Designing and Delivering Rhetorical Education" seminar, the reviewers and series editors who improved our thinking, the colleagues and friends whose work inspired us, and our families who always supported us.

Introduction: Why a Rhetorical Listening Education?

Have you ever found it difficult to listen to someone with whom you disagree? For example, have you ever changed the TV channel while someone was speaking, closed a website to avoid reading what someone had written, kept your mouth shut at work or school so as not to make a scene, or decided not to visit a friend or family member just so you didn't have to discuss that one topic that triggers you both? While avoiding such conflicts may work in some instances, in many others, people who disagree must live together in communities, workplaces, and homes. To navigate such situations, people who disagree need to find ways to listen to each other, especially given that current US educational systems generally provide lessons in only three of the four classical rhetorical arts: reading, writing, and speaking . . . but not listening.

The above difficult-to-listen-to situations are examples of rhetorical problems. Though you may not be accustomed to thinking about such situations as rhetorical problems, that is exactly what they are. *Rhetorical problems* may be defined in two ways: first, as situations in which speakers/writers must express their ideas, feelings, values, and beliefs in ways that their audiences can actually hear them, especially across differences; and second, as situations in which listeners/audiences must open themselves to actually hear ideas, feelings, values, and beliefs, even those with which they disagree. In such cases, the people involved must navigate, *through language*, all the contextual factors surrounding a rhetorical problem.

Rhetorical problems are tricky to navigate because ideas, feelings, values, and beliefs always connect a personal opinion with a broader

1

cultural discourse, which is simply a set of common words, claims, and ways of reasoning echoed among a group of people who may or may not know each other. For example, suppose someone claims that wearing a mask is a personal choice that affects only the wearer. Realistically, that "someone" is not the only person who has ever made this claim; indeed, that personal opinion echoes a chorus of other people's similar claims, all of which create a discourse about not wearing masks that is situated in a particular time and place, the COVID-19 pandemic.[1] Conversely, "someone's" personal opinion may also encounter another person's competing opinion, which is also linked to a larger cultural discourse, such as one claiming that wearing a mask affects many people by preventing the spread of disease. Within this context of competing opinions, "someone's" personal opinion about wearing a mask is suddenly implicated not just in "someone's" own thinking and not just in the discourses of those who agree but also in a cultural conflict. And with such a conflict, rhetorical problems ensue.

Rhetorical problems have haunted humans throughout recorded history (and no doubt before). At best, people seek to understand those who think and act differently, as when different countries create alliances, when competing political parties value compromise, when workplaces or schools champion diversity in teamwork, and when family or friends attempt to bridge their differences. But at worst, people enact violence against those who think and act differently, as when different countries go to war,[2] when political leaders deny basic human rights to women and under-represented groups, when workplaces or schools refuse to recognize or engage people's differences, and when friends and family throw abusive language, or punches, at one another.

Just as rhetorical problems have haunted human history, so too have attempts to resolve them, and these attempts are both structural and personal. To effect resolutions via structural change, societies have created cultural structures, such as Athenian democracy in fifth-century BCE Greece or the Truth and Reconciliation Commission in 1995 South Africa. To effect such resolutions via personal efforts, individuals have forwarded arguments for the collective good, an example being arguments promoting the education of women from Ban Zhao's writings in first-century CE China to Mary Wollstonecraft's versions in eighteenth-century England. If people are to live together as peacefully as possible and to afford everyone the best opportunities possible, then they must learn ways to recognize, analyze, and engage rhetorical problems. One way, this book argues, is by learning to listen rhetorically.

While *Rhetorical Listening in Action* will not solve all the world's problems, it does offer a rhetorical education grounded in rhetorical listening that cultivates writers who can listen across differences in preparation for communicating and acting within and across those differences. To articulate the need for this education, this "Introduction" makes the following moves: 1) identifies and analyzes one cultural conflict (the 2020 US Presidential election) to exemplify how rhetorical problems function; 2) argues what rhetorical listening offers rhetorical education; 3) explains a concept-tactic approach to this education; 4) defines a rhetorical listening mindset, which writers may adopt as they study concepts and tactics in subsequent chapters and engage various writing tasks in their everyday lives; and 5) describes what to expect from subsequent chapters.

What Does a Cultural Conflict Tell Us about Rhetoric Problems?

The 2020 US Presidential election generated many rhetorical problems. Families and friends stopped talking to one another as everything became politicized (again, wearing masks comes to mind). As such, the election exposed the need for a rhetorical education that cultivates writers who can listen across differences. During this election period, people disagreed not just about what roles government should serve and who should be elected but also about how to grant women respect and equality (arguments about #MeToo), how to achieve racial justice (arguments about #BlackLivesMatter), and how to end a pandemic (arguments about masks, social distancing, and vaccines). Immediately after the November election, the nation was further divided by arguments about alleged voter fraud despite the judicial system's finding no legal proof for it. Consequently, many people in the US could not, or would not, communicate with those they deemed on "the other side." The result was polarization.

This polarization was fueled by yet another underlying and complicated rhetorical problem: people's disagreeing about facts. That is, people who disagreed with one another did not simply disagree about issues and candidates; they disagreed about what was designated a fact. By embracing competing sets of facts, people ended up talking past one another. This rhetorical problem of competing facts amazed many people, from politicians to newscasters to family members. And this problem puts into play an interesting question: *is it possible to disagree over what constitutes a fact?* As evidenced by people's amazement and by cultural commonplaces such as "just the facts, ma'am," the common-sense answer seems to be, "No, people cannot disagree about facts." The reasoning for this claim unfolds something like this: facts exist either objectively or self-evidently; interpretations are the meanings that people lay upon facts; thus, while people may disagree about *how* they interpret facts, they cannot disagree about *what* constitutes a fact.

Rhetoric, however, tells a slightly different story about facts. If *rhetoric* is imagined as the study of *how we use language* and *how language socializes us to think and act*, then this focus on *how* suggests that rhetoric is concerned with processes. Consequently, the study of rhetoric offers a place where the process of selecting, naming, and employing facts can be questioned. This questioning is possible, Karlyn Kohrs Campbell argues, because the study of rhetoric intersects with epistemology (the study of how we know what we know) and ontology (the study of how we "be" in the world) ("The Ontological" 105).[3] But what exactly does that mean for understanding the function of facts?

On the one hand, when rhetoric intersects with epistemology (how we know), then rhetoric offers a space for imagining language use as a way of knowing, whether that language use includes the four classical rhetorical arts of reading, writing, speaking, listening, or Cheryl Glenn's addition of silence. Within a space of imagining language use as a way of knowing, it is possible to question the common-sense logic of "just the facts, ma'am." As Kenneth Burke explains, "since the 'fact' is believed to be 'speaking for itself,' people fail to note that there *is* no 'fact' before them; there is nothing but the *report* of the 'fact,'" and people also fail to notice "the critical framework in which [the fact] is to be judged" (*The War of Words* 170). Tharon Howard further explains this point in a Clemson University video entitled "In Defense of Rhetoric": if "epistemic rhetoric means adjudicating between competing knowledge claims," then within such an epistemic frame, "facts are not solid, monolithic, unchanging things; they are the results of processes, and rhetoric is one of the processes we use to construct facts." Steve Katz concurs: "A fact is raw data plus interpretation . . . not totally objective" ("In Defense" 10:36–11:27). In short, a person's interpretive lens affects *how* a person sees the raw data and, thus, affects *what* a person selects, names, and knows to be a fact.

With their comments invoking interpretive lenses, Howard and Katz implicitly invoke Kenneth Burke's terministic screens, the lenses created by words (or terms) that shape our perceptions. Burke claims these screens are inescapable: "We *must* use terministic screens, since we can't say anything without the use of terms; whatever terms we use, they necessarily constitute a corresponding kind of screen; and any such screen necessarily directs the attention to one field rather than another" (*Language* 50). Thus, terministic screens affect what is named as fact.

To understand how terministic screens work in relation to facts, consider sunsets. If *fact* is conceptualized as "raw data plus interpretation," then sunsets are "raw data." The "plus interpretation" depends on viewers' terministic screens: when poets view a sunset, they likely see an inspiring image; when meteorologists view a sunset, they likely see atmospheric data; when environmentalists view a sunset, they likely see levels of pollutant particles in the atmosphere; and when sailors view a sunset, they likely see predictions about the next day's sailing conditions. In this way, viewers are not simply generating different conclusions based on a set of identical facts; rather, they are looking at the same sunset (raw data), generating a different set of knowledge culled from the sunset (interpretation), and constructing different sets of facts.

On the other hand, when rhetoric intersects with ontology (how we "be" in the world), then rhetoric offers a space for imagining language use as a way of being. This space also makes possible the questioning of "just the facts, ma'am." As Thomas Rickert argues, "rhetoric is itself ontological, having to do with being and not just knowing" (xv). From this stance, he directly invokes Burke to demonstrate that humans experience facts not simply as objective or self-evident things but as result of people's living and being within language:

> As Burke puts it in *Attitudes toward History*, "our primeval ancestors, by learning language, no longer experienced a sensation solely as a sensation" (382). As he goes on to explain, we may like the warmth of a fire, and such warmth is certainly a sensation, but as soon as we start putting such experience into language, the words come to "*tell a story*"; as a result, attitudes (or affective stances) can emerge and be deployed across

various forms of discursive interaction, such as the movement from "that feels warm" to the observation that someone is "warm-hearted" (Burke, *AH* 383). (Rickert 167)

In short, how people are "attuned" to the world through language affects what they deem to be facts of the world (Rickert 13). Vorris Nunley expands this link between rhetoric and ontology to include ideology in order to argue that facts are not self-evident: "to tether ontology and being to rhetoric and ideology is not to deny the corpo-reality of the body and the physiology and biology necessary to life. Instead, it is to make legible that being is more than merely existing, and that ontology and meaning and what we think of as human are not self-evident" (18).

Of course, feminist theory has long informed rhetorical studies in ways that challenge "just the facts, ma'am," interrupting the idea of a neutral, objective identity or stance by offering a feminist version of interpretive lenses. Early standpoint theory posed by Nancy Hartsock[4] and others may be read as gendering terministic screens. It claims that people's identities and perspectives are influenced by people's individ-ual lived experiences in particular times and places within the cultural categories of sex and gender. In short, early standpoint theory argues that because women experience the world differently from men, they see the world, including facts, differently from men. Intersectionality theory further complicates how terministic screens influence people's selection of facts. Initiated by Kimberlé Crenshaw to describe particu-lar issues of identity that Black women face within the US legal sys-tem[5] and subsequently adapted by feminist and ethnic studies scholars for other contexts, this theory posits humans' identities and perspec-tives as compilations of multiple, intersecting cultural categories (gen-der, race, class, nationality, sexuality, athletic ability, etc.) that inform people's experiences and, thus, identities. That is, a person may iden-tify as a woman but also as a Chicana, a mother, a daughter, a CEO, an American citizen, a homeowner, a political activist, etc. More recently, feminist theory about non-binary gender identity further challenges the idea of "just the facts, ma'am" because it questions the common-place assumptions about words like *women* and *men* and about cul-tural categories like gender, thus reimagining the "facts" surrounding gender both in culture (Thompson) and in rhetoric and composition and communication scholarship (Patterson and Spencer). In sum, feminist-rhetoric scholars-teachers interested in rhetoric's intersections with both knowing and being have engaged feminist theories while keeping a focus on how knowing and being are mediated by language and discourses. This focus, too, informs the story of rhetoric.

So where does the story of rhetoric and its questioning of facts leave people as readers, writers, speakers, and listeners? Well, they are not left with a simple set of easy binaries: truth versus lies, real news versus fake news, or reality versus conspiracy theories. But neither are they stranded in a relativistic world where anything goes and where all ideas are equal. Rather, people are left with rhetorical problems within shared situations and situated discourses—all of which are comprised of facts (raw data plus interpretations) constructed differently based on people's individual and collective terministic screens.[6] But recognizing this story of rhetoric is not enough.

This story of rhetoric demands that people act.

Acting with purpose in a rhetorical world requires certain commitments. People need to recognize the situatedness and the constructedness of their belief systems and cultural systems, which are mediated through language and discourses. People need to articulate for themselves and others the possibilities and the limits of these systems. Finally, people need to argue for what they deem to be good, true, and possible, arguing not just to the choir who agrees but also across differences with those who disagree.

An example of such action is posited by Cheryl Glenn in *Rhetorical Feminism and This Thing Called Hope*: "Public, political, activist women—those Sister Rhetors who speak, work, and theorize their activism in the private, pedagogical, and public spheres—embody the best of feminist rhetoric, a set of long-established practices that advocates a political position of rights and responsibilities that certainly include the equality of women and Others" (5). One such "Sister Rhetor" is described by Jacqueline Jones Royster in "To Call A Thing by Its True Name: The Rhetoric of Ida B. Wells": "In calling the act of lynching by its true name, an act of terrorism, an outrage, a crime, a sacrilege against 'truth, justice, and the American way,' Wells established herself as a bold, outspoken woman, a woman who was willing to risk everything for the sake of her principles, for the sake of truth" (174).

But there are many, many, many other examples of people arguing for and acting to promote the truth of their own world views—from feminist to hypermasculinist, from conservative to liberal, from religious to atheistic, etc. It is not surprising, then, that these different experiences within language result in competing terministic screens that, in turn, result in competing claims, competing ways of reasoning, and, yes, competing sets of selected facts about what is truth and what are lies, what is real news and what is fake news, or what is reality and what are conspiracy theories. The story of rhetoric tells us that negotiating such competing differences is the never-ending story of people's knowing and being in the world with one another within language. Burke calls this story "the Scramble" and later "the War of Words"[7] (*RM* 23; *War* 240).

This story of rhetoric is difficult to plot and challenging to negotiate in daily life. Many problems abound.

One problem is physical and emotional weariness that manifests differently for different people and communities. For example, as Ersula Ore notes in *Lynching: Violence, Rhetoric, and American Identity*, which recounts, among other things, her experience with police brutality, "I've expelled a great deal of affective labor both in the writing of this book and this note, so I currently lack the bandwidth to elaborate on how these alterations force me to commit rhetorical violence to talk about the physical and material violence systematically enacted against blacks by the state" (xiv). With this sentence, Ore voices a weariness that echoes many, many people across many, many centuries. Michael Eric Dyson defines Black weariness in *Long Time Coming*: "It is a way of saying that many Black folks are exhausted: worn out by the cumulative injuries, quiet indignities, loud assaults, existential threats, microaggressions, macro offenses, and unceasing bombarding of our bodies and psyches in the name of white comfort" (198). Dyson then explains how this weariness may signify and how it should be received: "This sheer Black exhaustion sometimes sounds like cranky disregard for white awakening when in fact it may only be our refusal any longer to consider white comfort" (199); moreover, "in order for white folk to surrender comfort and claim a true awakening they must hear and not be defensive about Black claims of exhaustion" (200). While there is no easy answer to this problem, there can be recognition, acknowledgment, and consideration of it.

A second problem that emerges from this story of rhetoric is the possibility that people do not act in good faith. The need to evaluate whether, and to what extent, people are acting in good faith is why the story of rhetoric intersects with ethics. To highlight this point, Kris begins her rhetoric classes by saying: "The first principle of rhetoric is that reasonable people may disagree. But an important corollary is this: be very attentive to who has the power to define *reasonable*." People not acting in good faith may knowingly ascribe false motives or assert false claims, which is very different from simply having a different perspective based on different lived experiences and terministic screens. Acting in bad faith, or intentionally lying, complicates any situation and hinders genuine problem-solving. Again, there is no easy solution. A person acting in bad faith can be called on it, reflect, and change. But if no change occurs, the other people involved in such a situation must brainstorm ways to expose the bad faith and/or limit its impact . . . and then act.

A third problem that emerges from this story of rhetoric is the possibility that people may close themselves to multiple, competing perspectives. In such cases, whether consciously or not, people retreat into confirmation bias, which the American Psychological Association defines as "the tendency to look for information that supports, rather than rejects, one's preconceptions, typically by interpreting evidence to confirm existing beliefs while rejecting or ignoring any conflicting data" (Noor). An NPR/Ipsos pollster who studies why some US citizens believe in conspiracy theories writes that a December 2020 poll "illustrates . . . how willing people are to believe things that are ludicrous because it fits in with a worldview that they want to believe" (Rose).[8] Though this poll focused on people who embraced right-wing conspiracy theories, confirmation bias does not take sides. It may exist across any political spectrum. When the degree of bias is extreme enough to preclude people's listening to anyone who disagrees with them, then confirmation bias results in an impasse. When at such impasses, people become so entrenched in their own ways of thinking that they disagree with others about what constitutes *fact*, *valid claim*, *proof*, and *truth* as well as about what constitutes *ethical action*. Once again, there is no easy solution. As with a person acting in bad faith, a person performing confirmation bias can be called on it, reflect, and try to be more open. But if no openness occurs, the other people involved in such a situation must brainstorm ways to expose the confirmation bias and/or limit its impact . . . and then act.

But how does one learn to brainstorm, design, and enact plans to solve the above problems? One way, according to Aristotle, is to study rhetoric with an emphasis on discovering common values and beliefs:

"it is necessary for [proofs] and speeches [as a whole] to be formed on the basis of common [beliefs]" (I.1.12). But what happens when common values and beliefs are hard to find? Although no concept and tactic of classical or modern rhetoric can magically solve this problem, rhetorical listening is one means to help writers address it.

What Does Rhetorical Listening Offer?

Rhetorical listening is a rhetorical concept and tactic that was introduced in Kris's book *Rhetorical Listening: Identification, Gender, Whiteness*. It invites listeners to assume open stances; to lay competing claims and cultural logics side by side; to pause and stand under the discourses of self and others to hear what Toni Morrison calls "the sound that [breaks] the back of words," or the sound that breaks through our normal ways of thinking (261); to reflect on their hearings to promote an *understanding* of self and others; and, when possible, to design win-win solutions. Such listening is useful when writers have to compose effective and civil communications across commonalities and differences, regardless of whether the communications are academic, workplace, public, or personal.[9]

But how exactly may rhetorical listening be performed at different sites by different writers? To answer this question, Kris has been invited to give talks and lead workshops at colleges, universities, and professional organizations in the US and abroad, extending the ideas in her book in terms of rhetorical listening's applications for pedagogy, writing, and leadership; Kyle, too, has been invited to present papers at conferences and conduct workshops for high school teachers. As one answer, Kyle invited Kris to give a workshop on the role that rhetorical listening plays in rhetorical education, particularly in understanding people's identifications with race. Subsequent conversations and teaching resulted in this book, which delineates a rhetorical education inflected by rhetorical listening whose purpose is to develop listening writers.

Who are these listening writers? They are multiple. This book is intended for audiences inside and outside educational systems who want to procure and perform a rhetorical education grounded in rhetorical listening. Such an education offers a set of "tools" for negotiating competing perspectives and cross-cultural communication, especially in the service of civil discourse and social justice. As such, this book may have different uses for different readers. Teachers in grades 9–12 as well as in colleges and universities may adapt a rhetorical education to their own local curricula and pedagogies. Students may engage a rhetorical education in writing classrooms but transfer it to other classes and also to their lives beyond the classroom. Administrators may employ a rhetorical education as a means of understanding and relating to people with whom they work. General readers may use a rhetorical education to understand competing perspectives in society and to develop civil communication in their homes, workplaces, and social lives. Whatever their locations, all audiences are invited to reflect on their own situated local conditions and imagine how a rhetorical listening education might fit their needs.

Further, this book makes certain assumptions about listening writers. First, they are capable of learning to write effectively for everyday writing tasks. Second, they are capable of sustained study of sophisticated rhetorical concepts and tactics. Third, they come to the study of a rhetorical listening education already equipped with concepts and tactics that inform their analyses and their writings, whether or not they are aware of them. And fourth, they want to engage the difficult topics facing our culture but often lack the language, concepts, or tactics for doing so.

To help develop listening writers, *Rhetorical Listening in Action* explains not just how rhetorical listening functions on its own but also how it may inflect other rhetorical concepts and tactics discussed in subsequent chapters. In this way, this book provides teachers, students, administrators, and other listeners a rhetorical education inflected by rhetorical listening that may be employed, first, for analyzing everyday writing tasks and then, second, for writing effective responses based on the analyses.

Although analyzing and writing are the focus of this book, analysis may be imagined as part of a larger network of critical thinking that includes the following moves (or stases[10]): 1) identify, 2) define, 3) analyze, 4) synthesize, 5) interpret, 6) evaluate, and 7) argue. *Identifying* means recognizing and naming rhetorical concepts and tactics in others' and one's own writings. *Defining* means explaining what these rhetorical concepts and tactics are. *Analyzing* means breaking the written texts into component parts to better understand how the rhetorical concepts and tactics function on their own as well as in relation to each other, to the whole text, and to things beyond a text. *Interpreting* means assigning meaning to the text based on the content as well as the rhetorical concepts and tactics employed. *Evaluating* means assigning value to how well the content as well as the rhetorical concepts and tactics work. And *arguing* means employing rhetorical concepts and tactics to forward a stance and take action about a rhetorical problem. In actual practice, these critical thinking moves are recursive and interrelated and provide a set of skills to listening writers so that they may be life-long learners, continually teaching themselves how to write as they encounter new writing tasks with new situations, purposes, and audiences.

The rhetorical education promoted by this book emerges from multiple traditions.[11] It draws on a 2,500-year-old tradition of Greco-Roman rhetorics and also on newly mapped traditions of women's rhetorics and other traditionally under-represented groups' rhetorics. The theories and practices of all these traditions offer rhetorical concepts and tactics that enhance critical thinking and facilitate everyday reading, writing, speaking, silence, and listening.

Although classical and modern traditions of Western rhetoric[12] differ from one another in that classical rhetoric focuses on a speaker/writer's conscious persuasion of audiences while modern rhetoric extends that focus to include non-conscious identifications, socialization, and complicated gaps in communication,[13] both classical and modern traditions are pervaded by a dominant metaphor: win-lose. One debater wins a debate; the other loses. One political candidate wins an election; the other loses. One lawyer wins the case; the other loses. This win-lose metaphor implies the ideas of sports or warfare wherein two opposing sides spar, develop strategic plans composed of effective tactics to beat the other side, and eventually concede that one side has won and the other lost, with the winner taking the prize and writing the history. While such agonistic communication has its place (Roberts-Miller), not all everyday writing tasks need be so confrontational. To that end, rhetorical listening offers an alternative metaphor: win-win. This metaphor does not mean that everyone involved gets everything they want; rather, it implies that all sides of an argument assume the goal of moving forward together and negotiate accordingly, getting and accepting the best deal possible.

How does win-win work?

In terms of teaching, the win-win principle of rhetorical listening facilitates affirmation-based pedagogies, which invite teachers to focus on what students can do, not what they cannot. For example, when teachers teach argument in high school or college, they should assume that students already know how to argue; indeed, students have been doing it for most of their lives. True, they may not be conscious of a lexicon or toolbox of tactics with which to build effective strategies for making arguments in academic situations. But they may have developed habits of argument that work well in non-academic contexts. To promote affirmation-based learning, teachers may help student writers bring these habits of argument to consciousness, name them. and then reflect on how well their tactics do or do not transfer to academic contexts. Self-taught writers often do this on their own. To promote affirmation-based learning, this book offers teachers, students, administrators, and general listeners a lexicon and a toolbox of concepts and tactics that they, in turn, may employ to help them bring their habits to consciousness, revise them when necessary, and develop new ones.

Rhetorical listening fosters such affirmation-based learning in listening writers in several ways. It encourages them to slow down learning so that they may pause and reflect on multiple perspectives about their topics. It encourages them to move beyond traditional academic argument ("here's what I think and why") and develop projects relevant to their own lives and real-world audiences. It encourages them to recognize, analyze, and respond to the gaps between a claim's intent and its effect. It encourages them to connect their individual opinions and claims to networks of larger cultural discourses. And it encourages them to conceptualize, analyze, and employ not just content but also rhetorical concepts and tactics.

WHY USE A CONCEPT-TACTIC APPROACH TO A RHETORICAL LISTENING EDUCATION?

Rhetorical Listening in Action advocates a concept-tactic approach to rhetorical education. Like any good story, this book has a cast of characters, but here, the characters are not people but *concepts*. Concepts are abstract ideas—such as freedom, quality, hospitality, honesty, justice, and joy—that serve as building blocks for people's thinking about the world. *Rhetorical concepts*, then, are abstract ideas within rhetorical theories that help writers to think critically when they both *analyze* and *write* texts. Myriad rhetorical concepts abound: consider, for example, the five canons (invention, arrangement style, memory and delivery), traditional elements of argument (main claims, reasons, evidence, unstated assumptions), the ever-popular Aristotelian appeals (*pathos, logos, ethos*), the rhetorical triangle (author, text, audience) and recent additions, such as Cedric Burrow's rhetorical crossover and Lisa Blankenship's rhetorical empathy. In this book, the controlling rhetorical concept is rhetorical listening as it functions both individually and in relation to other rhetorical concepts of agency, rhetorical situation, identification, myth, and rhetorical devices. These six concepts help listening writers generate and select rhetorical tactics to employ when completing everyday writing tasks.

Rhetorical tactics are rhetorical concepts in action. As sets of critical thinking moves, rhetorical tactics make visible not just the content of a rhetorical problem but also the methods of thinking about that problem. For example, when employing the concept of rhetorical listening, writers may perform sample tactics presented in Chapter 1, or (and this is important) they may generate tactics of their own. As modelled in the following chapters, tactics are not finite, paint-by-number propositions; rather, they are generative sets of invention moves that may be employed (or not) and adapted (or not) to address rhetorical problems. Knowledge of many different tactics plus the knowledge of how to generate new tactics provide writers a set of invention options. But knowledge of how to employ and how to generate tactics is not enough to produce effective writing. Just as important is the knowledge of how, in any given situation, to select and employ effective rhetorical tactics strategically.

Rhetorical strategies are created when writers respond to a particular rhetorical problem or writing task by weaving together rhetorical tactics into an effective overall plan. Consider, for example, a young man who wants to enter a social media debate about a political topic, but the debate includes some mudslinging. If he wants to intervene, what should he do? He could fling mud back. Or he could frame the topic as a rhetorical problem and develop a strategy for addressing it. If he chooses the latter option, he must first distinguish for himself the difference between a topic and a rhetorical problem. While topics simply name issues that writers write about (for example, the environment), rhetorical problems are contextualized topics that must be acted upon in relation to specific audiences (for example, proposed federal climate change legislation must be negotiated among members of Congress). As such, rhetorical problems invite writers to respond to specific audiences by selecting and combining rhetorical tactics into plans that are strategic.[14]

The ability to develop rhetorical strategies for individual writing tasks while remaining open to the serendipity of writing processes is an important literacy skill. Why? Given that purposes, audiences, and contexts almost always change from one writing task to another, a writer must be able to adapt tactics from one writing task to another. This imperative to adapt makes writing (and communication more generally) challenging and intriguing. This imperative to adapt sometimes generates resistance, as manifested by people's desire for quick and easy solutions to writing problems, whether these "solutions" be five-paragraph themes, modes-based templates,[15] or hard-and-fast grammar rules. The problem with these solutions is not the impulse to identify form and structure; rather, the problem is to proceed as if only form and structure are important and as if one form and structure fits all situations, regardless of purpose, audience, or context. If simple formulae or sets of rules would always work, then communication problems that have perennially haunted humanity would have been solved eons ago. The imperative to adapt is precisely why the theory and practice of rhetoric is so important for writers to learn and, frankly, so challenging at times to implement.

Rhetorical concepts and tactics work together. Focusing on concepts and tactics helps writers and audiences to "see" not just the content of a rhetorical problem but also its rhetorical concepts in play as rhetorical tactics. A concept-tactic approach translates into different areas of life. For example, writing students can use rhetorical concepts and tactics to succeed in a writing class where they learn to analyze people, texts, institutions, and cultures and also to compose writing projects. Students can then carry their knowledge of rhetorical concepts and tactics with them from class to class, adapting the concepts and tactics when writing essays in philosophy classes, lab reports in chemistry classes, or business plans in entrepreneurship classes. Just as importantly, students can carry this rhetorical knowledge beyond the university into their workplaces, public engagements, and personal lives. When working at a job, serving on a community board, or even negotiating with a life partner, they will need to solve problems by thinking critically and communicating with other people. In those moments, they may find that using rhetorical concepts and tactics to function as a listening writer may help them strategize workable (and we hope, win-win) solutions to their problems.

Though useful, rhetorical concepts and tactics are never neutral. For better or worse, they are always implicated in the systems (educational, political, cultural, etc.) in which they function. And because even the best rhetorical concepts and tactics cannot address every facet of a rhetorical problem, they are necessarily partial; thus, concepts and tactics employed within systems are also subject to an imperative to adapt. This imperative can be evidenced by two problems in rhetorical scholarship.

The first problem is that existing rhetorical concepts and tactics sometimes stop being useful. For example, in *On African American Rhetoric*, Keith Gilyard and Adam Banks explain that sometimes existing concepts "do not match" current perceptions, in which case such concepts and their associated tactics may need to be rejected, redefined, or newly imagined; as means for doing so, the authors invoke Foucault's *epistemic break* (a rupture, rather than a progression, in a culture's thinking) and Burke's *perspective by incongruity* (oddly juxtaposing symbols in ways that lead to new perspectives) (2–3). Gloria Anzaldúa describes this disconnect between concepts and current perceptions in terms of metaphor: "The resistance to change in a person is in direct proportion to the number of dead metaphors that person carries. But we can also change ourselves through metaphor" (122), which includes, of course, the creation of new concepts.

The second problem is that rhetorical concepts and tactics and the methods that employ them determine the types of research that is produced. In *Feminist Rhetorical Practices* Jacqueline Jones Royster and Gesa Kirsch call for new concepts of *feminism* as well as new tactics and methods of rhetorical research to imagine scholarship not yet produced. Similarly, in her "Foreword" to *Re/Orienting Writing Studies*, Pamela Takayoshi celebrates the book for imagining new ground, for "offering guidance in how to navigate queer research questions and subjects in ways traditional research methods do not address and which traditional methods do not scaffold" (xiii).

Attending to rhetorical concepts and tactics while being attentive to their non-neutrality helps foster a rhetorical listening mindset.

WHAT IS A RHETORICAL LISTENING MINDSET?

The key to effective uses of rhetorical concepts and tactics is for listening writers to develop a rhetorical listening mindset. A rhetorical mindset may be defined as a facility, a flexible way of thinking that Quintilian calls *facilitas*, which is the ability to use and adapt rhetorical concepts and tactics *effectively* for different contexts, purposes, and audiences. A rhetorical listening mindset is simply the grounding of this *facilitas* in rhetorical listening; such a mindset may help listening writers address a host of rhetorical problems.

To develop a rhetorical mindset, listening writers may incorporate into their writing processes the following ten moves:

1. *Assume a Writerly Stance of Rhetorical Listening.* This move helps writers be open to multiple, competing perspectives; it, in turn, inflects all subsequent moves.

2. *Identify Situations, Purposes and Audiences.* This move helps writers contextualize their analyzing and composing of everyday writing tasks within situated discourses.

3. *Frame a Topic as a Rhetorical Problem.* This move reveals not just the content but the actions that must be taken. It helps writers recognize that a) the way in which a problem is posed influences what "solutions" may be imagined; and b) win-win solutions are possible more often than commonly imagined.

4. *Engage Multiple, Competing Perspectives.* This move encourages writers to use research when necessary, as a way to generate greater understanding of a rhetorical problem as well as its many stated claims and unstated assumptions.

5. *Ask Questions Generated by Competing Perspectives.* This move helps writers find ways to engage and focus their writing tasks.

6. *Develop Main Claims* (or Thesis Statements). This move helps writers understand that all claims or assertions are answers to (often unstated) questions.

7. *Select Rhetorical Tactics to Use.* This move helps writers make visible for themselves how they are engaging rhetorical concepts and tactics while analyzing and writing.

8. *Identify Forms as well as Flexibility within Forms.* This move helps writers recognize both that they are choosing forms and that their choices of form in turn affect how they select, organize, and link claims, reasons, and evidence, thus moving writers beyond formulaic notions of genre.

9. *Stylize Sentences.* This move encourages both invention and revision of ideas, not just proofreading and editing, at the level of the sentence with the main criterion for evaluating style being effectiveness, not correctness.

10. *Repeat moves as needed.* This move helps writers recognize that writing is both recursive and situated and that it requires revision to clarify connections between competing ideas, forms, and styles.

Developing a rhetorical listening mindset provides listening writers a more complex understanding of their everyday writing tasks, whether academic, workplace, public, or personal. In this way, this mindset informs listening writers' writing processes, which are discussed in more detail in Appendix B.

What to Expect in Subsequent Chapters

Rhetorical Listening in Action introduces a rhetorical education composed of rhetorical concepts and tactics that will help writers to develop capacities for rhetorical analysis and for writing within a rhetorical listening mindset. Subsequent chapters are organized around the following six rhetorical concepts and their associated tactics:

1. Chapter 1: Rhetorical Listening—the capacity of writers to listen to multiple, competing perspectives in claims and cultural logics.

2. Chapter 2: Agency—the capacity of writers to negotiate the agencies of people, discourses, cultures, and material objects/spaces, all of which influence how people think and act.

3. Chapter 3: Rhetorical Situation—the capacity of writers to recognize and negotiate contexts or sedimented ecologies of writing.

4. Chapter 4: Identification—the capacity of writers to assign properties to people, things, and situations and, in the process, find common ground or non-identifications with audiences.

5. Chapter 5: Myth—the capacity of writers to recognize culturally-grounded stories that capture, share, and pass on cultural values and beliefs and, in turn, explain where human motives originate and, thus, how people come to embrace certain beliefs or to act in particular ways, either in conjunction with or against others.

6. Chapter 6: Rhetorical Devices—the capacity of writers both to recognize and employ situated, habitual repetitions of argumentative moves that coalesce into unnoticed argumentative patterns that shape perceptions, influence judgments and, in the process, become associated with users' identities, with writers either using existing devices, such as those defined in Burke's *War of Words*, or inventing their own.

As the title of this book indicates, rhetorical listening is not simply the first concept studied in Chapter 1; it also inflects all the concepts studied in subsequent chapters. Each chapter, then, is developed by defining a rhetorical concept from a rhetorical listening stance, discussing why the rhetorical concept should be studied, and modelling how rhetorical tactics may be used. Although rhetorical listening is obviously not the only way to ground a rhetorical education, it does provide one productive option for learning how to analyze and compose with differences in mind.

In this spirit, we invite you to read on and join us in the important (and fun!) study of rhetorical concepts and tactics, with an emphasis on rhetorical listening in action.

1 Rhetorical Listening

For centuries people disagreed about the design of the known universe. In 1632 Galileo Galilei published his now famous *Dialogue Concerning the Two Chief World Systems*, which lays out two competing world views: 1) a religious theory that positions the earth at the center of the known universe, and 2) a scientific theory that positions the sun at the center.[1] A year after the publication of his book, Galileo was summoned to Rome for interrogation by the Inquisition. His rhetorical problem was how to defend his use of the sun-centered scientific theory to Inquisitors intent upon upholding Church doctrine and punishing what they deemed heretical. Galileo was not successful: his scientific explanations were judged "vehemently suspect of heresy" ("Galileo"). Escaping the worst punishments, he was not subject to water torture or the rack, nor was he was hanged or burned at the stake; however, his book was banned (a ban not lifted until 1835), and he was sentenced to prison and then house arrest for the rest of his life ("Galileo").

When considering this episode in history, we might simply echo the Vatican's 1992 official proclamation that "Galileo was right" (Cowell). The end. After all, we now know that our sun does lie at the center of our solar system although neither the earth nor the sun lies at the center of our known universe. Or, conversely, we might listen rhetorically to this episode, pausing to ask, "What do we learn when we lay the religious and scientific arguments in Galileo's situation side-by-side and reflect on them?" The Indigo Girls responded with a 1992 hit song, "Galileo."[2] We might respond by reflecting on how the past circles into the present, exposing contemporary issues haunted by conflicts between religion and science, such as climate change, genetic engineering, gender identities, COVID-19 vaccines, racial equity, abortion, and women's rights in different countries.

One means for engaging such conflicts and trying to resolve their associated rhetorical problems is rhetorical listening. To demonstrate this claim, Chapter 1 defines rhetorical listening as a rhetorical concept, discusses why it should be studied, explains the importance of cultural logics and unstated assumptions to the project of rhetorical listening, and models sample tactics of rhetorical listening for everyday writing tasks.

What Is Rhetorical Listening as a Rhetorical Concept?

Rhetorical listening is defined and theorized as a rhetorical concept in Kris's book *Rhetorical Listening*. Like all rhetorical concepts, it may be used to identify and navigate rhetorical problems and their situations, which are either situations in which speakers or writers must express their ideas, feelings, values, and beliefs in ways that their audiences can actually hear them *or* situations in which audiences must open themselves to actually hear ideas, feelings, values, and beliefs, even those with which they disagree.

Rhetorical listening invites listeners to make the following moves, which, though listed sequentially, are often recursive:

- Assume an open stance.

- Lay competing claims and cultural logics side by side.

- Pause to stand under the discourses[3] of self and others in order to hear claims and cultural logics that may break through usual ways of thinking.

- Analyze and reflect on what is heard in order to promote a deeper understanding of self and others.

- Design, when possible, win-win solutions, which are not conceptualized as victories but, rather, as situations wherein participants feel as if their stakes have been heard, considered, and factored, however possible, into decisions.

Such listening is useful for composing effective and civil communications for audiences who agree and, especially, for those who disagree, whether the communications are academic, workplace, public, or personal.

Rhetorical listening works by inviting listeners to reposition themselves—to move from stances of dysfunctional silence toward stances of rhetorical listening. While not all silences are dysfunctional, as Cheryl Glenn powerfully argues in *Unspoken*, some are, and they hinder or prevent personal reflection and interpersonal communication about rhetorical problems. Dysfunctional silences are perpetuated via stances of denial ("I do not see a problem"), defensiveness ("I had nothing to do with the problem"), and guilt/blame ("I am not responsible for creating the problem and should not be blamed for it") (Ratcliffe 23–24). Notice how all the dysfunctional stances position "I" as the subject of their sentences, which encourages an inward-looking, not outward-looking, perspective on the problem. If the subject of the sentences were shifted from "I" to "the problem," then rhetorical listening becomes easier to perform via stances of recognition ("The problem concerns some people even if I have not thought about it before"), critique ("The problem may function in different ways in different situations for different people"), and accountability ("Even if the problem is not something I created or experience, its existence in the systems I inhabit makes me accountable for analyzing it and acting to address it") (96–98).[4] Movement from denial to recognition opens up the capacity to acknowledge a problem; movement from defensiveness to critique opens up the capacity to analyze a problem; and movement from guilt/blame to accountability opens up the capacity to see oneself and others as both implicated in and acting upon systems (whether educational, economic, social, etc.) whose functions may need to be reinforced or revised or, in some cases, dismantled.

To fully comprehend how to reposition to a rhetorical listening stance, listeners must understand the following four terms: 1) competing claims, 2) multiple or competing cultural logics; 3) dominant tropes; and 4) key tropes.

Competing claims. Called "thesis statements" in many educational systems, claims are assertions of people's arguments. These assertions fall along a wide spectrum of motives: in the best cases, claims are what people know or believe to be true and the greatest good for all; in the worst cases, claims are what people know or believe to be in their own self-interests, regardless of what is true or good for others. When competing claims emerge in a situation, they expose disagreements about ideas. In the Galileo example, competing claims include: "Our universe is earth-centered" and "Our universe is sun-centered." In addition, competing claims often signal competing cultural logics.

Multiple and competing cultural logics. Cultural logics are ways of reasoning common to groups of people who come together based on common knowledge, beliefs, or goals and who share their ideas through discourse. Political parties, non-profits, professions, sports fans, and families are just some examples of groups that generate cultural logics. Multiple cultural logics usually surround any topic under discussion, and these multiple cultural logics may compete with one another as evidenced by Galileo's situation where religion and science clashed. Because cultural logics influence how people see and interpret the world, they influence both how people state claims and how they hear them (Ratcliffe 10, 33). Whether a claim is heard as true or not depends on the cultural logic within which a listener stands. In Galileo's situation, because religious leaders in 1633 reasoned that the earth was the center of God's creation based on revelations in the Bible, they heard the earth-centered claim as logical and the sun-centered claim as heretical. Conversely, because scientists in 1633 reasoned that the sun was at the center of the known universe based on observation and mathematical calculations, they heard the sun-centered claim as reasonable and the earth-centered claim as non-scientific or superstitious. And for scientists who were believers, they had to reconcile these two competing cultural logics in their own minds, a move that many religious institutions would not attempt until much later.

Dominant tropes. A *trope* is a word or phrase or image that signifies differently in different contexts. For the project of rhetorical listening, *dominant tropes* (whether stated or implied in claims) are terms that name cultural logics. In the Galileo situation, the dominant tropes are *religion and science*, each signaling a different way of reasoning about the universe. Dominant tropes take on different meanings within different cultural logics; for example, in 1633 the trope *science* was heralded within a scientific cultural logic but questioned within a religious one. Interestingly, one dominant trope may generate multiple cultural logics and invite them into conversation with one another, as when a dominant trope like *religion* invites different ways of reasoning about religion (Christianity, Hindu, Islam, etc.) or a dominant trope like *feminism* invites different ways of reasoning about feminism (e.g., first-wave, second-wave, etc.).

Key tropes. While a dominant trope names a cultural logic, key tropes are additional key words or phrases associated with a cultural logic. Whether key tropes are stated or implied, they often indicate unstated assumptions. In the Galileo situation, one key trope implied by both cultural logics of religion and science is *authority*. But their definitions of *authority* differ. Within the cultural logic of religion, *authority* signifies a sacred, all-knowing power of God as represented by the Inquisition. Within the cultural logic of science, *authority* signifies a rational human practice, the scientific method.

But what makes a person willing to listen to claims, cultural logics, dominant tropes, and key tropes? There is no magic formula. But certain capacities that people possess may be invoked to encourage their own listening and to invite the listening of others These capacities include presence, curiosity, suspension, association, focus, generosity, accountability, perseverance, and gratitude.

Presence involves assuming an open stance by committing to being fully present in a moment of listening. It, in turn, generates *curiosity* about any problem under discussion. Curiosity encourages *suspension*, or people holding two or more competing ideas simultaneously in mind without a rush to judgment. Suspension enables both listeners' *association* (analyzing across multiple contexts) and their *focus* (analyzing deeply within a specific context). This understanding of the breadth and depth of a problem offers listeners the opportunities both to perform *generosity* or choosing to grant charitable, not just highly critical, interpretations of a problem and to determine their own *accountability* for a problem, recognizing that while they may not be responsible for its origin, they may have an ethical imperative to act based on its effects on them or others. Because performing the aforementioned capacities can be difficult, another important capacity is *perseverance,* or the stick-to-it-ness needed to initiate both short-term and long change. Finally, *gratitude* entails listeners' choosing to be thankful for the moment of listening, for knowing what they know, and for being able to do what they can to address the problem. Because gratitude grounds people squarely within a moment, it returns them to presence, and this return establishes conditions for future rhetorical listening and highlights the recursivity of these capacities.

Will everyone choose to perform these nine capacities and listen? No. Nor should they. Not all problems require listening. But many do. And as the 47th President's inaugural address notes about important moments in US history, "enough of us came together to carry all of us forward" (Biden). The same principle applies to the use of rhetorical listening and, honestly, to the use of any other rhetorical concept and tactic.

Knowing the above terms and capacities help listeners generate a greater understanding of a rhetorical problem—what it is, why it exists, what is stated, what is assumed, how and why different groups think about the problem differently, and what is at stake in these different ways of reasoning. As such, rhetorical listening offers listeners one means to engage competing perspectives and, in many cases, to engender respect among reasonable people who disagree.

WHY STUDY RHETORICAL LISTENING?

When conflicts arise, they often tempt or trap people into employing agonistic debates, too often performed as "I'm right, you're wrong" arguments. People with power in a particular situation may be tempted to invoke such arguments because, well, they can, and people without power in that same situation may often feel trapped because, to an extent, they are (for while there are always choices, there are not always good ones). Such adversaries may feel resented or resentful, powerful or powerless. Of course, that does not mean that all "I'm right/you're wrong" arguments should be avoided. As Trish Roberts-Miller argues in her work on Hannah Arendt, agonistic rhetoric has a long and legitimate scholarly tradition that attests to its effectiveness (585). But more often than you might think, "I'm right/you're wrong" arguments may be converted to listening ones in order to approach win-win outcomes.

One problem with "I'm right; you're wrong" arguments is that they risk rendering an issue too simplistic by assuming only two sides, by expecting clear winners and losers, and by presupposing right and wrong. When such dualistic thinking becomes entrenched, confirmation bias may follow and prevent any understanding among those who disagree (Jonas et al 557). The result? Gridlock. At best, such gridlock causes two people simply to retreat into their respective stances of "Well, that's just my opinion"; at worst, it results in demonizing opponents as evil, which can lead individually to violence and collectively to war.

Another problem with "I'm right; you're wrong" arguments is that they obscure the fact that multiple perspectives exist, as illustrated by this "Four-No Three" cartoon.

Figure 1. "Four-No-Three" cartoon. Inspired by Bryan Ridgley. Screenshot from "3 or 4 ??? Funny Optical Illusion Drawing." © 2018 by DK Drawings.

In such cases, our own standpoints may render us myopic, unable to *see* that multiple claims might be valid. For example, relativity theory and quantum theory both claim to explain how the world may be measured, but these theories are valid only in their respective realms. Einstein's theory of relativity measures our observable universe of matter and energy, with gravity defined as an object's curving of spacetime. Quantum physics measures a subatomic realm of probability where particles and waves may be measured but where gravity cannot (yet) be clearly defined. So which theory is the true description of how the universe works? Both . . . at least according to current scientific thought. They just work at different scales, which is why physicists are still attempting to complete and, if possible, reconcile these theories.

Clearly, "I'm right; you're wrong" arguments signal a rhetorical problem where multiple perspectives are in play. When engaging them, listeners should be prepared to model the stance of openness that distinguishes rhetorical listening. In some cases, this modeling may mean engaging claims and cultural logics that listeners believe to be false or even know to be dangerous; for example, US government agents may listen to terrorists' chatter to better understand their reasoning in order to prevent an attack on the US. Sometimes, however, listening is not the ethical choice (people must make that decision situation by situation), but when it is the right choice, listeners should treat the false or dangerous claims and cultural logics as objects of inquiry, keeping in mind (it is worth repeating) that investigating a false or dangerous claim or cultural logic is not commensurate with sanctioning it or authorizing it.

In such cases, listeners may engage for a variety of purposes.

First, studying rhetorical listening helps listening writers understand multiple perspectives. When performing rhetorical listening, listeners should recognize that entertaining multiple perspectives does not preclude the existence of truth. Multiple perspectives might indicate the truth can indeed be clearly discerned and one perspective is decidedly right (e.g., we live in a sun-centered solar system, not an earth-centered one). Multiple perspectives might indicate that truth is larger than any one perspective can comprehend (e.g., the meaning of life). Or multiple perspectives might indicate that multiple truths really do exist and we just don't know enough yet to figure out how to reconcile them (e.g., relativity and quantum physics or even Democratic and Republican interpretations of US political landscapes).

Second, studying rhetorical listening helps listening writers find points of entry not just for common ground but also for counterarguments. Though listening to understand may generate points of commonality, it does not equate understanding with agreement. For example, understanding how Nazism gained traction in the first half of the twentieth century does not mean students of World War II embrace fascism whose functions are defined as follows:

> Fascism is the idea that politics is about will and emotion rather than reason and interests. It denies the factual world in favor of myths, it defines politics as a matter of us and them, portrays globalization as a conspiracy rather than as a set of challenges, and postulates a mythical union between the ("real" "us") people and a Leader that requires no mediation by laws or institutions. (Snyder qtd. in "The Global Rise")

Understanding these functions of fascism in one iteration such as Nazi Germany helps citizens recognize its rise in other iterations When leaders who ignore laws and institutions are recognized in contemporary politics, then understanding that particular function of facism may become a place to invent counterarguments, a place to use understanding as resistance.

Recognizing multiple, competing perspectives may not make arguments any easier to counter in the heat of the moment; however, pausing to imagine competing perspectives can be calming, enabling listeners to recognize that other people are not simply being unreasonable (although sometimes that is the case) but, rather, may be reasoning from within a different set of knowledge, beliefs, and goals. Listening to and reflecting on these differences can make clearer to listeners both the reasons and the cultural logics that explain why people (both ourselves and others) think and act as we do.

WHY ARE CULTURAL LOGICS IMPORTANT TO RHETORICAL LISTENING?

After listeners lay competing claims side-by-side and pause to consider them, they need to discern how individual claims connect to larger group perspectives. For example, suppose you meet a person at a party, she makes a claim about taxes, and then you think, "She sounds like a Republican." How do you know that? The person is simply expressing her personal opinion about taxes, right? Well, yes . . . and no. Do all Republicans think exactly alike about taxes? Of course not. But there exists enough of a common pattern of reasoning about taxes among Republicans, at any given place and time, that such thinking is rendered recognizable as, well, Republican. Kenneth Burke explains it this way: "the so-called 'I' is merely a combination of partially conflicting 'corporate we's,'" or group identities (*Attitudes Toward History* 264). One way to conceptualize group identities and ways of reasoning is via the concept of cultural logic.

As noted earlier, cultural logics are ways of reasoning common to groups of people who come together based on common knowledge, beliefs, or goals and who share their ideas through discourse. As such, cultural logics influence how people see and interpret the world as well as how they argue and act (Ratcliffe 10, 33). Cultural logics abound in our everyday lives. They haunt discussions of any topic: US politics (Greens, Democrats, Republicans, Independents, etc.), football (Viking fans, Packer fans, Chicago fans, etc.), gender (binary, nonbinary, etc.), religion (Christianity, Islam, Judaism, Buddhism, etc.). Subsets within cultural logics also exist: for example, subsets of Christianity include the cultural logics of Catholics and Protestants, and subsets within Protestants include Methodists, Presbyterians, Quakers, etc.

A focus on cultural *logics* as ways of reasoning does not deny the presence or importance of emotions. Indeed, Kris's book *Rhetorical Listening* grew out of a classroom moment when emotions among students ran high during a discussion of Cornel West's *Race Matters,* with classroom debate degenerating into polite but emphatic "I'm right, you're wrong" arguments. Dissatisfied with the fact that students had left class that day without seriously considering any views other than their own, Kris developed rhetorical listening as a rhetorical concept and pedagogical tactic that invites students to pause, step back from their emotions and personal opinions for a moment to examine cultural discourses, claims, and cultural logics and to analyze what makes the claims and cultural logics possible. Then students can reflect on both their emotional reactions and their discourse analyses, laying them side by side and reflecting on what these two types of knowing have to say to one another.[5] The goal in creating rhetorical listening tactics was twofold: to create a less charged but equally engaged classroom and, even more importantly, to provide students with a lexicon and tactics for talking about and reflecting on gender and race.[6] It is incumbent upon teachers to figure out what works best, given the contexts, talents, and predispositions of the students in their classes as well as of the teachers themselves. Rhetorical listening is simply one option.

To be effectively employed within the project of rhetorical listening, cultural logics may be best understood when studied in terms of their 1) elements, 2) structures, 3) functions, and 4) purposes.

As for elements of cultural logics, if we accept Burke's claim that rhetoric has a socializing function that moves people to adopt certain "attitudes and actions" (*RM* 41), then cultural logics may be imagined as discursive formations comprised of three elements: 1) a dominant trope; 2) associated beliefs, and 3) cultural scripts. As discussed earlier, a *dominant trope* is the main term, either stated or implied in a claim, that names a cultural logic. Again, in Galileo's seventeenth-century case, the dominant tropes are *religion* and *science. Associated beliefs* signify attitudes associated with a dominant trope. For example, attitudes associated with the trope *religion* are faith and obedience while attitudes associated with *science* are curiosity and experimentation. *Cultural scripts* signify actions that derive from both a trope and its associated beliefs, actions that become embodied as they are enacted and, when embodied, identify a person—to one's self and to others—with particular cultural logics. For example, a cultural script for a religious leader is to preach about faith and obedience and offer counsel to parishioners; a cultural script for a scientist is to question the world, posit a hypothesis, conduct experiments to prove a hypothesis, build a scientific theory, and publish results so other scientists may replicate the experiment and thus validate the theory. But these cultural scripts, then as now, are neither neutral nor objective, for the seventeenth-century scientific revolution was gendered not just in terms of the number of women participating but also in terms of the concept of science itself being masculinized as a rational process that explains and masters a feminized, observable nature (Tonn).[7]

The structure of cultural logics may be conceptualized as the three elements forming an if-then-therefore chain of reasoning where *if* signifies an assumed *definition of a dominant trope, then* signifies a resulting *belief or attitude,* and *therefore* signifies a resulting *cultural script or action.* Consider the Galileo example: in 1633, *if science* (a dominant trope) is defined as a valid way of generating knowledge of the universe via reason and experimentation, *then* it is believed that scientific observations and experimentation should be pursued (a belief) and, *therefore,* scientists perform observations and experiments to prove hypotheses and to write up their results as scientific theories (a cultural script). Again, no cultural script is objective or neutral or unmarked by cultural categories such as gender.

Five important functions of cultural logics explain how they work. First, cultural logics *change over time*; for example, US cultural logics of gender in 2022 are not the same as US cultural logics of gender in 1800 or even 1968. Second, cultural logics *change from place to place*; at any one time, cultural logics of gender may differ in, say, the US and Saudi Arabia. Third, multiple cultural logics *haunt every rhetorical problem*; when Galileo defended his book, he was dealing with cultural logics of religion and science, yes, but also with those of gender, parenting, nationality, etc. Fourth, cultural logics *intersect* in complicated and messy ways that affect people's thinking and acting and, thus, people's lives; for Galileo, his reasoning about gender, profession, social status, and religion precluded his being listed on the birth certificates of his three children by a woman whom he never married and resulted in his putting his two daughters in a convent but adopting his son. Fifth, cultural logics *become embodied* and, thus, inform people's identities and actions; for example, someone might vote for a certain candidate because the voter grew up in a home that identified with that candidate's political party. The question is: did the voter act on conscious beliefs or non-conscious family identifications? Identifying and reflecting on such embodiments help listeners to act intentionally, that is, to bring embodiments of multiple cultural logics to consciousness and then choose the ones with which they actually want to be affiliated.

If the purpose of a cultural logic is to make visible a group's collective thinking, then listening writers may realize this purpose in two ways. First, listeners may demonstrate that competing tropes (e.g., *science, religion*) can generate competing cultural logics. Second, listeners may demonstrate that one dominant trope (e.g., *race*) can generate multiple cultural logics (White supremacy, colorblindness, separatism, multiculturalism, critical race studies, etc.). Once listeners understand elements, structures, and functions of cultural logics, then when confronted with competing perspectives, they can for their own purposes build taxonomies of cultural logics. Using these taxonomies, listeners can map and analyze not just claims about a rhetorical problem but also cultural logics within which these claims function. This knowledge will help listeners better understand rhetorical problems as well as how to respond to them.

In sum, mapping a taxonomy of cultural logics is important to the project of rhetorical listening because it helps listeners identify stated claims and articulate unstated assumptions that haunt arguments.

WHY ARE UNSTATED ASSUMPTIONS IMPORTANT TO RHETORICAL LISTENING?

Unstated assumptions have long been part of rhetorical education. Aristotle's *Rhetoric* offers a concept and tactic for naming and employing unstated assumptions: the *enthymeme,* defined as a rhetorical syllogism (p. 4; I.2.8). In philosophy, a syllogism is a method of deductive reasoning that includes a major premise, a minor premise, and a conclusion (Smith). Here's a famous example:

Major Premise: All men are mortal.

Minor Premise: Socrates is a man.

Conclusion·   Socrates is mortal.

For philosophical syllogisms to be valid, all parts must be present, clear, and structured as a strict geometric proof that proceeds via substitution of terms.

In rhetoric, however, a rhetorical syllogism or enthymeme[8] assumes this same syllogistic structure but leaves premises or conclusions intentionally *unstated* for the audience to supply, thus rendering audience participation important while rendering the enthymeme messier than the syllogism. The claim "Socrates is mortal" is an enthymeme because it leaves its reasons (major and minor premises) unstated for the audience to fill in, either consciously or unconsciously. The claim, "Socrates is mortal because he's a man," is also an enthymeme because, while it states a claim and a reason, it leaves the major premise unstated for the audience to supply. This unstated function is a silence that, as Cheryl Glenn might argue, is "as powerful as speech" (*Unspoken* xi).

Aristotle argues that the enthymeme is the most effective rhetorical tactic that a speaker or writer can employ to persuade his or her audience, but only if it is used well (40–47; I.2.8–22). Why? Enthymemes provide a shorthand for communication. Audiences can simply fill in their own ideas for the unstated assumptions and, thus, participate in a speaker/writer's argument, constructing common ground in the process of thinking together. For example, when President Obama ran for President and used the slogan, "Change We Need," that slogan was an enthymeme because voters could fill in their own definitions of *change*, *we*, and *need*. The same thing happened when President Trump ran for office and used the slogan, "Make America Great Again"; different voters could fill in their own definitions of *great* and *again*.

As these political examples demonstrate, unstated assumptions function in rhetorical listening in two ways. First, all claims are haunted by unstated cultural logics. In the President Obama example, *change* was often haunted by the cultural logics or ways of reasoning among moderate and liberal Democrats; in the President Trump example, *great* was often haunted by the cultural logics or ways of reasoning among financially conservative Republicans and white nationalist groups. Second, cultural logics themselves are often haunted by unstated assumptions. The Democratic cultural logic about change is haunted by the assumption that the federal government should provide solutions to the country's problems, and the Republican cultural logic is haunted by the idea that the federal government should provide help only when absolutely necessary.

Granting hearings to claims, cultural logics, and their key tropes expose unstated assumptions that haunt arguments. Such exposures help listeners understand *how* and *why* others with whom they agree and disagree think, feel, believe, and act as they do. For listening writers, learning to understand perspectives different from their own serves three important purposes: one, listeners may anticipate counterarguments and actions of audiences whose cultural logics differ from their own; two, listeners may persuade such audiences to think and act differently; or three, listeners may decide to think and act differently themselves.

WHAT ARE TACTICS OF RHETORICAL LISTENING?

What follows are four sample tactics mentioned in Kris's *Rhetorical Listening* but not but not unpacked in as much detail as here. These tactics include: 1) building cultural logics, 2) eavesdropping, 3) listening metonymically, and 4) listening pedagogically. These tactics have grown out of our classroom teaching, our administrative experiences, and our lives outside of work. As two white scholar-teachers, we are ever mindful of Asao Inoue's caution in his "Foreword" to Frankie Condon and Vershawn Ashanti Young's *Performing Antiracist Pedagogy in Rhetoric, Writing, and Communication*: "Any teacher[s] who . . . may enforce rules of propriety that are meant to enact antiracist practices in the classroom are looking for rules that promote fairness, equality, and safety. The impulse is the right impulse. It's the method that messes up things, and how and by whom the method is enforced" (xii). Along with Inoue's questions of "how and by whom," we are also ever mindful of Adrienne Rich's warning and exhortation about people's (especially white people's) writing about race and ethnicity: "My ignorance can be dangerous to me and to others. Yet we can't wait for the undamaged to make our connections for us; we can't wait to speak until we are perfectly clear and righteous. There is no purity and, in our lifetimes, no end to this process." (123). As Rich suggests, such engagement may be an ethical imperative; as our "Introduction" suggests, this engagement represents the very story of rhetoric that we all inhabit, together yet differently.

To model engagements with the story of rhetoric, the four tactics of rhetorical listening below serve simply as samples. Each tactic is simply one means, not *the means*, for helping listening writers both articulate and perform their analytical and writing moves. Other tactics could and should be imagined by listening writers who possess the capacity to develop their own tactics, adapting them to their own rhetorical problems, situations, audiences, and stakes.

Tactic #1: Build a taxonomy of cultural logics around a dominant trope.

1. Identify a dominant trope.

2. Build multiple cultural logics around the selected dominant trope, using the three elements (definition of trope, associated beliefs, cultural scripts) in an if-then-therefore structure.

3. Analyze each cultural logic in terms these questions:

    a. What does a cultural logic offer to its proponents?

    b. What problems does it cause?

    c. What meanings does a single claim accumulate within different cultural logics?

Building a taxonomy of cultural logics takes more space in this book than any other tactic, but taking this space is important. Why? There are several reasons. To grant only one cultural logic a hearing would imply that there exists only one way of reasoning about a rhetorical problem and, thus, would compromise its complexity, the people involved, and the situations that frame it. To grant only two cultural logics a hearing risks reifying *either/or* thinking that is already too dominant in Western agonistic debates. In addition, because one cultural logic may be best understood in terms of its differences from others, building a taxonomy of cultural logics offers a deeper, networked understanding of any topic or rhetorical problem.

The rhetorical problem used here to exemplify this tactic is: talking about race in the US. When Claudia Rankine invites White men to tell her what they think about privilege, she asserts that talking about race in the US is difficult. Such conversations are difficult not just because our nation's history has a fraught relationship with race (although it does), nor simply because US citizens lack shared ways to talk about race across communities (although we often do), but because different definitions of *race* and different cultural logics of race confuse the issue. As a result of competing definitions and cultural logics, people often talk past one another, as illustrated in this Drew Sheneman cartoon.

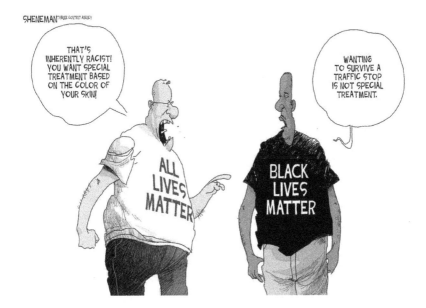

Figure 2. White Lives/Black Lives cartoon by Drew Sheneman. 13 July 2016.
Tribune Content Agency. Used by permission.

The white man wants to be blind to race (one cultural logic) and so
claims "All lives matter," and the Black man cannot afford to be blind to
race (a different cultural logic) and so argues "Black lives matter."

Taking Sheneman's cartoon as a starting point for building a taxonomy of cultural logics, listeners can identify the rhetorical problem represented and then identify a dominant trope (race) (#1); build a taxonomy
of different US cultural logics of race (white supremacy, colorblindness,
multiculturalism, and critical race studies)[9] (#2); and then analyze the
effects of these cultural logics via a set of questions (#3).

A Cultural Logic of White Supremacy offers a consciously combative and violent approach to US race debates.[10] When listening writers
choose to grant a hearing to such a dangerous cultural logic, they should
do so keeping three important points in mind. First, (it is worth repeating) tracking a dangerous cultural logic does not sanction, justify, nor
authorize it. Second, refusing to engage such a dangerous cultural logic
may be a personal choice for listening writers at any given time or place
based on their personal situations; however, such refusals do not make
that cultural logic, or its material traces, disappear from culture. Thus,
third, dangerous forms of argument require careful attention if they are

to be challenged, for as Burke argues in his famous essay "The Rhetoric of Hitler's 'Battle,'" the goal of such inquiry is to understand what makes dangerous cultural logics such as Nazism effective so that their violent beliefs and cultural scripts may be interrupted whenever and wherever they emerge (165).

To build a cultural logic of white supremacy so as to analyze how it functions, listening writers may define its three elements (dominant trope, beliefs, cultural script) within an if-then-therefore structure.

- IF (*assumed definition of dominant trope*):

    If *race* is defined as a biological, God-given essence that defines a person's body, mind, character, and value and results in a racial hierarchy with "whites" on top, . . .

- THEN (*associated beliefs*):

    Then racial differences, it is believed, should be acknowledged and maintained by whatever means necessary, individually and structurally (legally, economically, socially, religiously, scientifically, violently, etc.).

- THEREFORE (*cultural script*):

    Therefore, a cultural script of white supremacy not only justifies but insists upon oppressive actions by individual people as well as by cultural structures. Such scripts have socialized people and institutions in the US to perform and sanction the following actions: slavery, lynching, land grabs, Jim Crow segregation, racist textbook production, preaching about the mark of Cain, white-only mortgage clauses, and travel bans.

Once built, this cultural logic may be analyzed, as we do with students, via the following questions about its effects.

1. *What does the cultural logic of white supremacy offer proponents?* Proponents, students often tell us, are assured a simplistic hierarchy for classifying and valuing people as well as a guarantee of their own superiority, given that most proponents are classified as white. Consequently, they are not required to reach across cultures, question their own thinking, or rethink their sacred myths

whether those myths are in the realms of history, economics, politics, religion, or science. Then we ask students, "What else?"

2. *What problems does this cultural logic cause?* White supremacy, according to students, promotes a problematic definition of *race* grounded in a version of biology that biologists have now rejected. Although *DNA variation* occurs among groups of people who live with one another and have children together over long periods of time, biological variation is not synonymous with *race* as historically used in the US. White supremacy promotes social structures with built-in barriers to the advancement of people identified as BIPOC as well as sanctions violence against them. As such, this cultural logic undermines the ideas of life, liberty, and individual freedom on which the US was based. After these common student responses, we ask, "What else?"

3. *How does this cultural logic affect a speaker's saying or a hearer's hearing claims, such as "Race matters"?* Students often agree that someone functioning within a white supremacy cultural logic would hear this claim as logical and think, "Yes, race matters in order to keep whites in positions of power as nature and God intended." And in the "All Lives"/"Black Lives" debate, they would position themselves with "White Lives Matter." Again, we ask, "What else?"

Having constructed this cultural logic of "white supremacy," listening writers may use the same tactic to map others.

A *Cultural Logic of Colorblindness* appears, at first, to counter the legal, emotional, and physical violence of white supremacy. Positioning race as a false and non-relevant category for evaluating character, motivations, or actions, colorblindness is exemplified by claims such as "I never think of you as non-white. I just think of you as a person." This cultural logic is often presented as grounded in a founding US principle that all people are created equal and, by extension, are to be treated equally. But in reality, as Octavio Pimentel, Charise Pimentel, and John Dean argue, colorblindness promotes a "meritocracy myth," the idea that individuals are solely responsible for their own accomplishments (109), an idea Victor Villanueva famously critiques in his best-selling *Bootstraps*. Reflecting on colorblindness, Patricia J. Williams argues that she accepts it "as a legitimate hope for the future" but believes that at our current moment it promotes a naïve "utopianism" that "constitutes an ideological confusion at best and denial at its very worst" (4). Toni Morrison deems such denial dangerous: in her analysis of Herman Melville's *Benito Cereno*, she argues that the "willful blindness" undergirding racial codings in our use of language both insidiously enables racism while absolving whites of responsibility and, thus, guilt for it.

To build a cultural logic of colorblindness so as to analyze how it functions, listening writers may organize its three main elements (trope, beliefs, and cultural script) into a chain of reasoning resembling the following:

- IF (*assumed definition of dominant trope*):

  If *race* is defined as a category that is not viable either biologically[11] or culturally and, consequently, cannot determine a person's mind, character, or value, . . .

- THEN (*associated beliefs*):

  Then race, it is believed, is an unimportant and even detrimental category if employed in our daily lives and, thus, should *not* be acknowledged individually or structurally (legally, economically, socially, morally, politically, religiously, etc.); rather, it is believed, people should be colorblind, or blind to color, and not see race.

- THEREFORE (*cultural script*):

  Therefore, this cultural script justifies and indeed insists upon treating all people the same. Such scripts have socialized people in the US to perform a wide array of actions: challenging affirmative action and other laws about protected groups in terms of college admissions, hiring, and promotions. But being blind to race results in actions that are not at all equal: filming Hollywood westerns without Indigenous points of view; even stocking products in stores for only one type of hair.

Once built, this cultural logic may be analyzed, as we do with students, via the following questions about its effects.

1. *What does the cultural logic of colorblindness offer proponents?* Proponents, students can offer, are assured a system for classifying and valuing people based on fairness along with a sense that they

are performing the principle of equality upon which the US is founded; they also receive a pass from having to deal with race. Then we ask students, "What else?"

2. *What problems does this cultural logic cause?* Colorblindness, students commonly assert, is heard, at best, as an ideal that does not yet reflect the reality of everyone's everyday lives and, at worst, as a passive consent for racism.[12] Then we ask, "What else?"

3. *How does this cultural logic affect a speaker's saying or a hearer's hearing claims, such as "Race matters"?* Students often conclude that someone functioning within this cultural logic would hear this claim as illogical and think or respond, "No, race doesn't matter," arguing instead that "All lives matter equally." Within this cultural logic, the claim "Race matters" is unutterable, and if a claim cannot be uttered, it cannot be addressed. Again, we ask, "What else?"

Building *more than* two cultural logics to lay side-by-side helps listening writers move beyond dualistic thinking and, thus, unlearn default agonistic tendencies such as assuming zero sum argumentation that often results in gridlock. With these ideas in mind, let's turn to a third cultural logic, multiculturalism.

A *Cultural Logic of Multiculturalism* celebrates *ethnicity* as a cultural category defined in terms of ancestral and cultural traditions and posits it as more significant than *race* for studying history, literature, people, cultures, etc. Younger college students have experienced K-12 curricula grounded in multiculturalism as the study of multiple cultures in order to appreciate their traditions and rituals. The trope *multiculturalism* itself generates two competing cultural logics: 1) a liberal, feel-good multiculturalism that elides discussions of race (Jay 100) and, 2) a critical multiculturalism that attempts to confront race. Here we concentrate on the former because it is the more pervasive version in K-12 schools and affords an opportunity to bring the study of cultural logics into sharper relief.

To build a cultural logic of liberal multiculturalism so as to analyze how it functions, listening writers may weave three elements of a cultural logic (trope, belief, and cultural script) into an if-then-therefore structure.

- IF (*definition of dominant trope*):

  If *race* is defined as an imaginary category that, when popularly used, is grounded in false science, false religion, and false history, . . .

- AND IF (*corollary tropes and definitions*):

  And if *ethnicity* is defined as an actual (viable) category that signifies ancestry and multiple cultural heritages that may be studied via *multiculturalism* as the study of multiple ethnic groups, . . .

- THEN (*associated beliefs*):

  Then *ethnicity* and *multiculturalism*, it is believed, should be the operative tropes in our daily thinking and actions because they are more pertinent than race to our understandings of daily life, literature, language, music, etc. Further, it is believed, these tropes should promote education grounded in the appreciation and tolerance[13] of multiple cultures, and ethnicity should be viewed as only one of many markers constituting a person's intersectional identity.

- THEREFORE (*cultural scripts*):

  Therefore, this cultural script justifies and insists upon valuing all ethnicities for their differences. Such scripts have socialized people to perform the following actions: naming people, artifacts, and institutions by their ethnicities, not race (e.g., saying African American literature, not Black literature); celebrating differences among ethnicities in education, the workplace, social situations, etc. (e.g., learning about, if not celebrating, Hanukkah, Christmas, and Kwanza rituals in December); and refusing stereotypes because they inaccurately and cruelly represent only one dimension of a person's complex identity and because they imply more about a user's fearful imaginings than about the stereotyped group's reality (e.g., not calling people derogatory racial epithets or making assumptions about an entire group's intelligence, food preferences, etc.).

Once built, this cultural logic may be analyzed , as we do with students, via the following questions about its effects.

1. *What does the cultural logic of multiculturalism offer proponents?* According to students, proponents are offered ways to identify with particular cultures and to lay multiple cultures side by side and acknowledge differences as an important element both across and within a community as a means of fostering appreciation and tolerance. And we reply, "What else?"

2. *What problems does this cultural logic cause?* Its emphasis on ethnicity, students often answer, too often backgrounds discussions about the effects of race and, like colorblindness, risks rendering proponents blind to individual and structural realities of racism in society. Then we ask, "What else?"

3. *How does this cultural logic affect a speaker's saying or a hearer's hearing claims, such as "Race matters"?* Students often argue that, although someone functioning with this cultural logic might utter the sentence, "Race matters," or hear it as logical, they most likely would follow up by quickly saying, "But ethnicity matters more." Again we reply, "What else?"

By repeating this sequence of questions, listening writers learn to complicate rhetorical problems and to generate information that helps them decide how to address different audiences, keeping in mind that the point is not to tell an audience what they want to hear but, rather, to present the listening writer's ideas in ways that their audiences can hear them. In the process, listening writers learn not just to identify multiple cultural logics but also to practice the structure of reasoning that defines an open stance associated with rhetorical listening.

A *Cultural Logic of Critical Race Studies* is placed last because it consciously opposes, to different degrees, the previous three cultural logics. According to the *Oxford English Dictionary*, the term *race* began being used in the sixteenth-century to classify people according to "color" and country of origin to promote a slave economy, and before that time, the term *race* functioned as a synonym for national/ethnic heritage, such as the Irish race or the Gallic race. As for critical race studies, Neal Lester (the Director of Project Humanities at ASU) explains that it is not a curriculum nor a rigid set of beliefs but, rather, an analytical perspective that focuses on structural representations of race ("Dr. Neal Lester"). Though critical race studies had its origins in critical legal studies, it now spans academic disciplines,[14] inviting the study of how representations of race function structurally (with effects on individuals) from the courtroom to the ballot box to classrooms to retail stores to *New Yorker* cartoons.

To build a cultural logic of critical race studies so as to analyze how it functions, listeners may braid the three elements of a cultural logic (trope, belief, and cultural script) into an if-then-therefore structure.

- IF (*definition of dominant trope*):

  If *race* is defined as an imaginary (false) category that, when popularly used, is often based in false science, false religion, and false history, . . .

- BUT IF (*corollary definition of dominant trope*):

  But if *race* is also defined as a socially constructed category that has real consequences, both positive (celebrations of cultural traditions) and negative (dangers of discrimination and violence), . . .

- THEN (*associated beliefs*):

  Then race, it is believed, is not a biological determinant of mind or character but, rather, a socially-constructed and embodied trope that informs people's daily lives both individually and structurally.

- THEREFORE (*cultural scripts*):

  Therefore, this cultural script rejects studying race as a biological determinant of mind, character, or value but insists upon studying race for antiracist purposes. Such scripts socialize people to perform these actions: e.g., identifying functions of race in law, the workplace, literature, architecture, sociology, etc.; interrupting negative functions in structural policies and practices as well as in individual actions; and researching what remains unstated in history, literature, rhetoric, etc., to remedy, as much as possible, centuries of misperceptions, oppressions, and violence.

Once built, this cultural logic may be analyzed , as we do with students, via the following questions about its effects.

1. *What does the cultural logic of critical race studies offer proponents?* Proponents , students often suggest, are given means to deny race as a God-given or scientific category and to assert, instead, race as a socially constructed category that informs the life of *everyone* in US culture, albeit differently. They are offered ways to lay all the "race cards" on the table and discuss them, with antiracist intent. And we ask, "What else?"

2. *What problems does this cultural logic cause?* By foregrounding racial categories, students caution, this cultural logic risks reifying these categories and inadvertently perpetuating the status quo (Mocombe). Critics are calling for it to be outlawed in school systems. And we query, "What else?"

3. *How does this cultural logic affect a speaker's saying or a hearer's hearing claims, such as "Race matters"?* Someone within this cultural logic, students tell us, would most certainly claim, "Yes, race matters." But the antiracist meaning of this claim would signify a vastly different idea from an identical claim stated by someone functioning within a white supremacy cultural logic. And we would ask, "What else?"

Having built and questioned this taxonomy of cultural logics of race, listening writers can use it to situate themselves and to identify the standpoints in texts (including their own writings), interpersonal interactions, and institutional policies. They can also ask what other cultural logics are not represented here, for example, how a global perspective might alter this taxonomy.

When listening writers begin identifying cultural logics on their own, they learn to identify and analyze two types of unstated assumptions. First, they learn how cultural logics function as unstated assumptions, haunting the meanings of all claims, such as "Race matters." Second, they learn how key terms may function as unstated assumptions, haunting cultural logics; for example, key tropes haunting cultural logics of race include *equality, individualism, fairness*. The second move is challenging for listening writers who lack a "trope-based" education; however, once they understand how tropes function, their ability to track the reasoning chains of cultural logics and to find key tropes in cultural logics increases exponentially. Once listening writers learn to identify and analyze tropes, build and analyze cultural logics, and hear and analyze unstated assumptions, they are ready to do the hard work of ethical eavesdropping.

Tactic #2: Eavesdropping on an Argument (positioning oneself as an outsider)

The origins of the word *eavesdropping* derive from the activity of standing outside a house under the eaves from which rainwater drops, overhearing what people inside are saying. Eavesdropping usually evokes a negative connotation of violating someone else's privacy. But as a tactic of rhetorical listening,[15] it can become an ethical activity *if* listeners imagine eavesdropping as a means of positioning themselves in the following ways: a) to listen to the discourses of others *that are available to them*; b) to hear over the edges of their own knowing; and c) to think what is commonly unthinkable within their own cultural logics. In this way, eavesdropping is not invading privacy but, rather, overhearing already-public discourses from an outsider's position, listening to learn. And after having learned how to build cultural logics via the previous tactic, listeners will be familiar with listening not just for claims but also for cultural logics and their key tropes, whether stated or unstated.

The rhetorical listening tactic of eavesdropping proceeds as follows:

1. Identify a public argument.

2. Position yourself as an outsider to one side (remember, multiple sides may exist)—that is, a) recognize that you are on the border of knowing and not knowing and b) grant others the insider position in terms of experience and/or knowledge.

3. Listen to what is stated and unstated in terms of claims, cultural logics, and key tropes, questioning and analyzing them (Ratcliffe 104–05).

4. List what you now know, after eavesdropping, about the argument.

5. Select three significant points from the list in #4 and explain why they are significant.

6. Reflect on how and why eavesdropping has altered your own stance—a little, a lot, or not at all—about the public argument.

To demonstrate how eavesdropping works, listening writers may return to the public argument represented in the "All Lives Matter"/"Black Lives Matter" cartoon by Drew Sheneman, which highlights the rhetorical problem and difficulty of communicating across cultural logics.

To determine their outsider position, eavesdroppers may choose one side of the cartoon's argument, a side with which they either disagree or agree. At this point, agreement is not as important as positioning oneself as an outsider to whatever side is selected. In this real or imagined outsider space, eavesdroppers acknowledge that they possess only partial knowledge of the argument and that people on other sides may have lived experiences or knowledge from which eavesdroppers may learn. In the process, they may learn how to wield the rhetorical empathy advocated by Lisa Blankenship, which she defines as "an effort to listen to and understand others, especially [but not only] those very different from us" (11).

For example, if people position themselves as outsiders to the "All Lives Matter" claim, they might try overhearing the unstated reasons haunting this claim:

> All lives matter
>
> > *because* all people are created equal under God.
> >
> > *because* all people should be treated equally under the law.
> >
> > *because* every consideration of race is inherently racist.
> >
> > *because* any consideration of race hinders progress.

When thinking critically about this list, eavesdroppers might ask: Is every consideration of race really racist? For example, is saying that blues music grew out of the Black experience racist? If so, why? If not, why not? And if it's not, then what are the conditions that must exist for a consideration of race *not* to be racist or to be racist? In this way, an outsider's position of not knowing generates a chain of questioning that complicates the argument at hand.

Conversely, if people position themselves as outsiders to the "Black Lives Matter"[14] claim, they might try overhearing the unstated reasons haunting this claim:

> Black lives matter
>
> > *because* Black people face specific problems in the US.

because "all lives" erases these specific problems that Black people face.

because "all lives" too often codes as only "white lives."

because there's a difference between the ideal and the real, a difference between the colorblind ideal of how Black people should be treated (All Lives Matter) and the reality of how they are actually being treated (Black Lives Matter).

When thinking critically about this list, eavesdroppers might ask: Does the phrase "All lives" always code as "white lives"? Does replacing "Black lives" with "All lives" deflect attention from the events affecting the Black community? If so, why? If not, why not? Also is there a difference between claims that replace "Black lives" with "All lives" and claims that replace "Black lives" with "white lives"? Such overhearing, while not always easy, helps finetune our thinking and generate more ideas with which to communicate across differences haunting a rhetorical problem.

Making a list of what is learned via eavesdropping is important as is being able to explain why this knowledge is significant. Both moves enable eavesdroppers to reflect on what was known previously, what was learned and, thus, how one's stance has changed or not. For example, someone positioned as an outsider to the "All Lives" stance in the cartoon might reflect and be willing to entertain some ideas (the impulse toward fairness) but dissociate from the cartoon's representation of that argument in terms of age (old), gender (masculine,) tone (combative), or potential (violence). Eavesdropping on such associations and dissociations provides additional entries into critical thinking not just about the topic (race) but about intersectionalities of identities composed of, among other things, race, age, gender, tone, and potential.

Tactic #3: Listening Metonymically (navigating intersectional identities)

Metonym is a rhetorical figure that describes when a part represents a whole. For instance, when a ship captain says, "All hands on deck," that's a metonym. Though she is ordering all hands on deck, she means sailors' entire bodies. In this case, *hand* is an appropriate *part* to represent the *whole person* of a sailor because a lot of sailors' work on deck is done with their hands. When used as a tactic of rhetorical listening, listening metonymically[16] entails a listener's reflecting on the effects of, first, assigning a person or a text only one identity category and imagining that one part as representing the whole and, then, assigning a person or text other identity categories and imagining those intersections as representing the whole

The tactic of listening metonymically may be performed via the following moves:

1. Identify a person or text that intrigues you.

2. Identify one important identity category associated with that person or text (e.g., a person's being an actor or a text's being a romance novel).

3. Analyze how seeing that person or text in terms of only one identity category enhances and limits your understanding of that person or text.

4. Consider a) what other identity categories are also associated with the person or text; and b) how the intersections of these identity categories complicate an understanding of the person or text generated in #3.

Listening metonymically proceeds via three assumptions. First, *a person or text is always a member of a larger cultural group*. For example, one mother is a *part* of a group of people called mothers, and one detective novel is a *part* of a genre called detective fiction. Second, *the identity of a person or text is always intersectional.*[17] A person is never just a mother, and a book is never just a detective novel. Rather, a person's or text's identity consists of multiple identity categories that intersect with one another: for example, a mother may also be a woman, a friend, a daughter, a neighbor, etc., and a detective novel may also be a book, a genre with a tradition, a commodity to be sold to a movie studio, an escape, etc. Third, *a person or text is not representative of an entire group*. Although one particular mother (say one who cannot cook but is a great hiker and loves her children) is a member of the cultural group called mothers, she does not represent the entire group because other mothers may have other talents (such as cooking really well). Likewise, Dana Stabenow's fictional character Kate Shugak is a detective, a woman, an Aleut, a resident of Alaska, and a dog lover; however, she does not represent all fictional detectives whose intersectional identity categories certainly differ from hers even as they are all detectives. Recognition of such intersectionality is important for getting a picture of the "whole person" (at least as much as possible) and for avoiding stereotyping.

When writers listen metonymically to the "All Lives Matter"/"Black Lives Matter" cartoon, they can avoid stereotyping the characters. They may *see* each character as more than just a white man and a Black man or more than just spokesmen for two competing causes. The characters might be imagined as men, of a certain age, class, and nationality, with common values (such as a belief in fairness and justice) and with individual histories (the unstated "more-to-their-stories") that *might* be haunting their claims. Suddenly the two men do not appear simply as one-dimensional caricatures speaking for one cause. They just might be complicated humans who need a nudge in how to talk to one another. In addition, listening writers should probably also eavesdrop on the "more-to-their-stories" that they are attributing to each character and question "why" they are imagining the characters as they do.

As with previous rhetorical listening tactics, listening metonymically invites listening writers to engage ideas that are unfamiliar to them. But such engagement has risks. A listening writer must be careful to ground his or her imaginings in cultural facts, not fantasy. That means doing the work, whether in research or in person, to justify the claims. Even so, culturally-grounded imagining can be difficult. That is why people sometimes resist it, which leads to the next tactic of listening pedagogically or resisting resistance.

Tactic #4: Listening Pedagogically (resisting resistance)

The term *pedagogy* refers to methods employed for teaching others and oneself, both inside and outside the classroom. *Listening pedagogically* entails identifying psychological resistance that prevents learning and determining when political resistance is needed to encourage learning.[18] *Resistance* is a trope that generates completely opposite meanings. On the one hand, *psychological resistance* refers to dysfunctional behaviors that get in the way of people's seeing reality in healthy ways (e.g., people's denying that they have a problem, or their being defensive when someone tries to help them). On the other hand, *political resistance* refers to advocating and making changes that promote justice, which is defined differently within different cultural logics and employed across political spectra. Both definitions inform this tactic, which helps listening writers interrupt a psychological resistance and promote a political resistance grounded in knowledge, imagination, and respect.

Examples of resisting resistance manifest in many sectors of daily life. For example, the online Merriam-Webster dictionary anticipates readers' psychological resistance to their including the nonbinary use of *they* "to refer to a single person whose gender identity is nonbinary." To counter this anticipated resistance, the dictionary includes the following note:

> All new words and meanings that we enter in our dictionaries meet three criteria: meaningful use, sustained use, and widespread use. Nonbinary *they* has a clear meaning; it's found in published text, in transcripts, and in general discourse; and its use has been steadily growing over the past decades. English speakers are encountering nonbinary *they* in social media profiles and in the pronoun stickers applied to conference badges. There's no doubt that it is an established member of the English language, which means that it belongs in Merriam-Webster's dictionaries. ("A Note")

Another example of resisting resistance occurs in April Baker-Bell's *Linguistic Justice*. She calls out resistance to the study and use of Black Language, a resistance she claims is driven by "Anti-Black Linguistic Racism and white linguistic hegemony and supremacy in classrooms and in the world" (7). To resist this anticipated resistance, she offers an Antiracist Black Language Pedagogy that fosters in students a *"Black Linguistic Consciousness"* (93–94),[19] which helps them counter "the linguistic violence, persecution, dehumanization, and marginalization that Black Language-speakers experience in schools and in everyday life" (11).

Listening pedagogically to resist resistance may be performed by listening writers via the following moves:

1. Identify, in relation to a rhetorical problem, an instance of *psychological resistance* such as denial or defensiveness (see list below) that you notice in another person, text, or yourself.

2. Analyze how this dysfunctional resistance hinders and/or helps people deal with this rhetorical problem, focusing on what this resistance enables to be or not to be said or heard.

3. Identify, in relation to this rhetorical problem, an instance of *political resistance* that you've noticed in another person, text, or yourself.

4. Analyze how this advocacy resistance hinders and/or helps people deal with this rhetorical problem, focusing on what this resistance enables to be or not to be said or heard.

5. Attempt to find places within both sites of resistance where dialogue across differences might begin.

If listening pedagogically entails listening for psychological resistance and determining when political resistance is needed, then listening writers must be able to recognize dysfunction and analyze such resistance.[20] As noted in *Rhetorical Listening*, below are a few types of psychological resistance that sometimes hinder listening writers' ability to listen and learn.

> *Denial*: refusing to acknowledge the existence of an idea/action
>
> *Defensiveness*: shifting conversation from idea/action to one's guilt/blame or lack thereof
>
> *Dismissal*: acknowledging but not engaging an idea/action
>
> *Indifferent Compliance*: going through motions of engaging but not genuinely engaging
>
> *Overidentification*: being so involved in an idea/action that only personal reactions, not cultural/systemic analyses, are possible
>
> *Nonproductive Guilt*: blaming oneself for current privileges afforded one by history and adopting a patronizingly helpful attitude for people one imagines less privileged
>
> *Speaking/writing block*: lacking a conceptual framework or lexicon for discussing an idea/action (Ratcliffe 138–39)

The above may work separately or in conjunction with one another.

In the "All Lives Matter"/"Black Lives Matter" cartoon, the white man performs denial and defensiveness, denying the "Black Lives Matter" claim and sounding defensive via his strident tone and closed fist, which echoes with the violence of white supremacy; these types of resistance do not invite dialogue with those who disagree. The Black man performs dismissal of the "All Lives Matter" claim, which invites dialogue only in that it throws the conversational turn back to the white man. The absence of genuine dialogue prevents the two men from communicating, let alone learning from one another. While their initial reactions might be accurate, their agonistic mode of exchange does not afford them an opportunity to test their initial reactions of each other or to build an alternate way of reasoning together. In this way, the cartoon captures the divisiveness haunting US culture.

To counter the psychological resistance performed in the cartoon (defensiveness/denial and dismissal), listeners may listen pedagogically to the cartoon, attempting to resist the characters' resistances and find ways to engage in genuine dialogue about this rhetorical problem. For example, if the men are viewed as functioning from different cultural logics (colorblindness and critical race studies), then they both may be heard as implying an interest in fairness and justice. Perhaps that common ground is a place to begin a conversation by asking: What is fairness? What is justice? Why are these values important? To whom? What do the values offer? What do they threaten? What might they transform? Yet listeners must also attend to the fact that, at the same time as the white man espouses a claim about "fairness," his closed fist echoes the potential violence associated with white supremacy; listeners must also attend to the fact that if this were an actual physical exchange and not simply a cartoon representation, then as a means of survival that fist might be the first thing that needs to be noticed before anything else is heard.

As a rhetorical concept and set of tactics, rhetorical listening can help listening writers listen to themselves and to other people, texts, and cultural institutions to enhance their own skills of analysis and everyday writing. To that end, rhetorical listening may serve as a grounds for engaging other modern rhetorical concepts and tactics discussed in this book: agency, rhetorical situation, identification, myth, and rhetorical devices.

2 Agency

In her 1993 Nobel Prize lecture, Toni Morrison asserts, "We die, that may be the meaning of life. But we do language, that may be the measure of it." The capacity to "do language" is one way to define rhetorical *agency*.[1] For Morrison, this agency affords humans both an ethical imperative and an ethical choice. People's relationship to language, Morrison explains, creates an imperative to allow language to multiply knowledge "unmolested" so that all accounts of human life are granted a hearing. To accomplish this task, each of us must choose our words, our silences, and our listening stances carefully; the relative success or failure of such choices, Morrison suggests, is how all of our lives will be measured. That is why the questions of *how* people define rhetorical problems and of *how* they address the problems are important.

Take, for example, the rhetorical problem faced by the author of *Braiding Sweetgrass: Indigenous Wisdom, Scientific Knowledge, and the Teachings of Plants.* Here Indigenous biologist Robin Wall Kimmerer must decide how to bring disparate knowledge systems together for herself and her readers in ways that her audiences can actually hear her and then be persuaded to act in ways that preserve the planet (x). To that end, Kimmerer's plan to address her rhetorical problem is to offer readers an experience of reading meant to invoke her community's experience of braiding sweetgrass. Her trope *braiding sweetgrass* evokes a process, a *how*, in which people work in concert with one another, which she describes as, "a reciprocity between you, linked by sweetgrass, the holder as vital as the braider," with the tension between the two, the push and pull, a part of the process (ix).

With her metaphoric gesture, Kimmerer gifts her readers with "a braid of stories meant to heal our relationship with the world. This braid is woven from three strands: indigenous ways of knowing, scientific knowledge, and the story of an Anishinabekwe scientist trying to bring them together in service to what matters most. It is an intertwining of science, spirit, and story" (x). As a writer, Kimmerer enacts Morrison's imperative to "do language" and invites readers to join her in this process, asking them to hold her three strands as she braids and also to recognize that their holding makes her braiding possible. Such a decision to "do language together" can only be made together, just as Kimmerer's invitational goal to heal our relationships with the world can only be achieved together.

After inviting readers to participate in the braiding ceremony in her "Preface," Kimmerer brings together in subsequent chapters her two different ways of knowing and being. In "Putting Down Roots," she reflects on language, education, and survival by describing a scene where she as a professor is working with a graduate student named Daniela on the latter's thesis project: "On the graduate school forms it says I'm her professor, but I've been telling her all along that it is the plant who will be her greatest teacher" (255). In one sentence, Kimmerer both acknowledges the time-honored professor-student relationship in Western education . . . and upends it. Likewise, in the same scene, Kimmerer portrays Theresa, "a Mohawk basket maker and . . . an integral part of our research team," singing a counting chant in the Mohawk language as they count the number of plants to record as part of their scientific data gathering (256), here laying two traditions of language and of gathering side by side. Kimmerer then notes:

> Pockets of the [Mohawk] language survived among those who stayed rooted to place. Among those remaining, the THANKS-GIVING Address was spoken to greet the day: "let us put our minds together as one and send greetings and thanks to our Mother Earth, who sustains our lives with her many gifts." Grateful reciprocity with the world, as solid as a stone, sustained them when all else was stripped away. (256)

In this passage, two traditions live side by side, with words signifying both similarly and differently within these traditions; for example, the trope *Thanksgiving* echoes gratitude in both traditions even while echoing a Western tradition of colonialism and reenacting an Indigenous tradition of speaking to the land (257).

Kimmerer's invitational braiding proposes a reciprocity of action, interaction, and reaction that suggests an agency inflected by rhetorical listening. This reciprocity allows agency as a rhetorical concept to be imagined, enacted, and facilitated via listening writers' capacity to use words so as to lay side by side their stories, their multiple claims and cultural logics, whether stated or unstated, while attending to the spaces between and beyond, all to construct new ways of knowing and being in the world. Of course, listeners' capacities to use language are encouraged or limited by the function of language itself, by policies and practices of cultural institutions, and by the materiality of our environments.

This vision of agency is not an impossible fantasy. It is the story of rhetoric that plays out in our daily lives in multiple ways in multiple contexts. For instance, as evidenced by the Constitution of the United States, by legislative amendments to the Constitution, and by courts' interpretations of the Constitution, the ways words are used in legal contexts set conditions for the daily lives of US citizens—from schools' no longer being allowed since 1954 to function as separate but equal to women's no longer being allowed since 2021 to access comprehensive healthcare in the state of Texas. And so it goes.

How people use words matters.

How people are encouraged and limited in their use of words matters.

The possibility of a listening writer's agency being employed and also being encouraged and limited suggests the co-existence of multiple agencies that may supplement and compete with one another. To demonstrate this claim, Chapter 2 defines agency as a rhetorical concept that may be classified into four types (personal, discursive, cultural, and material), discusses why each agency should be studied in conjunction with rhetorical listening, and models sample tactics that focus on how these multiple agencies interact.

WHAT IS AGENCY AS A RHETORICAL CONCEPT?

The concept of agency offered in Morrison's Nobel Prize speech, with its ethical imperative and ethical choices, has long permeated the history of rhetoric. Even at the beginnings of codified rhetorical education in fifth-century BCE Greece, the sophists and Socratics argued with one another, as Susan Jarratt explains in *Rereading the Sophists*, about what constitutes ethical uses of language (88–89). Such agency is often construed as a personal agency, the capacity of an individual person to make choices about how he, she, or they attempt to persuade audiences. This idea of personal agency, while not always named as such in rhetorical theories, is always assumed insofar as the theories assume that people can make choices when performing the rhetorical arts of reading, writing, speaking, silence, and listening.[2]

Recent theories in rhetoric and composition studies have complicated this idea of personal agency.[3] In *The Animal Who Writes*, Marilyn Cooper defines agency as "relational" (131), located among people instead of just within individual people, a point similar to the one Kimmerer makes with her metaphor of braiding sweetgrass. Thomas Rickert extends this concept of relational agency beyond humans, echoing Bruno Latour to argue "that, first, agency is no longer the sole preserve of humans so that 'actants' proliferate (in the laboratory, in social life, in deliberation); and that, second, these actants, dispersed through networks, undermine the notion that humans have privileged, impartial access to the world; so that third, knowledge production becomes the result of technological craft involving practical, political, material and rhetorical resources" (24). By reframing *material resources* as *gifts*, Kimmerer suggests yet another take on "relational": "Strawberries first shaped my view of a world full of gifts simply scattered at your feet. A gift comes to you through no action of your own, free, having moved toward you without your beckoning. It is not a reward; you cannot earn it, or call it to you, or even deserve it. And yet it appears." (23–24), thus ascribing agency to that which exists beyond the human and over which humans may have little or no control.

Such a relational concept of agency among and beyond humans may, when inflected by rhetorical listening, be classified into four types that work singly, relationally, and intersectionally:

1. *Personal agency* is the capacity and willingness of a person to act, which creates an opportunity to be heard[4]; it is the power of people to think and act in relation to other people and things as well as other types of agencies, when addressing rhetorical problems.

2. *Discursive agency* is the capacity of language itself via the functions of words and discourses (defined as situated networks of words) to act upon and be heard by people; it is the power of words and discourses (as processed in human brains consciously and unconsciously) *to socialize* people[5] and, thus, influence people's personal agency for thinking and acting in relation to rhetorical problems; it is also the power of language *to play*, which enables socialization to be consciously reflected upon and then

confirmed or interrupted.[6] In short, words and discourses are the means through which a person's ideas and actions are mediated, and they matter because they affect *how* a person's ideas and actions are mediated.

3. *Cultural agency* is the capacity of cultural systems (political, economic, educational, etc.) via their institutions (government, markets, universities) and institutional practices (policies, rituals, traditions, events, etc.) to act upon and be heard by people; it is the power of cultural systems to inflect words and discourses and to dictate laws, rules, policies, scripts, etc., that may encourage and/or constrain people's personal agency for thinking and acting in relation to rhetorical problems.[7]

4. *Material agency* is the capacity of objects, places and spaces, human and non-human bodies, and physical resources to act upon and be heard by people; it is the power of material reality to affect people's personal agency to define rhetorical problems and imagine how to address them.[8]

As these four agencies imply, a listening writer's personal agency does not exist in a vacuum but always exists in the presence of other people's personal agencies as well as in the presence of other types of agencies, whether discursive, cultural, and/or material.[9] These four relational and intersecting agencies inform writing processes of listening writers.

Personal agency, with its relational focus among people and things, is enacted, for example, by Kimmerer the writer when she invites the stories of other people and things such as sweetgrass and maple trees into her book and also when she invites readers into the meaning-making process of her book. Personal agencies of other people, with whom she is inextricably linked, supplements Kimmerer's personal agency when their voices come to the fore, such as the story in which her parents model how to serve a community, her father's words echoing in her memory, "Good communities don't make themselves" (169).

Discursive agency, with its focus on the capacity of words and discourses to influence people via socialization and play, enables, for example, Kimmerer's personal agency, as when she riffs on the influence of existing tropes and discourses in defining her identity and her methods for investigating the world. Early in her career, she names herself "an enthusiastic young PhD colonized by the arrogance of science" (222), but by the time *Braiding Sweetgrass* is written, she names herself not just *scientist*, not just *Anishinabekwe*, but *Anishinabekwe scientist* (x), a braiding of tropes that opens up discursive space for the cross-cultural work performed in her book.

Cultural agency, with its focus on the capacity of cultural systems and their institutions to inflect words and discourses and, thus, to influence people, grounds Kimmerer's discursive space by offering two systems and institutions of knowing and being within which to study nature: her Western scientific training in biology at university and her Indigenous holistic approach to nature in her community. Cultural agency also locates her within a publishing system and institution, Penguin Press, within which she must shape her writing for it to be published. And the cultural agency of her Indigenous beliefs encourages her to see community as more important than individual, thus shaping her concept of personal agency.

Finally, material agency, which focuses on the capacity of physical surroundings to influence people, intersects with the above agencies to inform Kimmerer's writing, adding the influences of nature and the environment such as sweetgrass and maple trees on her knowing, being, thinking and writing. For readers of Kimmerer's book, material agency manifests in the fact that they may rhetorically listen to her book while holding it in their hands, viewing it on a screen, or hearing it over Audible.

Given these multiple, relational, and intersectional levels of rhetorical agency, listening writers may approach everyday writing tasks by laying these four different types of agency side by side and negotiating their intersections. In this way, listening writers may develop a deeper understanding of particular writing tasks and contexts and also a greater appreciation of the power of agency as a multi-faceted rhetorical concept and set of tactics.

WHY STUDY PERSONAL AGENCY?

For listening writers, personal agency is the capacity and willingness to act in relation to other people, things, and other agencies when addressing a rhetorical problem. In US culture, however, the problem with personal agency is that it is typically conceptualized as unlimited or unfettered, as an assertion of individualism that Victor Villanueva famously debunked in his bestseller *Bootstraps* (xiv). When agency is imagined as unfettered individuality, its power is imagined as a *possession* that some (the few) have and can wield over others (the many). When the power of personal agency is conceptualized exclusively as a possession, people tend to view argumentation as a zero-sum game that is weighted in favor of the powerful few who will not give up their possessions. When functioning from this view, people with power are tempted to adopt an "I'm right, you're wrong" stance, which encourages an "I'm right" assertion and sometimes coercion. People at the "you're wrong" end of such arguments reasonably recoil at the thought of learning more about argumentation, even if it promises to recalibrate the situation.

But learning about argumentation, rhetoric, and agency is important because as Villanueva reminds us, power is hegemonic (132), and "[h]egemony is rhetorical" (128). In other words, if dominant power may be built via rhetoric through multiple agencies, it may also be dismantled by multiple agencies, though not without consequences. Martin Luther King Jr., for example, challenged the hegemony or dominant power of white supremacy in mid-twentieth-century US culture with multiple agencies, invoking powerful rhetorics of words, images, and bodies; the consequences were enhanced Civil Rights for all, physical harm for some supporters, and death for himself.

Rhetorical listening helps listening writers challenge the concept of personal agency as unfettered individuality by helping them find alternative cultural logics for defining power. Echoing scholars who explore agency within feminism,[10] critical race studies,[11] and rhetorical education,[12] rhetorical listening emphasizes that personal agency comes in multiple ways and in multiple degrees at different sites for different people at different times. Some listening writers, by virtue of their identity markers (e.g., race, class, gender, sexuality, ability, ethnicity and their intersections), have more or less personal agency in certain circumstances, whether those circumstances be academic, workplace, public, or personal. In this way, the "power as possession" cultural logic may be countered with a "power as situational" cultural logic. The latter contends that everyone circles in and out of places of power on a daily basis, albeit to different degrees. For example, a student may have limited personal agency in a college course (after all, a teacher decides what is read, what is assigned, and how assignments are evaluated, and the school system decides how the course counts toward graduation requirements), but that same student may have a greater degree of personal agency at her job if she also works as a manager of a sports store although that manager's personal agency may be limited by the business's policies as well as US labor law.

Helping listening writers think critically about the situatedness of personal agency is important for the following reasons.

First, studying the situatedness of personal agency helps listening writers grasp that the degree *to which one's personal agency is necessarily related to other people's personal agencies.* A listening writer who uses personal agency to persuade other people must study and contend with the audience's personal agencies. As Aristotle and Cicero have taught us in discussions of *ethos*, in some situations a person's individual character will make it possible to be more or less persuasive to an audience:[13] a generous person can inspire others to be generous but can also make others feel uncomfortable. Similarly, a person's cultural position (think: parent, president, teacher, boss, student, etc.) can be a powerful influence in certain situations but a liability in others: for example, parents may hold sway over their children at home but not in the workplace, unless of course they own the workplace.

Second, studying the situatedness of personal agency helps listening writers understand the quality *of a listening writer's personal agency in terms of how personal agency is dependent not just on effects that are visible but also on motives that are conscious and unconscious.* If an imbalance of power exists between a boss and an employee, for example, the quality of an employee's use of personal agency may be measured by observing effects, or *how* he, she, or they respond to a set of directions, and also by observing motives, or *why* he, she, or they respond in a certain way to a set of directions. If an employee disagrees with a boss's directions but chooses to follow them, it could be argued that the employee has ceded personal agency; conversely, it could be argued that the employee uses personal agency to keep a job and, in the process, creates more opportunities for agency outside the work situation. This example demonstrates why listening writers should remember that motives may be more complicated than visible effects suggest, which may affect how listening writers define rhetorical problems and compose responses.

Third, studying the situatedness of personal agency helps listening writers comprehend how personal agency regularly intersects with other types of agencies in different ways. Personal agency may be enhanced or limited by discursive agency, or the power of situated words to influence people's

actions and perceptions. If people are defined as *US citizen*, that classification affords them the right to vote in a US government election; conversely, if people are defined as *not a US citizen* or as *resident alien*, that
classification prevents them from voting in a US government election,
regardless of how much effort the person has put into understanding
candidates' positions on issues or persuading others how to vote. Further, such labelling affects how other people view them, in both positive
and negative ways. Personal agency may be enhanced or limited by cultural agency, too, as when people follow rules of cultural systems such as
schools (showing up at 7:30 am) or national laws (paying taxes) even if
they would prefer not. Personal agency may be enhanced or limited by
material agency, as when food, shelter, writing tools, and personal health
affect how well a person can complete writing assignments for a course.
And personal agency may be affected by all the other agencies simultaneously: for example, even as students may use their personal agency to
consider skipping class, they may also listen to cultural agencies (families,
schools, workplaces) that pressure them to attend by promoting claims
and cultural logics of duty and success, two tropes that carry powerful
discursive agency in US culture. In this way, personal agency may be encouraged or limited by the agencies of other people, discourses, cultural
systems, and material conditions.

WHY STUDY DISCURSIVE AGENCY?

Within US culture, words are often imagined as neutral tools that people
simply learn and use. But in actuality, words are never neutral. They
carry a history accrued through their various uses; this history informs
their definitions and the conventions of their situated usages. Moreover,
words work together in networks called discourses, which are always
situated in and inflected by time and place even as they may travel from
one time and place to another. For listening writers, discursive agency is
the capacity of words and discourses to act upon and to be heard by people or, more specifically, the capacity of words and discourses to socialize
people and to enable a language play within human brains that makes
possible a critical reflection that may interrupt such socializations. Thus,
listening writers may mine discursive agency for their own ends. Given
its situatedness, discursive agency never occurs in a vacuum; it always
works hand in hand with cultural agency. But distinguishing between

the two is important so that discursive agency, or the power of words and discourses, is not rendered invisible.

Studying discursive agency influences listening writers' abilities to analyze rhetorical problems and to compose possible responses. For example, moviegoers have for many years been socialized by a discourse of technological etiquette, which primes them to perform and expect certain behaviors and to respond to violations of this etiquette in particular ways. A moviegoer sitting in a movie theater will probably be prompted during previews to silence her cell phone, and because this prompt is familiar, she will likely comply without giving the action too much thought. If halfway into the film another patron's phone rings, she is likely to get irritated, especially if he answers the call and carries on a loud conversation about the big game. She might even later write an on-line review of the theater, complaining that someone interrupted her movie experience by failing to adhere to basic technological etiquette. In such a situation, she would be using the discourse of technological etiquette to think through this problem and to communicate her concern. Alternatively, if she hears in that loud conversation the other patron mentioning a family emergency, she might conclude that the situation warrants the other patron's breaking the "rules" of the technological etiquette at movies. It all depends.

Helping listening writers think critically about discursive agency is important for the following reasons.

First, studying discursive agency—with attention to words—reminds listening writers that words are not neutral tools that people simply pick up and employ. Instead, words function as tropes: they take their meanings from their contexts, the cultural logics in which they are produced and received, and their relations to other words, all of which change over time and place. For example, in 1920 US the word *professor* would code as male; not so in 2020.

Second, studying discursive agency—with attention to discourses—reminds writers that discourses are networks of words about any topic. There are religious discourses, education discourses, gender discourses, national discourses, sports discourses, philosophical discourses, automobile industry discourses, family discourses, etc. Discourses perpetuate categories that describe the world and ground cultural logics.[14] By studying how multiple discourses socialize people to think and act in certain ways, listening writers learn to track how networks of words are associated with and function within *specific* contexts: for example, studying religious discourses in Catholic churches and in Buddhist sanghas may render both different and similar conclusions about how practitioners should think and behave.

Third, studying discursive agency helps listening writers understand how words accrue meanings within situated discourses. A good example is the words *black* and *white*, which in the US have long signified evil and purity as well as two racial groups. Thanks to Kenneth and Mamie Clark's 1940's "Doll Tests," *Black* and *white* played a crucial role in the 1954 *Brown vs. the Board of Education* decision that rendered unconstitutional the doctrine of "separate but equal" in education ("The Significance"). These tests demonstrated that US children associated negatively with Black dolls but positively with white dolls because they lived in a society where the words *Black* and *white* had accrued negative and positive meanings, respectively. The "Doll Tests" served as evidence, helping the Court determine how racial segregation affected US children's self-esteem. Today within US culture, the terms *Black* and *white* have accrued additional meanings, from the Black Is Beautiful movement that began in the 1960s (Adesina) to the current Black Lives Matter movement. Yet traces of the Doll Tests definitions still haunt US culture; otherwise, these two more recent movements would not be necessary.

Fourth, studying discursive agency also helps listening writers understand that, within discourses, associations between words and meanings are not natural or even inevitable. To appear natural or inevitable, a word's discursively manufactured meanings must be circulated ad nauseum. Take, for example, the words *Mr., Mrs. and Miss.* Though commonly used today, they all have a history. According to the *Oxford English Dictionary* (*OED*), *Mr.* appeared circa 1500 CE to abbreviate *master* and later in the seventeenth-century to abbreviate *mister*, signifying a man who did not hold the rank of knight or above. *Mrs.* and *Miss* both abbreviate *mistress* but differentiate the marital status of women, with *Mrs.* used circa 1500 CE and *Miss* used in the mid- to late-1600s. Adding to this list of sanctioned titles, the *New York Times* announced in 1986 that it would use *Ms.*, a term that had been in play since 1901, so as to offer women an option that mimics *Mr.* in not indicating marital status. Then in 2015, the *New York Times* used *Mx.* as a term for people who identify as *gender nonbinary*, the *OED* followed suit the same year, indicating in its entry that *Mx.* had been in use since 1977.

By recognizing how words and their meanings are not fixed but ever organic, listening writers can track all kinds of words and discourses and determine how this discursive agency may be tapped to enhance[15] or limit their own personal agencies in positive or potentially harmful ways. Again, discursive agency never occurs in a vacuum; it always works hand in hand with cultural agency.

WHY STUDY CULTURAL AGENCY?

Cultural agency is the capacity of cultural systems (political, economic, educational, etc.) via their institutions (government, markets, universities, etc.) and institutional practices (policies, rituals, traditions, events, etc.) to act upon and be heard by people.[16] Cultural systems with their institutions and institutional practices are, of course, built and perpetuated through discourses and the possibilities of discursive agency. Yet studying cultural agency is important: it foregrounds how contexts situate words and discourses, and it clarifies, as Villanueva argues, how "we are—all of us—subject to the systemic" (xviii). That is, individuals are always implicated in larger cultural systems that are mediated by language and through which people's daily lives are structured and socialized. As such, cultural systems and their agencies influence how listening writers think and act as well as how they analyze and compose everyday writing tasks.

One way to study cultural agency is to identify and analyze the workings of culturally-situated discourse communities and their associated discourse conventions.[17]

Discourse communities are groups of people with common goals who use and are socialized by language in similar, though not identical, ways. For example, accountants belong to a professional discourse community whose members use a specialized set of words and discourses to complete their work, so specialized in fact that clients must pay them to translate and advise about terms such as *tax codes, amortization,* and *future value of money.* In addition to professions, examples of discourse communities include nations, political parties, religious groups, ethnic groups, sports teams, sports fans, music lovers, friends, families, etc. The key point is that each person belongs to multiple culturally-situated discourse communities and learns different discourse conventions in each community, code-switching among the different conventions, sometimes with great difficulty and sometimes with great ease.[18]

Discourse conventions are organic "guidelines," not fixed rules, for how members of a discourse community communicate with one another; as such, these conventions distinguish one group from another. Myriad discourse conventions exist. They include, for example, *what* can be said (topics) and not said (silences) as well as *how* something may be said and not said (tone and word choice) and *how* something may be delivered (platform, genre, formatting, sentence style, etc.). Because listening writers already participate in a number of discourse communities (families, friends, work, school, nation, etc.), they learn to track how they and others adapt to using conventions from group to group. Once grasped, this literacy helps listening writers understand that when they talk differently to their bosses and to their friends, they are not being two-faced but, instead, have simply learned to code-switch so as to speak effectively within different discourse communities. Recognizing their and others' code-shifting practices provides listening writers an easy entry point into discussions of rhetorical listening.

Helping listening writers think critically about cultural agency is important for the following reasons.

First, studying cultural agency helps listening writers unpack how cultural systems shape identities. Words and discourses that a culture assigns people affect how people think of themselves and act as well as how other people think of them and act.[19] For example, a newborn baby is given immediate multiple cultural identities simply by being labelled with a series of terms: a *US citizen, African American, male, healthy, middle class, Westerner, one of three siblings in a two-parent family*, and *cute*. These terms with their discursive agency function as cultural identity categories that immediately immerse the baby into cultural systems of nation, race, sex, gender, health, socioeconomic class, region, family, and beauty. Only a few moments old, the baby has done nothing to earn these identities or systemic affiliations. As the baby grows, he learns to negotiate these unearned identities and systems, based on his family's and society's expectations. In addition, he *earns* by his own actions (in relation to others, of course) other identities such as *friend, athlete, college graduate*, and *good son*, which are all associated with situated discourses and systems of friendship, sports, education, and family. And of course, some cultural identity categories may be both unearned and earned; for instance, a person deemed an *Olympic athlete* may have natural talent (unearned) at the same time that she practices intensively to develop that talent (earned) within systems of Olympic training and of gender, to name only two.

Second, studying cultural agency helps listening writers identify how cultural systems shape intersectional identities. In 1991 Kimberlé Crenshaw first published her theory of intersectionality in the *Stanford Law Review* as a means for helping lawyers conceptualize how issues surrounding discrimination, harassment, and violence against women of color were handled in the US legal system; in 2017 she published a book of her collected writings on the topic. The brilliance of her theory is how well it serves her original intent and yet may be extended beyond that intent. For example, the baby from the previous paragraph, though male, is more than just a male. Though a US citizen, he is more than just a US citizen. It is the intersectionity of his identities, earned and unearned, and his experiences within affiliated cultural systems that create the complex human identity that is uniquely his. To identify a person in terms of only one cultural identity category (e.g., male) or only one system (e.g., citizenship) is to reduce the potential of the person and to risk stereotyping.

Third, studying cultural agency helps listening writers pinpoint how cultural systems ascribe scripts for identities. Discourses situated within specific cultural systems socialize people into thinking in certain ways and, thus, performing certain scripts. For example, the script of *US citizen* within the US system of government may encourage, among other things, the performance of voting, following the laws of the land, upholding the rights of others, etc. The script of *African American woman* within the US racial system may encourage, among other things, the performance of taking pride in cultural heritage but, for safety's sake, paying extra attention to how other people perceive them and their families; the script of *African American woman* within our US gender system may further complicate the former. People may perform cultural scripts without realizing it or without recognizing the systems in which they are functioning, as when people order food at a restaurant without thinking about the *customer* script they are performing within a consumer culture. Or people may perform a script consciously, such as when they enter a new, unfamiliar workplace and must learn how to perform as an *employee* within a particular company's culture. Or, they may think about a script only when it is in their best interest to do so, such as when they become reflective about their living habits and adopt the script for a *healthy lifestyle* that is championed within a US medical system, which may be different from that which is championed within a Chinese medical system. Changing words and discourses then is not always simply a case of nominalism, or changing language without changing reality. Instead, changing words and discourses may be a way to generate more inclusive thinking and acting within systems, such as the changes in 2020 US political discourses and the script associated with the position of *Vice President within the systems of US politics, history, and race.*

Fourth, studying cultural agency helps listening writers determine how cultural systems provide a means for people to identify with one another, either knowingly or unknowingly. People may be aware of how they react to words and discourses within cultural systems. For example, shouts of "Go Pack" may energize Green Bay football fans (one discourse community) but irritate Minnesota Viking fans (another discourse community); the chant causes members within each group to knowingly identify with the other members within their group. But in other cases, people may not be aware of their reactions to words and discourses or of systems within which words and discourses function. For example, if a small child is brought up in a home where immigrants are feared, then the child may think that such fear is the normal way to think and feel. And when the child becomes an adult and encounters different discourses and becomes aware of the political and economic systems in which he, she or they and immigrants function, then the child-now-adult must decide whether to reaffirm or interrupt this inherited cultural script of fear.

Fifth, studying cultural agency helps listening writers understand how culturally-situated words and discourses mediate the writers' ways of knowing and being in cultural systems, including how power circulates broadly as well as among personal, cultural, and material agencies. Listeners must learn to identify the discourses they encounter, the discourse communities they and others inhabit (or not), and the discourse conventions they and others employ (or not), including the cultural logics common to different communities and their affiliated systems. Such awareness offers listeners conscious choices when speaking and writing: these choices include whether to continue working within a system and its discourses, whether to revise a system and its discourses, or whether to reject a system and its discourses altogether (although the latter may be more difficult than it first appears). Such choices raise ethical concerns, as evidenced by the arguments in and the reception of the 2021 special edition of *College Eng-*

lish on pluriversal rhetorics grounded in discourses and research methods of decoloniality (Cushman et al, 8).

Developing a listening mindset renders cultural agency visible to listening writers who can then decide how to proceed with a writing task. In the deciding, a listening mindset creates spaces that allow speakers and writers to assert personal agency over cultural agency, but with an awareness of individual and systemic consequences, both positive and negative.

WHY STUDY MATERIAL AGENCY?

Material agency is the capacity and power of objects, places, spaces, bodies, and physical resources to act upon people and be heard. Studying material agency helps listening writers understand how they are implicated in the material and, thus, how material factors influence their analyzing and composing of everyday writing tasks. As Cooper argues, "[p]osthumanism, new materialism, and the nonhuman turn from epistemology to ontology challenge the assumptions that writing is simply a cognitive activity of symbol use" (4).[20] While rhetorical listening maintains a focus on listening in order to understand (an epistemic function), it also acknowledges the constraints and limitations on such knowing, thus positing epistemology, ontology, and ideology as intersecting ways of being/acting/believing in the world of everyday writing.

Helping listening writers think critically about material agency is important for the following reasons.

First, studying material agency challenges listening writers to reflect on how writing tools (objects) affect their writing processes. Listening writers can ask how efficient it would be to write multiple revisions of an essay using a pen or pencil rather than a computer. Maybe a writer has a high-tech stylus for his tablet, and he can write efficiently that way. Imagine, then, having to replace the tablet with an old-fashioned typewriter or with an ancient stylus and wax tablet. How might this change of tools affect writers' writing processes? And how does access to technology affect writers' writing processes as well?

Second, studying material agency challenges listening writers to reflect on how place affects their thinking and writing. Virginia Woolf called attention to this problem for women writers in her 1929 *A Room of One's Own*, where she argues that women need £500 and a room of one's own if they are to have the space and stretches of time and silence needed to imagine and write fiction. Alice Walker in her 1974 "In Search of Our Mothers' Gardens" extends Woolf's argument, calling out the class and racial codings in Woolf's text by asking "What then are we to make of Phillis Wheatley, a slave, who owned not even herself?" and by arguing that traces of a mother's artistry may have been found in her gardens, her art, and her progeny (235). Kimmerer extends the idea of place from garden to ecosystem in terms of how place affects writers' ways of knowing and being in the world. On a field trip to the Great Smoky Mountains with college students, she laments not being able to communicate deep truths to her students: "I had given them so much information, all the patterns and processes laid on so thick as to obscure the most important truth . . . How will people ever care for the fate of moss spiders if we don't teach students to recognize the world as gift?" (221). But on the way down the mountain, the students started singing "Amazing Grace," creating a moment that leads Kimmerer to conclude that deeper understandings of nature may be accessible through different knowledge systems, her epiphany being that "it wasn't naming the source of wonder that mattered, it was wonder itself. Despite my manic efforts and my checklist of scientific names, I knew now that they hadn't missed it all. *Was blind, but now I see.* And they did. And so did I . . . The rush of waterfalls and the silence of mosses have the last word" (222). The students heard these "words," as did Kimmerer, because they were listening to their environment, "receiving the gift with open eyes and open heart" (222). This experience provides Kimmerer with content and a stance for writing her book.

Third, studying material agency challenges listening writers to reflect on how it intersects with other agencies. For example, material agency may work with cultural agency to explain 1) how certain objects 2) organize public spaces in order to 3) encourage cultural values and beliefs that 4) redefine or reaffirm how personal, discursive, and cultural agencies may be performed. For example, in the web article "How the Female Body Evolved in Art," the medium of paint and the delivery platform of the internet combine to present Western artists' renderings of women's bodies in ways that challenge viewers to listen for the cultural values of the artists' times as well as the cultural and personal values haunting their own viewings (Spaggiari).

　　In engaging these four types of agencies, rhetorical listening assumes that listening writers possess *enough* personal agency to choose a listening stance and to be accountable for their actions—that is, for their using certain discourses, for their navigating cultural systems, and for their negotiating material conditions. But at the same time, rhetorical listening assumes that sites of listening are not always equal and, consequently, that the ease of listening is not always equal. Present in such relational and intersectional agencies are competing desires to be heard as well as consequences, both positive and negative, for granting or receiving hearings. At stake is power. To ascertain the power afforded the different agencies, listening writers might ask: In particular situations, which agencies have the power to make their desires heard? How? Why? And how do each of these agencies enhance and/or constrain the other agencies, especially personal agency?

Once listening writers understand how the four agencies—personal, discursive, cultural, and material—may be defined and analyzed as relational and intersectional, it is time to turn to tactics of agency in everyday writing tasks.

WHAT ARE TACTICS OF AGENCY?

The rhetorical concept of agency generates many tactics for rhetorically analyzing how agencies function individually, relationally, and intersectionally. But rhetorical analysis alone will not make effective writers. Listening writers must learn to employ the results of their analyses to compose texts that are rhetorically effective, given the writers' purposes, audiences, and rhetorical situations. Exemplified by sample topics related to the #MeToo movement, the following tactics model how to listen rhetorically to multiple agencies in order to articulate analytical moves and to generate writing for everyday writing tasks.

Tactic #1: Analyze Personal and Discursive Agencies via Intersecting Cultural Identity Categories.

1. Select a person, text or situation as a topic to analyze.

2. Identify five cultural identity categories associated with that topic.

3. Pick one of the identity categories and discuss whether it is earned, unearned, or some combination of the two.

4. Pick a second identity category and discuss how it intersects with the first.

5. Discuss how this intersection complicates your initial understanding of your topic.

Analyzing identity categories associated with people, texts, or situations helps, first, to identify how discursive agency (the power of words, of categories) intersects with cultural agency and, second, to determine whether identities are unearned, earned, or both. For example, consider Tarana Burke as a topic to analyze (#1). In 2006 she founded a "Me Too" movement to call attention to the problems of sexual abuse for underprivileged African American women. This action exemplifies her personal agency being used to address systematic abuse. In October 2017 Alyssa Milano tweeted #MeToo in response to stories of Hollywood sexual harassment/assault, and it went viral on Twitter and then travelled to other social media. When informed of Burke's movement, Milano quickly paid homage to her. Although Milano exerted her personal agency and took advantage of material agency in tweeting on her phone, her tweet also gained power from the discursive agency of Burke's already-existing term *Me Too* as well as the fact that the phrase is a common refrain of identification in daily conversations.

In terms of identity categories, Burke is a woman, an African American, a college graduate, a civil rights activist, and a 2017 *Time* person of the year (#2). While her first two identity categories are initially unearned, she has spent her life taking actions to build pride and agency within these categories and their intersections; her third through fifth identity categories are definitely earned (#3). Her commitment to women's rights explains her creation of the Me Too movement; intersecting that commitment with her commitment to civil rights (#4) helps us understand her vocation and also explains why it was imperative that Milano later tweeted an acknowledgment of Burke's earlier movement and that *Time* selected Burke as a person of the year, so as not to repeat a US cultural pattern of erasing African American women (#5). Because no movement can be all-encompassing, erasures are ever present dangers; for example, how well has the #MeToo movement highlighted harassment of people who identify as LGBTQIA?

Tactic #2: Analyze Cultural Agency via Cultural Logics.

1. Identify a dominant trope (word) associated with a topic (a person, text, or situation) that you are analyzing.

2. Identify two different cultural logics or ways of thinking associated with the dominant trope.

3. In these two cultural logics, analyze (a) what can be said and why and (b) what cannot be said and why.

4. Discuss how laying the two (or more) cultural logics side-by-side generates (or not) a more complex understanding of the topic.

Analyzing competing cultural logics that inform the #MeToo movement demonstrates how cultural agency informs people's everyday lives. Two dominant tropes in the #MeToo movement are *sexual harassment* and *sexual assault* (#1). Two competing cultural logics that surround these terms are patriarchy and feminism (#2): *patriarchy* is a way of reasoning that argues men are superior to women and, thus, society should be organized with power flowing from and through men; *feminism* is a way of reasoning that argues women are equal to men and, thus, society should be organized with equal opportunities, rights, and power for women and men. The #MeToo movement, it could be argued, emerges from a cultural logic of feminism to interrupt a cultural logic of patriarchy. Echoing Burke's 2006 Me Too message, Milano's #MeToo tweet in October 2017 opened up a discursive and cultural space in social media for people to break their silences and to share their harassment and assault stories. As a result, people are now talking about sexual harassment and assault on the news, at work, over drinks, and with family in ways they have not done before (#3).

Corollary questions include: what stories of sexual harassment and assault can and cannot be shared—and why? (#3). What remains unspoken in this social media space of #MeToo are stories of people who are not yet ready to share and stories of people whom society is not yet ready to hear; what remains unwelcome in this cultural space are excuses for the perpetrators; and what remains hard but necessary to discuss in this space are false charges. Interestingly, the #MeTo movement demonstrates that people can agree across cultural logics and work together for a common cause (#4): that is, people who do not usually embrace feminism are joining the chorus of #MeToo, calling for the end of sexual harassment and assault as a basic human right for women and men. While building a coalition with feminists to end this problem, such people are often functioning from a cultural logic of egalitarianism, which is a way of reasoning that argues all people are equal and, thus, society should protect everyone's rights while being blind to gender differences. This cultural logic provides a site of common ground with feminism because it echoes principles of equality in US founding documents, yet this cultural logic also provides a site of suspicion for feminists because the trope *all men* in the founding documents originally meant white male property owners.

By laying the pro's and con's of all these cultural logics side by side, listening writers will gain a deeper understanding of the complexity of #MeToo discourses and actions.

Tactic #3: Analyze Discursive & Cultural Agencies via Cultural Scripts.

1. Identify a prominent discourse present in a text (book, film, tv show).

2. Identify a main trope of that discourse.

3. Analyze the implied definition of that trope.

4. Identify the implied cultural script associated with that trope.

5. Analyze what is encouraged and what is inhibited by this cultural script.

6. Analyze the implications of this script.

7. Repeat with one or two different discourses.

Analyzing discourses of the #MeToo movement shows how discursive and cultural agencies intersect within cultural scripts. This tactic can help listening writers articulate a statement of the problem they want to address. For example, in the #MeToo discourses that emerged on social media (#1), one main trope is the hashtag *#MeToo* (#2). Its implied definition (#3) is that anyone writing it has also experienced some form of sexual harassment or sexual assault and that sharing this information empowers both writers and readers.

The cultural script associated with this hashtag (#4) is that women and men should tweet or post "Me Too" and then share as much or as little information as each feels comfortable doing. What is encouraged in this cultural script is the sharing of survivors' stories, not defenses of abusers (#5). The implications of this script include: #MeToo invites survivors to speak out; in speaking out, survivors and their audiences need not feel ashamed or alone; the volume of responses makes the degree of sexual harassment and assault visible; and this visibility, it is hoped, will expose the secrecy (both personal and systemic) that protects abusers and will thus end sexual harassment and sexual assault (#6).

Of course, if the discourses selected to be analyzed using this tactic were associated not with social media but with Title IX law (legal discourses) or the Promise Keepers (discourses of a men's rights group) (#7), then different rhetorical problems would emerge, especially concerning #MeToo. This tactic is a useful invention strategy because it generates competing perspectives for everyday writing tasks.

Tactic #4: Analyze Material Agency in a Writing Tasks (via Objects and/or Spaces).

1. Identify an object (computer, iPad, hammer, book) or a space (room, city, hiking trail, nation) regularly used for writing.

2. Reflect on how the use of this object or space, particularly on how writers' being in this space affects their thinking and writing process.

3. Determine how the object or space affects a final written product.

4. Discuss how writers gained access to this object or space, whether other people have comparable access, and the implications of both.

5. Analyze the power of this material agency and its impact on other agencies (personal, discursive, cultural).

To understand material agency as it affects writing about the 2017 #MeToo movement, writers should analyze objects such as cell phones and social media platforms. The cell phone (sometimes a computer) was the main object used in this movement to open up a social media space for discussing sexual harassment and assault (#1). A tweet's limit of 280 characters guarantees only brief responses or a string of brief responses, not in-depth, nuanced thinking; however, this technology enables a viral speed for sharing information (#2, #3). Obviously, those who can afford cell phones and computer access are more likely to participate (#4). While the personal agency of truth telling by abused women and men fueled the movement, the material agency of social media to move the message widely and quickly helped. So too did the Twitter's limit on words because slogans like #MeToo, #NeverAgain, #BelieveWomen gained power from being short, catchy, and easily remembered. It is important to note, however, that social media was not the only space for #MeToo discussions: tweeted stories were picked up by newspapers, magazines, cable news, the police, workplaces, etc., and further investigated. So the cultural agency of these institutions and their rituals as well as the material agency of their resources were invoked as well (#5).

Tactic #5: Analyze Intersections of Rhetorical Agencies

1. Select as a topic one person, text, event, or place.

2. Identify how each of the four agencies—personal, discursive, cultural, and material—are manifest in writing about this topic.

3. Explain significant intersections of agencies.

4. Analyze and evaluate the effects of these intersections.

By 2018, the #MeToo movement had gone global, and its impact is best understood in terms of intersecting agencies (#1). The personal agency of Tarana Burke (who first used "Me Too" in a 2006 MySpace post) promoted "empowerment through empathy" among sexually abused women of color. Relationally, the personal agency of Alyssa Milano resurrected the term in a 2017 tweet to ask women who had been "sexually harassed or assaulted" to reply with the words "me too." The discursive agency of the trope *me too* resonated because it invited readers of social media to identify with the *me* in the "me too" and, in the process, identify with one another. The collective me's helped people find the courage to speak out; in the process, they mapped a cultural problem. The cultural agency of the term *me too* became an important factor, too, because the 2017 tweet of a famous white woman actress went viral and initially erased the 2006 term's usage by an African American woman activist. The echoes of the earlier usage were heard, though, and offered an occasion for cultural reflection on whose voices are heard or remembered and why. The material agency of social media became a source for reflection too; the technology afforded a "space" where women could talk with one another, be freed from the need for detailed depositions, and demonstrate the immense numbers affected in the US and globally (#2).

Taken together, these agencies help listening writers understand not just the topic of #MeToo more deeply but also the intersectionality of rhetorical agencies. For example, personal agency is easier to perform when material agencies, such as social media, make speaking out *en masse* both possible and less direct. Discursive agency closely aligns with cultural agency when uses of terms are studied contextually to determine how they function differently at different times for different groups of people across the globe. And personal agencies of people within systems (schools, businesses, governments, etc.) engage cultural agencies of institutions, encouraging both the finetuning and the enforcement of sexual harassment and sexual assault policies (#3, #4).

As this chapter has demonstrated, agency is an important concept and tactic of a modern rhetorical education inflected by rhetorical listening. It makes visible the capacity, willingness, and power of an individual to respond to a writing task as well as the capacity of other people, discourses, cultural systems, and material realities to act upon and influence listening writers' lives and writing tasks. As a concept defined by its multiple iterations, agency holds people accountable for their actions while also accounting for limitations to their own personal agencies. As a set of tactics, agency challenges people to affect change in the world and affords them means for doing so. To affect change, however, listening writers must combine the concept and tactics of agency with an ability to define and negotiate the situations within which multiple agencies and potential changes operate. To that end, the next chapter addresses the concept and tactics of rhetorical situation.

3 Rhetorical Situation

In late summer of 1955, Mamie Till Mobley found herself in one of the most horrific situations possible for a parent: having to decide whether to approve an open or closed casket for the viewing of her murdered son, Emmett Till. On August 28, 1955, this young Black man had been abducted and brutally murdered in Money, Mississippi. His murderers—two white men named Roy Bryant and J. W. Milam—were subsequently acquitted of their crimes, which they later detailed in *Look* magazine under the legal protection of double jeopardy (meaning once they had been declared innocent in court, they could profess their guilt and not be retried for Till's murder). On September 6, 1955, Till's family laid the fourteen-year-old's body to rest in Chicago, Illinois. According to Bryan Stevenson[1] who narrates *Time* magazine's documentary short entitled *The Body of Emmett Till*, Mamie Till Mobley resisted the social conventions of the time and made the "really unorthodox choice of having a funeral with an open casket." She made this decision knowing that her son's grotesquely disfigured body would be unrecognizable both to those who knew him and those who did not: "she told the funeral director, 'Let the people see what I've seen.'" ("Emmett Till | David Jackson 1955"). She wanted funeral-goers to bear witness to what had happened to her son.

To broaden the audience for this witnessing, Mamie Till Mobley invited David Jackson to the funeral home to photograph her son's body and publish the pictures in *Jet* magazine. These harrowing pictures circulated across the US and served as a catalyst for the Civil Rights Movement. As the Mississippi Development Authority later noted, Till's murder and funeral gave "'Rosa Parks the strength to sit down and Reverend Martin Luther King Jr. the courage to stand up'" (Tell 1). But the influence went beyond major Civil Rights icons. As Till Mobley later claimed, "When people saw what had happened to my son, men stood up who had never stood up before . . ." (*Emmett Till Legacy*). Indeed, the pictures of Till's mutilated body redefined the rhetorical situation that characterized racial politics in that mid-century US moment.

The redefined rhetorical situation of US racial politics was made possible by a confluence of agencies in the moments immediately following Emmett Till's death. Mamie Till Mobley marshalled her personal agency to challenge systemic racism through the memorialization of her son's murder.[2] By permitting the publication of Jackson's photos in *Jet*, she helped expose the coarse brutality of racial violence associated with the US's dominant cultural logic of white supremacy. Her willingness to expose the brutality of Till's murder photographically also served as a call to action for cultural institutions and viewers to employ their own agencies. On the national front, US institutions, communities, and citizens were given an opportunity to challenge white supremacy, to replace it with a more just cultural logic about race, and to act for justice. On the home front, families across the country were given the choice to look at the pictures and to address the saturation of racial violence throughout the country, not ignore it. For white families who had previously turned a blind eye toward racial violence, the wide circulation of Till's images made it impossible for them to look away, impossible "to stay indifferent, to stay neutral" ("The Body"), at least in that moment.[3] For BIPOC families who had been victims of racial violence for centuries, the wide circulation of the *Jet* photographs served as proof of their claims. What also made Till's experience so catalytic was the material agency of the technologies of photographs and magazine circulation. His bloated, unrecognizable body was literally placed before everyone's eyes.

This redefined rhetorical situation of midcentury racial politics may be understood more deeply by laying these agencies surrounding Emmett Till's murder alongside the histories that haunt it. Tragically, his mother's resistance to his murder at the hands of white racists did not occur in a vacuum, for witnessing racial violence was not new. In the late nineteenth-century noted Black journalist Ida B Wells had written in *Southern Horrors* and other articles about the then-present US lynchings as well as the long US history of white people's lynching Black men, women, and families.[4] From a 2022 location, writers may extend Wells's map of historical hauntings, including the time since Emmett Till's murder. In 2019, rhetorical scholar Ersula Ore updated Wells's history in *Lynching: Violence, Rhetoric, and American Identity*, including contemporary iterations. And in 2020, witnesses of George Floyd's death circulated online videos that went viral, including the nine minutes and twenty-nine seconds he was held down with a white police officer's knee on his neck.

To describe how the history of Emmett Till and the history of the Civil Rights Movement more generally are organized rhetorically, Dave Tell offers the term *ecology of memory* (*Remembering* 5). This term, Tell argues, challenges distinctions between history and memory because "both are little more than the selective appropriation and recirculation of narratives of Till's death" (31). In this way, the term *ecology of memory* implies that all rhetorical situations involve memory (and its "connotations of impermanence") and also that all memory is history and all history, memory (31). Further, Tell's term champions the "ecology of memory and the rhetorical power of place" (31), making an argument for "rethink[ing] the role of place" (32). According to Tell, the ecology of public memory about Emmett Till is composed of an "interanimating force of race, place, and commemoration" (5). Thus, the US's commemorating the place where Emmett Till died entails naming everyday sites like white-owned grocery stores (where Till shopped prior to his abduction) and everyday occurrences like speaking with someone from another race (as Till did before his murder). Tell's argument about rethinking the rhetorical role of place echoes claims made by Malea Powell in her CCCC Chair's address where she defines *place* as follows: "I mean a place that has been practiced into being through the acts of storied making, where the past is brought into conscious conversation with the present and where—through those practices of making—a future can be imagined" ("Stories" 388).[5]

Rhetorical listening complements Tell's and Powell's ideas of place by positing history as an ever expanding past comprised of both public, private and unstated memories, with a past imagined as "both a cultural structure and an individual embodiment of that structure, with the embodiment being different in different people depending on their experiences and identifications within the cultural structure" (Ratcliffe 110). In this way, people construct and experience the past in ways that "not only identify some of our identifications [especially our troubled identifications such as racism] but also find ourselves accountable to ourselves and to others not for the *then* [e.g., Till's murder and the systems that enabled it] but for the *then-that-is-now*" (111). These concepts of place-based ecologies of memory and accountability join the continued fight for racial justice, a fight whose purposes are to honor Till, to memorialize the people who were murdered before and after him in the name of race, and to protect the very real people alive today who are threatened by racial violence.

With an ecological view of rhetorical listening's *then*-that-is-now, listening writers may analyze the rhetorical situations of their rhetorical problems (such as how to commemorate Emmett Till) by including the public memories of the place and also the private and the unstated ones that haunt the rhetorical problems (such as how discourses of race, lynching, gender, etc., haunt Emmett Till's murder). Listening writers may also analyze the rhetorical situations of their own places of writing, recognizing the importance of their own places and all the memories that historicize and haunt the task at hand. This focus on historicization and unstated hauntings of rhetorical situations is one argument for the necessity of research in most writing tasks. Analyzing rhetorical situations enables listening writers to connect to the pasts, the presents, and the futures they can imagine.

Rhetorical listening benefits from engaging rhetorical situations as a rhetorical concept and tactic because the engagement not only deepens considerations of context and history but also raises questions of politics, ethics, and action. To understand and potentially alter rhetorical situations for more fair and just outcomes, listening writers must, as W. E. B. Dubois urges in *The Souls of Black Folk*, confront their existing discursive practices "with careful inquiry and patient openness to conviction" (48). By approaching rhetorical situations with an open stance, listening writers may stand under the discourses of public memories that historicize rhetorical problems as well as under the private and unstated memories haunting them, allowing considerations of all these discourses to "wash over, through, and around us and then letting them lie there to inform our politics and ethics" (Ratcliffe 28).

To demonstrate how and why the concept of rhetorical situation is important to a rhetorical education grounded in rhetorical listening, this chapter defines rhetorical situation as a rhetorical concept, explores why it should be studied, and offers model tactics for analyzing and composing.

WHAT IS RHETORICAL SITUATION AS
A RHETORICAL CONCEPT?

Traditionally, the term *rhetorical situation* refers to contexts that frame everyday writing practices. For classical Greek rhetoricians, context was theorized as *kairos*, a term that signifies not just an argument's time and place but also its "timeliness, appropriateness, decorum, symmetry, [and] balance" (Pantelides). For theorists of modern rhetoric,[6] context has been theorized via a chicken-and-egg debate about rhetorical situations, with Lloyd Bitzer arguing that an external situation "invites" responses (5)[7] and Richard Vatz counterarguing that people's interpretative lenses determine whether they "choose or do not choose" to construct situations and exigences for writing (160).[8] By focusing on how a rhetor either responds to or constructs situations, both Bitzer's and Vatz's concepts champion rhetorical agency but reduce it mostly to personal agency, with the writer being the respondent to or constructor of situations.

To understand the implications of this focus, consider again the work of Ida B. Wells. When in the 1890s this Black journalist wrote anti-lynching pamphlets and editorials, she was invoking her personal agency to protest white people's agency to lynch as vigilantes as well as the discursive, cultural, and material agencies of lynching as they existed at that time.[9] Bitzer's lens might invite writers to argue that Wells is responding to specific situations; thus, they would focus on the lynching scenes about which she writes, which of course are important. Vatz's lens might invite writers to argue that Wells constructed the situations for her writing by selecting certain scenes to emphasize, narrate, and offer evidence for her argument; thus, writers would focus on the scenes Wells created via her writing. But this argument about whether situations invite rhetoric or whether rhetoric invites situations is a false binary of cultural logics (objectivist vs. phenomenological). Both offer elements of truth. And that is why rhetorical situations and their attendant agencies are complicated.

Indeed, other rhetorical theorists have complicated the personal agency that undergirds Bitzer's and Vatz's concepts of rhetorical situation. To shift this focus from personal agency and invite discursive agency into the conversation, Barbara Biesecker argues that deconstruction provides a productive means for thinking about/with/in rhetorical situations: released from a "logic of influence" (110), rhetorical situations are imagined as discursive fields of possibilities in which unstable subjects (writers and audiences) play and in which "identities and social relations" are always already being formed and deconstructed (126). To shift this conversation to invite considerations of cultural and material agencies, Jenny Edbauer 2005 article and Dave Tell's 2019 book offer the concept of *ecology*.[10] Edbauer reimagines rhetorical situations as "rhetorical ecologies" (9)—a concept that "radically revises" the "one-way flow" of situation-to-writer (Bitzer) or writer-to-situation (Vatz):

> Rather than replacing the rhetorical situation models that we have found so useful, however, an ecological augmentation adopts a view toward the processes and events that extend beyond the limited boundaries of elements. One potential value of such a shifted focus is the way we view counter-rhetorics, issues of cooptation, and strategies of rhetorical production and circulation. Moreover, we can begin to recognize the way rhetorics are held together trans-situationally, as well as the effects of trans-situationality on rhetorical circulation. (20)

Thus, Edbauer argues that in everyday writing, "rhetorical ecologies are already spatially, affectively, and conceptually in practice" and focus on public creations of discourses and attention to *"material effects and processes"* within systems (23). What Tell's concept of *ecology of memory* brings to Edbaurer's is the idea of memories and commemoration, those public memories and the private and unstated memories that commemorate a place and time. What rhetorical listening brings to this conversation about ecology is a consideration of multiple agencies and their identifications as well as a consideration of the ecological *then*-that-is-now.

Drawing on these scholarly conversations, this chapter offers a concept of rhetorical situation that attends to Edbauer's concept of *ecology* as a means of complicating Bitzer's and Vatz's concepts of rhetorical situations, even as it honors their contributions; this chapter also attends to Tell's concept of *ecology of memory* as a way to think about the *then*-that-is-now. As such, a concept of rhetorical situation may be imagined as a scene where this *then*-that-is-now is analogized to experiencing the Grand Canyon, where an observer can stand at its edge, be encompassed by the scene, and feel both awe and small. Such a scene invites the observer to appreciate the grandeur of the canyon as well as the observer's small place within it and within the cosmos scaled large. Simultaneously, the scene invites the observer to appreciate the visible, physical sedimentation of the past written in the walls of the canyon as well as its hauntings by the peoples, discourses, cultures, and material agents no longer readily visible.

Rhetorical situations, then, instead of being flattened sites, are deeply sedimented scenes with hauntings. As such, rhetorical situations may be imagined as 1) grounded in rhetorical problems, 2) grounded also in writers' moments of writing about the problems, 3) marked by audiences' concerns, 4) haunted by public, private, and unstated histories and potential futures, 5) scaled for various scopes of analyses, and 6) informed by multiple and often competing agencies (personal, discursive, cultural, material) that delimit discursive actions.

If rhetorical listening demands that agency be imagined not just as personal but also as discursive, cultural, and material, then a more complicated (read: sedimented and haunted) concept of rhetorical situation must recognize a multitude of scenes, sometimes overlapping, sometimes compressed, which make a discursive place for performing all these agencies as well as for negotiating their hauntings. For example, when the rhetorical situations associated with Wells's journalism are imagined from a rhetorical listening stance, they may include 1) the scenes of the lynchings that some whites had instigated (a material reality) and that had inspired Wells's reporting; 2) the scenes of Wells's own writing as well as the scenes of all the agencies in the situations, including all their purposes; 3) the scenes of multiple audiences such as her readers reading (then and now), including other writers writing in response to her (then and now); 4) scenes of pubic, private, and unstated hauntings of previous lynchings and an imagined future that does not repeat them; 5) the scenes scaled from one instance to national patterns across time; and 6) the scenes of discourse, culture, and material reality that generated competing cultural logics of lynching[11] *either* as a viable trope and a viable act for lynchers who embraced vigilante justice and for authorities who looked the other way *or* as an unacceptable trope and heinous act for those who deemed lynching murder.

Thus, sedimented and haunted, rhetorical situations include the following seven elements. These elements may intersect and be prioritized in different ways for different writing tasks:

1. *Exigences.* Exigences, as Bitzer noted, are rhetorical problems that demand a response in speech or writing (5).[12] These rhetorical problems may involve a person's action, discourses, cultural patterns, or material events that writers believe need to be reinforced, revised, or interrupted.

Take, for example, the Keystone XL Pipeline. Those in favor of the Pipeline's development define their rhetorical problem in terms of economics and national security, specifically the need for billions of dollars in potential tax revenue as well as a reduced reliance on foreign oil. The rhetorical problem for Indigenous peoples, however, is how to convey to audiences with decision-making power their concern that the pipeline poses a legal, environmental, and sacred threat to ancestral lands. And the rhetorical problem for President Biden is how to use the power of his office to address this issue (he issued an executive order to revoke permits for constructing this pipeline).

2. *Times and places.* Times and places are interrelated, referring to situated moments that are always located in memory because as soon as a present moment is observed, it is rendered historical, existing in the observer's immediate past and subsequently in some distant past. In either case, this situated moment is accessible only through memory. Such situated moments are where rhetorical problems are located, where speaking or writing about them occurs, where audiences receive information, and where sedimentary histories and potential futures haunt the previous three. The time President Biden issued the executive order banning the pipeline construction was on January 20, 2021, the first day he assumed the office of the US President, indicating the importance he placed on the problem. The sedimentary history that led to this order and haunted his signing include white land grabs, white-Indigenous land treaty negotiations and renegotiations, previous pipeline negotiations, US-Canadian deals, etc. The place of his signing was the Oval Office in Washington DC, a symbol of power; however, the places he affected were much broader, given that this executive order stopped work on the pipeline in a number of US states from Montana to Texas to Illinois and also triggered the dissemination of information via news outlets in both domestic and international locations.

3. *Multiple agents.* Agents in rhetorical situations include a) human and non-human actors associated with the scene, b) speakers or writers as observer-participants in the scene, c) everyone (including institutions) involved in the production of the speaking and writing at the scene, d) existing discourses available at the scene, and e) systems (gender, race, political, economic, etc.) within which the aforementioned all function. Moreover, these agents may be present at the scene or implied by the scene but do their work behind the scene. For example, to produce the

scene of President Biden's signing an executive order on TV, many people had to have worked behind the scenes to shape the content. A number of Indigenous activists lobbied against the permits issued by former President Trump, questioning both their legal and moral integrity. The State Department worked alongside President Biden's team to review his predecessor's permit and determined it to be not in the best interest of the nation. And Prime Minister Justin Trudeau had to respond to President Biden's executive order because the permit had been issued to the Canadian government. In addition, the television signing invited into the scene other agents such as other politicians, TV production people, communication staff, reporters, political advisers, legal precedent, etc. While writers cannot address all agents in any rhetorical situation, they can keep in mind that there is always more to the story than what they are focusing on and then make their writerly decisions accordingly.

4. *Multiple purposes.* A purpose in rhetorical situations is an *outcome* encouraged by a) speakers and writers, b) institutions, c) existing discourses and/or d) systems. Most situations entertain more than one purpose with some being prioritized by different agents as more important than others. Purposes can take the form of *projections*, as when a person says, "I intend to take responsibility for the harm that I have caused you," projecting on the audience the feeling of having been harmed. They can take the form of *rationalizations*, as when a person says, "I did not mean to cause you harm." And they can take the form of *inferences*, as when a person observes, "I think he was not aware of his underlying motivation to cause harm." Regardless of its form, purpose is judged not in terms of *intent* but in terms of *effect*. When President Biden signed the executive order, he invoked purposes associated with different sites—for example, his individual intent, the institution of the Presidency, his political party, and discourses and systems already in play. Such purposes are measured according to their effects: to perform personal and party values; to use the power of his office responsibly; to condemn and redress illegal issuing of government permits; to curb dangerous effects of climate change; to show respect for Indigenous peoples and their ancestral lands that were disturbed by the project; and to reinforce the value of science for decision-making about adapting to environmental change.

5. *Multiple audiences.*[13] Audiences include the interrelated addressed and invoked audience roles described by Lisa Ede and Andrea Lunsford (165–66). For addressed audiences who live outside the text, Ede and

Lunsford stipulate six roles (self, friend, colleague, critic, mass audience, and future audience). For invoked audiences who function as traces within a text, the scholars stipulate the same six roles. Although more than six roles may be imagined for each of these two audience categories (addressed and invoked), listening writers may benefit from considering these categories as long as they also recognize two things: one, they are mediating their addressed audiences through their own listening at particular times and places even as, two, they are constructing invoked audiences within their own texts at particular times and places. Because, as Bitzer claims, some audience roles may have more power than others to solve problems, listening writers may prioritize some roles so that they are addressed and invoked in a particular writing task even as other roles may haunt the writing or the final written text. Because some audience roles overlap, listening writers may need to negotiate these lines that blur. Such audience concerns are present in President Biden's writing his executive order. He and his writers/advisers had to determine how different addressed audiences—for example, Indigenous peoples, leaders of other nations, citizens of other nations, scientists across the world, businesses with legal and economic interests in the project, and economic systems (such as the stock market)—might interpret the executive order differently and, thus, what they might want or need to hear from him in his written text. The resulting conclusions and their priorities in turn inform writerly decisions made by Biden's writing team. These conscious decisions (as well as unconscious ones) inform the ways that audiences are invoked and addressed in the executive order.

6. *Constraints.*[14] Constraints, as Bitzer noted, are discourses or objects that hinder decision-making and actions when speaking and writing (8). For listening writers, constraints may be their or their audiences' personal resistance, a lack of a lexicon or methods for writing about the rhetorical problem, the cultural systems in which they function, or even to material objects. For example, some constraints that President Biden faced when producing his executive order include: dissatisfaction from laborers hired to work on the Keystone XL pipeline; formal and political expectations associated with executive orders from the President of the United States; cultural logics associated with the dangers of climate change; the poten-

tial of deteriorated foreign and economic relations between the US and Canada; and so on.

7. *Objects and spaces.* Objects and spaces are the physical or material surroundings that influence everyday speaking and writing tasks. Although they may function as exigences or constraints, objects and spaces are important enough to emphasize on their own because they can, singly or in concert with others, influence rhetorical situations. For listening writers, such influence is key to understanding how effective writing works. Because all objects are associated with histories that either facilitate or prevent listening, listening writers should track how objects and spaces are haunted by memories. For example, the executive order is an object itself, a historical document that serves as evidence about the pipeline decision. Its visual image on TV concretizes President Biden's action. His signing the order and our reading it depend, in part, on the objects/spaces associated with his signing (such as broadcast equipment, televisions, computers, webpages, his desk, and even his clothes) and also the objects/spaces associated with our reading or listening to reports of the signing (such as our computers, smartphones, radios, cars, living rooms). Questions that haunt objects/spaces are, for example, ones of access, quality, and ethics.

While all seven elements of rhetorical situations are probably present in each everyday writing task, listening writers must learn to navigate these sedimentary elements and to choose which ones should be addressed, invoked, or unstated in particular times and places.

WHY STUDY RHETORICAL SITUATIONS?

Studying rhetorical situations[15] from a listening stance helps writers explain how sedimentary scenes and their hauntings influence everyday writing tasks, which, in turn, helps writers to analyze and to write more effectively. When negotiating comfortable scenes or rhetorical situations, listening writers do not have to think too hard about what to include and what to omit in their writing for their audiences because they are, to invoke a common metaphor, preaching to the choir. But when desiring to have the choir think beyond their own songs or when negotiating uncomfortable scenes or rhetorical situations where competing perspectives seem to be at an impasse, listening writers may benefit from studying rhetorical situations.

Helping listening writers think critically about rhetorical situations is important for the following reasons.

First, identifying individual elements of a rhetorical situation (such as agents) helps listening writers explain why a situation is uncomfortable, an important move if a situation is later to be mediated and negotiated. Consider, for example, a classroom scene from a *New Yorker* cartoon with two agents in conflict with one another: a white teacher is standing in front of her desk holding a student paper; a white student named Paige stands opposite with her backpack on, sulkily crossing her arms; the teacher is saying, "I'm sorry, Paige, but grades are based on the quality of the writing, not on your Klout score." This classroom scene represents an uncomfortable conflict between these two actors wherein the student's folded arms suggest that the conversation has reached an impasse. One reason for this impasse is that each actor is functioning from a different definition of *good writing*. Paige defines *good writing* in terms of its relevance in social media—hence, the appeal to her Klout score, which measures the level of influence a social media post has on its audience: the higher the score, the more relevant the post. Paige's teacher defines *good writing* in terms of the academic criteria used to grade all students' work. The teacher's definition and resistance to Paige's definition is a problem for Paige because, even if she is forced to revise her essay, she will not be persuaded that her teacher's view is correct. Paige's definition and resistance is a problem for her teacher because Paige is refusing to learn the literacy skills of making one's writing appropriate to different situations, whether academic or social media.

Second, identifying intersecting elements of rhetorical situations (such as agents and exigences) also helps listening writers to understand competing cultural logics in play in any situation. For example, though both *actors* in this cartoon (the teacher and the student) are functioning from the *exigence* of wanting Paige to succeed in her assignment, their competing cultural logics of success shape their debate. Paige desires to succeed in school, as evidenced by her wanting her teacher to raise her grade. If Paige succeeds in school, so a common cultural logic goes, then she is more likely to succeed in her future profession and find happiness in her personal life. To address her situation, she knowingly or not draws on this existing cultural logic. Simultaneously, however, Paige desires to succeed in her social media network, as evidenced by the reference to her Klout score. According to this cultural logic of social impact, the more relevant a person's social media posts, the more the person is identified as a trust-worthy source of information or entertainment. The competing ways of reasoning about success appear on the surface contradictory but can be reconciled, at least a bit, by reflecting on different situations for writing that engage discourses of school and social media.

Third, understanding the competing perspectives and cultural logics that haunt rhetorical situations helps listening writers devise tactics that yield more effective responses to specific audiences. For example, Paige's teacher's know-ing how exigences of success influence Paige's perspective and motiva-tions may help the teacher address Paige more effectively. By understand-ing Paige's perspective and motivations, the teacher may quickly discover that Paige's frustration is more complicated than not earning a high grade and that Paige is motivated by cultural logics about educational success, by her parents, by her social network, and by her sense of identity as a good student and a good social media influencer. By understanding how these factors motivate Paige's actions, the teacher can decide on the best way to counter Paige's argument: in other words, the teacher can resist the impulse to simply assert her authority and force Paige to follow the rules stated in the teacher's own terms. Instead, the teacher could find ways to help Paige respond effectively to her overlapping exigences while still teaching the importance of code-switching for writing in different situations and for determining what makes a piece of writing persuasive given the situation in which it is distributed.

Fourth, understanding their own rhetorical situations also help listening writ-ers generate more effective responses to their audiences. For example, what is the teacher's perspective and motivation? Is she simply on a power trip in this situation to assert her criteria over Paige's? An argument could be made along these lines. But power might not be her only motivation. Per-haps she feels pressure to use her authority to maintain school standards, to grade equitably among students in the class, to teach according to the best practices in her field, and so on. She also probably feels pressure to maintain a relationship with Paige because administrators demand good working relationships between teachers and students. Regardless, the concept of rhetorical situation may help listening writers to become more self-aware in ways that make them, in turn, more aware of others.

Fifth, such self-awareness may help listening writers help audiences become more aware of writers' rhetorical situations. For example, because the teacher is the adult in this situation and is being charged with educating students, it is incumbent upon her to articulate her points to Paige in a way that Paige can actually hear them. She might help Paige recognize that the teacher's perspective ought not to be disregarded as a calloused, unfair use of authority. Like Paige, the teacher's actions are shaped by institutional and cultural pressures that, in many ways, are out of her control. Yet, if the teacher can help Paige articulate all the points above, then they will have mapped a much larger terrain for negotiation than they initially had.

When listening writers and their audiences map a larger terrain for negotiation, they not only better understand competing perspectives in rhetorical situations but also may find places of common ground while simultaneously recognizing the "coercive function of common ground" (Ratcliffe 58).[16] This understanding and recognition is an incredibly important lesson to learn if listening writers want to compose effective texts. Why? Because being an effective writer is not always about simply expressing oneself clearly or writing the best formal argument; rather, being an effective writer is more often about demonstrating an aware-ness of the complexities in any given rhetorical situation for all actors and audiences involved. This awareness can help listening writers more frequently imagine and compose win-win responses.

With such awareness of rhetorical situations, listening writers can an-alyze and compose not just how overlapping exigences function but also how time/places, agents, purposes, audiences, constraints, and objects/spaces affect their audiences, and thus, their own writing. The sample tactics below are designed to help listening writers employ these seven elements of rhetorical situations to create effective responses to everyday rhetorical problems and writing tasks.

WHAT ARE TACTICS FOR RHETORICAL SITUATIONS?

Rhetorical situations suggest the following tactics for listening writers to employ when analyzing sedimentary, haunted scenes while compos-ing everyday writing tasks. These five tactics are, of course, not the only ones associated with rhetorical situations; they are models. Indeed, writ-ers might create tactics of their own. To illustrate how these five tactics work, the following discussion focuses on the topic of the domestic at-tack on the US Capitol on January 6, 2021.

Tactic #1: Analyze how a rhetorical situation has definable, overlapping, and evolving purposes grounded in different cultural logics.

1. Identify a rhetorical situation associated with a text, a person, or a cultural event that you want to analyze.

2. List cultural logics performed by actors in the rhetorical situation.

3. Determine the purposes of the actors within their cultural logics.

4. Analyze the actors' purposes in light of their probable audiences.

5. Determine multiple consequences of the actors' purpose(s) being achieved in this rhetorical situation.

During a joint session of Congress held on January 6, 2021, US citizens led a domestic attack on the US Capitol. Marching to the Capitol from a "Rally to Save America," the rioters broke across police barriers and stormed the Capitol building, targeting people and vandalizing offices, such as the one occupied by House Speaker Nancy Pelosi. They also assaulted police officers and reporters, illegally occupied the Senate floor, and posed for pictures (#1). In this rhetorical situation, the two dominant cultural logics at play were those of rioters and legislators: rioters believed that the November 2020 Presidential election had been "stolen," and legislators believed that the election was valid and should be certified (#2), although as is the case with cultural logics associated with groups, not all members within each group, whether rioters or legislators, agreed with each other on every detail.[17]

As desired outcomes, purposes are used by actors in a rhetorical situation to justify or explain their actions to their audiences and to themselves, and their rhetorical projects are judged by audiences and history on how principled the purposes are and how successfully their intent becomes an effect. The main purpose within the rioters' cultural logic was stated in their chant, "Stop the Steal," which indicates the perpetrators' belief that they had witnessed a corrupt election process and needed to march on the Capitol to persuade the Senate to correct the results ("Pro-Trump"). The main purpose within the legislators' cultural logic was seen in their action to certify the election and in their comments about their Constitutional duty, including Vice President Pence's claim that he was not empowered by the Constitution to stop the certification (Haberman and Karni) (#3). On the day of the Capitol attack, the intended purposes of each group played only to the choirs because the cultural divide between these two groups often prevented them from hearing one another: rioters felt the certification was illegal, due to the defeated candidate's calling the election illegal; the majority of legislators felt the election and their certification of it were legal actions, due to state governmental oversight of the elections and due to legal precedent (#4).

The consequences of this divide's hauntings are multiple. The majority political party may have to go it alone and forego unity; families may have to forego discussing politics; advertising campaigns such as the Jeep/Bruce Springsteen Super Bowl ad may take advantage of this divide economically even as the ad calls to end it. On the other hand, pragmatic politicians who actually want to get work done and deem the divide bad for the country might actually look for ways to find a common ground of dual purposes that could be translated into concrete action and effects (#5).

Tactic #2: Analyze competing perspectives in terms of definable and overlapping exigences that are grounded in different cultural logics.

1. Select a rhetorical situation associated with a text, a person, or a cultural event that you want to analyze.

2. Identify competing actors associated with this rhetorical situation.

3. Determine the exigences associated with the competing perspectives of the rhetorical situation (i.e., the problems associated with people, institutions, or discourses that demand an urgent response).

4. Connect the exigences associated with the competing actors to the broader cultural logics that organize the rhetorical situation.

5. Evaluate how such exigences and cultural logics shape responses to the situation from actors and audiences.

To understand the attack on the US Capitol as a rhetorical situation from the perspectives of a spectrum of US citizens (#1), listening writers may identify competing groups weighing in on this situation. For example, four groups could be addressed: rioters, advocates for the Black community, Republicans who condemn the attack and hold former President Trump responsible for it, and Republicans who condemn the attack but do not hold the former president responsible (#2). To determine the exigences associated with the different groups, listening writers may identify problems associated with people, institutions, or discourses that demand an urgent response. For rioters, one exigence was the January 6 deadline for certifying the election. For advocates for the Black community, one exigence was the visuals of police treatment of white rioters compared to previous visuals of police treatment of Black protesters. For Republicans who hold the former president responsible for the attacks, one exigence is defending the Constitution's separation of powers and their party's conservative principles. For Republicans who do not hold the former president responsible, one exigence is the continued success of their party and the loyalty of its base (#3).

Listening writers may connect the groups' exigences to broader cultural logics in order to understand how these exigences are reasoned about and acted upon (#4) and to evaluate the resulting responses (#5).

First, if, as the rioters argued, the election process was corrupt and if the US Government, which is charged with safeguarding the process, certified the states' results without considering rioters' concerns, then the rioters would use aggression and violence to draw attention to and redress the perceived corruption. They assumed that their aggression should be proportional to the severity of the perceived corruption, that concerned citizens should assert their will on government procedures when the procedures are perceived to be unfair, and that political strength is best articulated in terms of physical threat. Such violent actions and assumptions would seem valid within rioters' cultural logic but probably not sound as reasonable in the other three cultural logics.

Second, advocates for the Black community such as Lebron James have argued that the Capitol attack signified that Black Americans "live in two Americas" (J. West). If, as he reasoned, Black men and women had believed that a presidential election had been corrupt and if they had protested such corruption with aggression proportional to the mostly white "Save America" rioters, then the Black protestors would have been exposed to much greater levels of counterforce, and the country would have witnessed considerably more violence. James's unstated assumption is that histories of violence against BIPOC peoples haunt US past and present. James's cultural logic would be rejected within the cultural logics of rioters and, probably, of Republican defenders of President Trump; however, it might be given a hearing within the cultural logic of Republicans who hold the former president responsible for the attacks.

Third, the minority of the Republican party who condemned the attacks and publicly blamed former President Trump for inciting them, such as Congresswoman Jaime Herrera-Beutler, have argued that the former president's actions warranted impeachment because they violated the US Constitution and compromised the values of the Republican party (Johnson). The unstated assumptions here are that words and processes matter and that elected officials are responsible for safeguarding the integrity of the US Constitution and preserving the organizing values of a political party, even if such a responsibility makes one unpopular with the base. This reasoning and action would be rejected by those functioning within the cultural logics of rioters and of Republicans defending the former president; however, this reasoning and action would probably be given a hearing by advocates for the Black community.

The majority of Republicans who condemned the attacks but did not blame President Trump for inciting them, such as Lindsey Graham, have argued that a process question (Can a former president be impeached?) precludes addressing the question of the former president's culpability (Did he incite the riots in ways that merit impeachment?) (Rutz). This reasoning and action would be seen as rational and as a skilled political maneuver within this cultural logic and even within the rioters' cultural logic; while other cultural logics might also recognize this reasoning as a political maneuver, they would deem it at best a dodge and at worst a political capitulation to the Trumpist wing of the Republican party.

Tactic #3: Analyze how a rhetorical situation has a definable time and place that is both sedimentary and haunted.

1. Identify a rhetorical situation associated with a text, a person, or a cultural event that you want to analyze.

2. Determine specific times and places associated with this rhetorical situation.

3. Identify the sediment and hauntings of those times and places.

4. Reflect key terms that mark the times and places.

5. Analyze how the times and places of the rhetorical situation explain the actions that unfold within it.

Prior to the Capitol attack, rioters met in front of the White House in Washington, DC, on January 6, 2021, and were addressed by former

President Trump at a "Save America" rally (#1, #2). The sedimentary and haunted elements of that time and place that made the subsequent attack on the Capitol possible include the Bill of Rights' assurance of free speech and the right to assemble, the previous year spent prepping Trump followers with the idea that a lost election would be a stolen election, the rise of social media as a forum for disseminating conspiracy theories, etc. (#3). The key terms in the rally and attack are those that encouraged rioters to "Save America," "stop the steal" and "take back our country . . . with strength" (Vallejo). Another key term is the one referring to the people who attacked the Capitol: were they *protesters* exercising their Constitutional rights or *rioters* illegally entering a secured national building to interrupt a Constitutional process for certifying an election in hopes of overturning the election's result? (#4). It could be argued that *protesters* attended the rally at the White House and marched down Pennsylvania Avenue to the Capitol but became *rioters* when they broke glass around 2 pm to storm the Capitol building, which was not deemed secure until after 5 pm (Leatherby et al) (#5).

Tactic #4: Analyze actors, both present and implied, that affect how actions are imagined and implemented in a rhetorical situation.

1. Identify a rhetorical situation associated with a text, a person, or a cultural event that you want to analyze.

2. List the agents present in this rhetorical situation.

3. List the agents implied in this rhetorical situation.

4. Analyze how the different actors in a rhetorical situation either make possible or limit actions.

At the January 6th US Capitol riot (#1), actors actually present at the rally scene consisted of former President Trump, his staff, the "Save America" rally organizers, invited speakers, and Trump supporters, including but not only alt-right extremist groups such as the Proud Boys, the Three Percenters, and the Oath Keepers. Actors actually present at the Congressional scene were Trump supporters who had marched from the rally to the Capitol, reporters from the Associated Press who covered the events, members of the US Congress, their staff and families, former Vice President of the United States Mike Pence, and the US Capitol Police as well as the Metropolitan Police Department (#2), with videos of the police capturing their heroic actions in the face of a mob who out-numbered them.

Given the violence of the riot, actors implied by the Capitol scene included a wide range of national and international viewing audiences. Most pertinent to the rioters were US citizens who were not present at the rally but were nevertheless persuaded by the false claims about election fraud made by the former president. Other implied actors also included US citizens who voted for President Biden, election volunteers, officials who certified the ballots, US citizens who did not vote during the election but may have a passing interest in US politics, and future generations of US voters (#3).

A focus on the rioters demonstrates how certain actors make actions possible or impossible. The us-versus-them nature of the former president's discourses about election fraud precluded any listening across political party lines. Choosing to believe the former president's discourses of election fraud, attendees of the "Save America Rally" felt they were protesting at the behest of their leader and mistakenly believed that their attendance at the rally and subsequent march to the Capitol could stop the certification of President Biden's election. Believing they were called to advocate for a just cause, many rally attendees got to the Capitol and were simply caught up in the riots. Some joined in, however, with other protesters who had come prepared to riot, as evidenced by their weapons, military-style maneuvers, and knowledge of the Capitol's layout. By the time the doors and windows were battened down, peaceful protest at the Capitol was no longer possible. Instead, when rioters unlawfully breached the US Capitol grounds, chanting "Hang Mike Pence" (Foreman), property damage and threats to working politicians were in play, as recorded live by national and international media outlets who ordered their reporters to cover the scene, a breaching of the Capitol that lasted for three hours. Another interesting focus for analyzing actors would be not focusing only on groups but rather focusing on themes, such as what ideas were invoked to justify raiding the Capitol or halting the raid ... and what ideas were not (#4).

In the rhetorical situation of the Capitol raid, the aggressive nature of the riot and the false political claims upon which the rioters' grievances were based made it impossible for reasoned political deliberation to take place. Insofar as the rioters' actions required organized protection, few if any opportunities for listening arose among participants. But afterwards, citizens, politicians, police, etc., should all reflect on the Capitol riots, listening to determine what different groups were thinking in order to prevent such an event from ever occurring again (#4).

Tactic #5: Analyze how different objects and spaces influence action in a rhetorical situation, especially as it relates to hauntings of the past.

1. Identify a rhetorical situation associated with a text, a person, or a cultural event that you want to analyze.

2. List the objects and spaces that are referenced in this rhetorical situation.

3. Reflect on how the objects and spaces associated with the rhetorical situation are haunted by historical injustices.

4. Analyze how objects and spaces make certain actions possible or impossible given how the rhetorical situation has been defined.

In the Capitol riot of January 6, 2021 (#1), the most notable objects that signaled rioters' willingness to enact violence against anyone who opposed their beliefs were clothing, banners, and weapons. As of this writing, 241 of 800 rioters have been arrested (Harrington, et al).[18] As the rioters marched and stormed the Capitol building, they wore, amongst other things, military fatigues, stocking caps, and MAGA gear. They carried a range of alt-right flags and paraphernalia such as "American flags with the stars replaced by the Roman numeral III, patches that read 'Oath Keepers' . . . Pepe the Frog masks, T-shirts urging people to 'Trust the Plan,' variants of the Crusader cross"; there were also flags that depicted "President Trump as Rambo" and flags that depicted "him riding a Tyrannosaurus rex and carrying the kind of rocket-propelled grenade launcher seen on the streets of Mogadishu or Kandahar" (Rosenberg and Tiefenthaler). As for weapons, some rioters constructed gallows, some converted flag poles into weapons, and some carried bear spray, assault rifles, crossbows, additional rounds of ammunition, explosive devices such as Molotov cocktails, brass knuckles, pocket knives, stun guns, and stinger whips (Shapiro) (#2).

Objects associated with rioters, when combined with some rioters' identifications with extremist groups, were haunted by cultural logics of white supremacy in the US and abroad. Some rioters carried a number of flags such as the Confederate flag, Pepe the frog, and "Kek" whose iconography borrows from the Nazi flag, thus invoking the horrors of US slavery, white supremacy, and the Holocaust. Some rioters erected a gallows and noose in plain view of the Capitol building, thus invoking the US history of lynching Black men, women, and children, a legacy of slavery and Jim Crow (#3). And some rioters openly displayed guns and ammunition, an act haunted by Second Amendment rights as well as by racial injustices of shootings of Black people. While the Second Amendment is supposed to be a universal right available to all citizens, regardless of race, as Lebron James's post-riot observations attest, this right has historically been unevenly applied. Thus, the ghosts of weapons used in service of white supremacy haunt the rhetorical situation created by the US Capitol riots. As such, the weapons at the Capitol attack on January 6, 2021, invite conversations about the origins and stakes in narratives of election fraud and also about the legacy of white supremacy that characterizes rhetorical situations within the US Capitol and its political history.

Listening writers must combine the concept and tactics of rhetorical situations with an ability to identify and negotiate the group identities within which people function. To that end, the next chapter addresses the rhetorical concept and tactics of identification.

4 Identification

The Human Rights Watch (HRW) takes as its mission the need to "investigate," "expose" and "change" international human rights abuses, with women's rights being only one of its many concerns. The 2021 HRW website describes as follows the current state of women's rights around the globe:

> Despite great strides made by the international women's rights movement over many years, women and girls around the world are still married as children or trafficked into forced labor and sex slavery. They are refused access to education and political participation, and some are trapped in conflicts where rape is perpetrated as a weapon of war. Around the world, deaths related to pregnancy and childbirth are needlessly high, and women are prevented from making deeply personal choices in their private lives. Human Rights Watch is working toward the realization of women's empowerment and gender equality—protecting the rights and improving the lives of women and girls on the ground. ("Women's Rights")

As an organization, the HRW's rhetorical problem is how to communicate the abuses they uncover in ways that will solicit donations through their webpage—donations that may, in turn, be channeled to effect social change. As with any charitable solicitation, the HRW's website asks audiences to identify with its mission, its leaders, or the people supported by their work because only then are audiences likely to donate funds. For audiences, seeing themselves in an organization's mission, leaders or people supported is a form of identification.

As a psychological concept, identification was first defined by Sigmund Freud[1] and later taken up by a host of twentieth-century theorists in various fields of study.[2] Simply put, identification is a process of seeing ourselves in other people, objects, ideas, nations, etc. More precisely, because identification is an encounter with other people, objects, ideas, nations, etc. that results in our projections of them within our own minds, identification is a process of seeing ourselves in *our projections of* other people, objects, ideas, nations, etc., including the properties we attribute to and share with them. In this way, identifications "emerge from encounters with forces both internal (ego-id) and external (self-other)" (Ratcliffe 61). Identifications, then, drive all our daily lives. But identifications are concerned not just with how individuals interact with other people and things but also with how individuals are interpolated by history and culture (Fuss 3). For each individual then, the sum total of his/her/their identifications (good and bad, conscious and unconscious, individual and collective) shapes each person's identity, and as a consequence of multiple identifications, each person's identity is, as Kimberlé Crenshaw argues, necessarily intersectional.[3]

Identification may be best understood via examples. We shop at the same grocery store time after time because we "identify" with it as "our grocery store," which can mean anything from "it carries the brands we like" to "it sits on the corner of our street" or "it is a site of habitual ritual that we find comforting." Or, we pursue certain jobs because we "identify" with the knowledge and skills needed to perform the jobs. We pick friends because we "identify" common interests about a host of issues from sports teams to ethical values to simply living next door to one another. And yes, we donate money to a charitable organization when we "identify" with its mission, its leaders and the people it supports. But identifications may have tragic consequences, too, as when children internalize what bullies call them and subsequently hurt themselves or as when young men and women become radicalized into terrorist groups (domestic or foreign) by internet propaganda.

While identifications fill our daily lives, disidentifications also occur. Disidentification is a process of *not* seeing ourselves in other people, objects, ideas, nations, etc., or more specifically, not seeing ourselves in the *projections* that we construct of them. For example, while people may watch certain TV news shows because they "identify" with the newscasters' perspectives, they may also watch competing news shows because they "disidentify" with these shows and simply want to know what the "other side" is saying. Interestingly, as Diana Fuss argues, disidentifications are prior identifications that have been "disavowed" (6) and then, echoing Judith Butler, rendered "abject" (*Bodies* 112).[4]

Since the publication of *Rhetorical Listening: Identification, Gender, Whiteness*, rhetorical listening has been invested in the relationship between listening and identification (47–77). This relationship benefits from Kenneth Burke's study of identification as a rhetorical concept and tactic because, much in the same way that rhetorical listening tracks the unstated assumptions of competing cultural logics, Burke's identification emphasizes the need to make identifications the subject of conscious attention. By bringing identifications "to *consciousness*," listening writers can perform identification as "a matter of *conscience*" (Burke, *War of Words* 143). To supplement Burke's thinking about identification, rhetorical listening also draws on Fuss's thinking about identification to invite concepts and tactics of disidentification into the conversation (Ratcliffe 62–63); it also offers a concept of non-identification (72–76).

To demonstrate how and why the concept of identification is important to a rhetorical education grounded in rhetorical listening, this chapter defines identification as a rhetorical concept, explores why it should be studied, and offers model tactics for analyzing and composing.

WHAT IS IDENTIFICATION AS A RHETORICAL CONCEPT?

Identification was introduced into rhetorical studies in 1950 when Kenneth Burke published his landmark work, *A Rhetoric of Motives*. His interest in identification arose because he was concerned that, as WWII ended and the Cold War ramped up, reporters and world leaders were promoting, however unwittingly, increasingly virulent forms of nationalist aggression that we now identify as Cold War rhetoric. He feared that such nationalist aggression would result in nuclear war, a common fear in the 1950s as evidenced by the popularity of bomb shelters and "duck and cover" exercises in public schools. To understand identifications with such nationalist aggression as well as to find ways of interrupting them, Burke spent the last half of the 1940s drafting and revising his *Rhetoric*. It argues that argumentative aggression does not occur simply because of inherent biases of certain people; instead, it occurs because of *how language is used* to identify and communicate these perspectives. In short, he made visible the role of language within identifications.

According to Burke, people and institutions use language to facilitate identifications by *assigning properties* to themselves, other people, objects, spaces, and rhetorical situations (really, *anything*) in order to bridge divides and establish relationships among people as well as among people and things (*Rhetoric* 20). For example, assigned properties may be identity categories. People and groups who assign the term *feminist* to themselves and others find themselves linked by beliefs and actions that advance women's rights. People and governments who assign the term *enemy* to other nations feel justified in fighting wars to defeat them. People and institutions who assign the term *US citizen* to individuals endow those individuals with certain unalienable rights and deny those rights to people relegated to the status of *non-citizen*. In addition, assigned properties may be qualities. If parents tell their young children that a public space is *safe* because it is well-lighted and supervised, they are granting their children agency to navigate the area with greater levels of freedom. In the future, using the same spatial property of *safe* in terms of *well-lighted* and *supervised*, the children may identify other public spaces as more or less safe and invite their friends to play in those they deem safe. Likewise, people who assign the term *fun* to a person may want to be friends with that person, and people who assign the term *dangerous* to an entire ethnic group are stereotyping that group. Such property assignments—whether grounded in identity categories, qualities, or something else—are designed to orient how people feel, think, and act, both individually and collectively. By assigning properties *through terms*, rhetorical identification facilitates identifications and disidentifications among people as well as among people and things.

Properties assigned in identifications may be deemed accurate or inaccurate, comforting or dangerous, or even real or imagined, etc., depending on the situation. Assigned properties may be deemed accurate as when someone traditionally identified as *quiet* typically behaves that way in public. But in other situations, the properties might be deemed inaccurate; a seemingly quiet person might become more outspoken in private conversations. Perhaps more importantly, assigned properties represent privileges or the lack thereof in different cultural locations as when a middle-aged white man may call his well-worn hoodie *comforting* but parents of young Black men must deem hoodies *dangerous*. Equally important is determining whether properties assigned in identifications are real or imagined. Real identifications are those that represent actual experiences or objects as when James Baldwin or Lilian Smith describe the state of racism in the mid-twentieth century. Imagined identifications, if grounded in the work done to warrant the property assigned can be fine; fiction, for example, may represent deep truths. But if built on false premises, prejudices or fantasies, imagined identifications may result in stereotypes as when women are deemed *too emotional* to be President or people within ethnic groups are assumed to be *all the same*. Because context is so crucial to understanding identifications, listening writers should think critically about properties assigned to people, objects, spaces, rhetorical situations, etc. Indeed, such critical thinking is an ethical imperative.

Importantly for Burke, assigning properties is done in the service of bridging divides. Indeed, identifications are necessary because people live in a natural state of division and conflict. As such, people desire to overcome this division and bridge their differences with other people or things:

> We need never deny the presence of strife, enmity, faction as a characteristic motive of rhetorical expression. We need not lose our eyes to their almost tyrannous ubiquity in human relations; we can be on the alert always to see how such temptations to strife are implicit in the institutions that condition human relationships; yet we can at the same time always look beyond this order, to the principle of identification in general, a terministic choice justified by the fact that the identifications in the order of love are also characteristic of rhetorical expression. (*Rhetoric* 20)

While humans are prone to verbal conflict, they are not destined to communicate only aggressively; they may also use language to reconcile conflict and seek alternatives to war. Indeed, both options are made possible by rhetorical identifications, or how people use language to name (assign properties to) the world and, in the process, identify their relationships to it.

With this insight, Burke's own rhetorical problem in his *Rhetoric* came into clear view: How to explain to 1950s readers how everyday citizens can learn to recognize and consciously counteract their impulses toward argumentative aggression so that, together, they can create a more peaceful and equitable existence in the future?

Over the years, scholars have taken up this rhetorical problem and, in the process, expanded how identification may be defined and implemented in rhetorical studies.[5] For example, in *Queer Migration Politics* Karma Chavez studies the rhetoric of Yasmin Nair, an academic, writer, activist, and organizer who has dedicated her life to fighting for (among other things) the rights of migrant workers who identify as queer. As Chavez explains, migration policies in the US have prevented such workers from receiving protections against exploitation because such policies overstress their sex-based identifications. To solve this rhetorical problem, Nair imagines a form of coalition building that is not reducible to unique identity categories such as "queer identity group" (Chavez 70). Specifically, Nair "focuses on queer migrants as unique subjects and also constructs identification (as opposed to identity) among workers" (70).

Nair's use of the phrase "and also" is a crucial feature of how rhetorical listening uses identification to affirm the complexity of identity formation. By resisting the urge to collapse difference into sameness via the creation of stable identity categories, rhetorical listening asks writers to lay differences (between one another and within themselves) side-by-side so that such differences may be negotiated with greater ethical responsibility. Nair's coalition building tactics show that an identification between undocumented queer and heterosexual laborers does not mean "that being gay is just like being undocumented" (Chavez 70). Instead, by focusing on "the material realities of workers, *some of whom* are undocumented and queer," listening writers may "consider how multiple dimensions of power interact to constitute the possibilities for belonging and viability" for all migrants (70, emphasis added). That is, listening writers may more precisely differentiate the points at which sexual and labor identifications converge and diverge from one another. By listening for such dimensions, listening writers can imagine solutions that foster "solidarity, coalition work, and alternative imaginaries" (72).

In *Rhetorical Listening*, identification is defined in terms of Judith Butler's claim that identification is "an assumption of place" (*Bodies* 99) a place both psychical (ego/id) and historical/cultural (self/other) (Ratcliffe 49). Conceptualizing identifications as place-based property assignments links rhetoric and ethics. Burke explains: "Metaphysically, a thing is identified by its properties. In the realm of rhetoric, such identification is frequently by property . . . In the surrounding of himself with properties that . . . establish his identity, man is ethical" (*Rhetoric* 23–24). For example, if people are ascribed as *old, wise, generous,* and *socially aware,* then what is being ascribed is not only intersectional identities but also the ethical values associated with those identities. But as the agency chapter taught us, an individual's personal agency does not exist in a vacuum; it is complicated by discursive, cultural, and material agencies as well as other people's personal agencies within rhetorical situations. In the same way, identifications do not exist in a vacuum nor depend solely on individual conscious choices; rather, identifications are contextually grounded in relations within and among people, discourses, cultures, and material things. In this way, identifications are both incredibly ordinary and incredibly complex.

Identifications may occur at varying degrees of a person's consciousness. Sometimes identifications are conscious actions or choices; that is, people consciously assign properties to themselves, other people, objects, spaces, rhetorical situations, etc., as when one person chooses to adopt an open stance and name themselves a *rhetorical listener*. Likewise, other people, objects, spaces, rhetorical situations, etc., may also make a person consciously aware of what properties they have had assigned to themselves; think, for example, about signs on public school buildings that declare the spaces *gun-free zones* and people within the zones as *gun-free*. Sometimes, though, identifications are wholly unconscious actions; for example, people unknowingly accept via socialization the properties assigned to people, objects, spaces, rhetorical situations, etc., as when a child born into a religious cult unquestioningly assumes the cult's beliefs to be true, at least until they are old enough to think for themselves. More often, however, identifications are non-conscious actions, occurring in a space between the conscious and the unconscious. As Burke argues, the tendency to assign properties to people, objects, spaces, and rhetorical situations manifests "in an intermediate area of expression that is not wholly deliberate, yet not wholly unconscious. It lies midway between aimless utterance and speech directly purposive" (*Rhetoric* xiii). Non-conscious identifications are not inherently bad and so should not necessarily be characterized as unthinking in quality.

Yet non-conscious identifications raise questions of ethics. They risk establishing relationships between a person and institutions or value systems that a person might otherwise consciously oppose. For example, shoppers may buy a certain clothing brand because they assign it the properties of *stylish* and *classy*, but what if this brand has also perpetuated dangerous labor practices in a third-world country? Or for another example, students may choose to attend a certain university because they assign it the properties of *excellence* and *prestige*, but what if its history includes examples of racism and sexism? In the first scenario, the shoppers' identification with the brand risks being deemed *unethical* or *dangerous* by others and, upon further reflection, possibly even by the shoppers themselves. In the second scenario, the students' identifications with the school also risk being deemed unethical or dangerous by others and, upon further reflection, possibly even by students themselves; or, the students' identifications might be deemed as ethical if the school has owned its history and is working on a better present and future.

When reflecting on the ethics of their identifications, listening writers benefit from studying the concept of disidentification (Ratcliffe 62–67). If disidentifications are identifications that have existed, been "disavowed" (Fuss 6) and rendered "abject" (Butler, *Bodies* 112), then listening writers must reflect on how their identifications led to their disavowals. For example, people cannot decide to hate brussels sprouts until they have identified with its taste and then declared they do not like it. In this way, disidentifications might be thought of as identifications to which negative values have been attached. The same principle applies to all other aspects of life, not just food. For instance, such disavowals are the basis for virtuous action via the negative as in the Ten Commandments' "Thou shalt nots"; such disavowals are also responsible for actions without virtue such as stereotyping groups of people. As with all rhetorical concepts and tactics, disidentifications may function for good or ill. But bringing them to consciousness helps listening writers determine if they should be reinforced or revised.

Likewise, listening writers benefit from studying non-identification,[6] a place of pause "wherein people may *consciously choose* to position themselves to listen rhetorically" (Ratcliffe 72). This place invites people to "recognize the partiality of our visions and listen for that-which-cannot-be seen, even if it cannot yet be heard" (73). As such, non-identification "maps a place, a possibility, for consciously asserting our agency to engage cross-cultural rhetorical exchanges across commonalities and differences" (73). It provides a space for "navigating (some of) our own identifications and disidentifications" (75). In short, it is a place for reflecting on assigned properties of any of the examples above, their consequences, and the ethical next steps.

WHY STUDY RHETORICAL IDENTIFICATIONS?

The study of identification as a rhetorical concept and tactic inflected by rhetorical listening offers listening writers ways to perform critical analyses so as to generate more details and thus deepen their understanding of particular rhetorical problems. Such understanding, in turn, offers listening writers more choices for composing responses to the problems. As such, the study of identification has many benefits.

First, the study of identification shows that a person's identifications are always made in relation to versions of one's self, other people, objects, spaces, rhetorical situations, etc. and thus are subject to change over time. For example, listening writers might assign the property *entertaining* to a music concert because it is *like* other music concerts they have found entertaining or *unlike* other concerts they have found boring. Such relations engender judgments that may be subject to change as writers gain more experience, as when they see more concerts and thus have more basis for comparisons. Indeed, a music concert that writers found *amazing* at a time earlier in their lives may leave them embarrassed that they ever liked it at all. In such a case, writers relate differently not just to the concert, but to earlier versions of their selves.

Second, the study of identification exposes how they haunt people's perspectives as well as the accompanying cultural logics. When listening writers analyze their identifications critically, they create opportunities to reassess the possibilities and limits of their existing perspectives about people, objects, places, rhetorical situations, etc. In other words, they also create opportunities to understand how their perspectives are haunted by cultural logics. Consider, for example, a cartoon where supermarket aisles are labelled not as *produce, meat, beverages,* etc., but, rather, as *lose, maintain,* and *gain.* Supermarkets do not post signs identifying foods by whether they cause people to *lose, maintain,* or *gain* weight. Instead, they post signs organizing products by types (produce, meats, snacks, etc.) or ethnic origin (Italian, Mexican, Chinese, etc.) or function (laundry detergent, household cleaners, etc.), thus signaling customers where to find particular products. Yet, the food classifications actually do imply associations with weight in that healthy foods such as fruits and vegetables are often grouped in one part of the store while snacks such as potato chips, candy, and soda are grouped in another section. The cultural logic haunting this organizational scheme argues that people who look for one type of grocery item will probably be interested in products that share similar properties and so said products should be grouped together—a first principle of marketing. And as customers walk through the supermarket, they non-consciously count on this assumed logic to find what they need.

Third, the study of identification offers opportunities for laying competing cultural logics side by side. When listening writers analyze their identifications critically, they create opportunities to develop new perspectives and embrace different cultural logics that may increase their potential for openness and understanding. Consider, again, the grocery store cartoon. The lessons of this cartoon are not just about how grocery stores are organized or how our nation obsesses on weight; the lessons are also about how identifications invoke competing cultural logics. The grocery store signs—*loses, maintains,* or *gains*—appear at first sight to assign properties to the food products, but they actually assign properties to bodies of shoppers. Indeed, this cartoon participates in a broader cultural logic of *health* that helps people identify the properties of their bodies (fat, slim, etc.) relative to the foods they eat. Do audiences of the cartoon make these identifications consciously? Some may. But most make these identifications non-consciously and simply laugh at the cartoon and then move on without analyzing too deeply. Of course, audiences could also respond to grocery "signs" by identifying with cultural logics other than health. For example, they could identify *loses, maintains,* or *gains* with cultural logics of *taste* or *class* as related to body type if these cultural logics were more important to some people than "health." When listening writers engage in rhetorical listening, it is important to lay these cultural logics side-by-side so that a variety of interpretations can be understood, negotiated or renegotiated.

Fourth, the study of identifications and competing cultural logics clarifies questions of ethical decisions and truth. For example, at sporting events circa 2016, different perspectives about the American flag presented an ethical decision for players, coaches, owners, and fans: whether to stand or take a knee when facing the flag during the playing of "The National Anthem." One cultural logic reasons that the flag overtly signifies patriotism, freedom, individual rights, and sacrifice—all of which are true. It is the dominant logic that has become naturalized (seen as normal or as just the way things are). Yet a competing cultural logic reasons that the flag also implies a history of slavery, colonization, the threat of direct violence via war or capitalist expansion, including a present of racial violence—all of which are also true. Depending on which cultural logic one prioritizes and recognizes as "the truth" (which *may* or *may not* include rejecting the other cultural logic), one decides to stand or to kneel. Or one attempts to construct a third way that embraces the complexity denied by most binary options.

Fifth, the study of identification provides a way to disrupt inadvertent violence associated with identifications. This function addresses Burke's main concern: how to prevent unwitting associations with unethical or dangerous identifications (such as Nazi or Cold War rhetorics) that engender violence, whether material, psychological or symbolic. Burke was concerned about a violence that played out on a national political and economic stage, as when Italians in World War II not only overtly embraced fascist leader Benito Mussolini's making the trains run on time but also implicitly sanctioned concentration camps. By thinking critically about their identifications, listening writers can safeguard against such rhetorical deceptions, which Burke defines as the use of rhetorical identification to "protect an interest merely by using terms not incisive enough to criticize properly" (*Rhetoric* 36). One means for thinking critically about identifications and safeguarding against rhetorical deceptions is for listening writers to grant hearings, via an open stance, to competing cultural logics and the identifications that haunt them.

In sum, the point of studying identifications is to bring them (as much as possible) to consciousness, to critique their effects, and to use them purposefully. In the process, listening writers learn not to jump to an immediate conclusion about which assigned property is right and which one is wrong but, rather, to recognize that people have opportunities to be more deliberate and ethical about the properties they assign and accept. Rhetorical listening is simply one means to that end.

WHAT ARE TACTICS OF RHETORICAL IDENTIFICATION?

The concept of rhetorical identification gives rise to multiple tactics that listening writers may employ for everyday writing tasks. Below are some sample tactics that have emerged from our own pedagogies, tactics that are intended to help writers envision their thinking moves as well as their ideas. These sample tactics are illustrated by the topic of *climate change*. But it is important to keep in mind that listening writers may develop their own tactics as appropriate to particular rhetorical problems and their writing tasks.

Tactic #1: Analyze how identifications are connected to tropes and values.

1. Select as a topic a person, text (image, video, advertisement, etc.), or cultural event.

2. Assign properties identified with your topic. (These properties are terms that function as tropes.)

3. Determine how the properties/tropes associated with your topic suggest certain values.

4. Explain how the identifications you've identified are designed to make people feel, think, and act about the topic.

As Chapter 1 on rhetorical listening notes, tropes may function as keywords within cultural logics that orient our perspective on a particular topic. Tropes (functioning as properties) are assigned to people, objects, spaces, and rhetorical situations, and these tropes represent identifications. Understanding the relationship between tropes and identifications helps writers to analyze and compose with greater precision.

Consider as a topic a cartoon in which one polar bear is holding a hairdryer and inadvertently melting ice nearby and another polar bear says, "I recognize that climate change is a complex subject with multiple causes, but this really isn't helping (#1). The caption claims that climate change is the result of "multiple causes." Yet even without the caption, we would probably conclude that this cartoon is about climate change. Why? Because writers and artists often use melting polar ice caps to represent climate change. A dominant trope used here is metonymy, which describes how a *part* represents the *whole*. Climate change affects not only ice caps but also other ecosystems such as rainforests, the great barrier reef, etc. Yet as a shorthand, writers use polar bears and ice caps so audiences will immediately identify the topic as climate change (#1).

Because many people have never been to the Arctic, they find it difficult to conceptualize how climate change affects that ecosystem. This cartoonist asks audiences to identify with the animals (in this case, polar bears) who will be affected by rising temperatures. The writer creates the audience's identification with polar bears by writing and drawing from the audience's point of view. Even if readers have never seen a polar bear, they have seen stuffed animals, watched films, and purchased products that make the polar bears seem *comforting, funny, and/or relatable* (all properties we assign to them) (#2).

The cartoon counts on our comfort and relatability with polar bears to communicate its values. To understand how tropes and their identifications suggest certain values, listening writers may examine the captions and the visuals. From the caption, listening writers may conclude that one of the cartoon's main values is an "even-handed assessment of complex issues." From the caption and visuals, listening writers may conclude that another main value is "environmental protection" (#3). In addition, although the cartoon recognizes that climate change has "multiple causes," it implies that people can control some causes such as the needless use of industrial products (the hairdryer) that speed up the melting process. Through this implication, listening writers are meant to identify with the hair-drying polar bear who is engaging in a dangerous activity without being fully aware of its broader implications (#3).

By establishing this identification, the cartoon asks audiences to view climate change personally. If audiences make the connection, they might feel guilty about how their actions have compromised the welfare of polar bears; they might think more carefully about the products they use or endorse in the future, knowing that their practices could be raising global climates; or, they might begin to support activist groups trying to combat climate change and to preserve compromised ecosystems. Or they might laugh and move on (#4).

Tactic #2: Analyze How Identifications Connect to Cultural Logics.

1. Select as a topic a person, text (image, video, advertisement, etc.), or cultural event.

2. List the beliefs identified with the topic.

3. Determine how these beliefs connect to broader cultural logics.

4. Analyze how the identifications established between the topic and cultural logics affect how we interpret the topic.

5. Reflect on the consequences of failing to recognize the relationship between the topic's identifications and its cultural logics.

6. Imagine ways of talking across cultural logics.

Chapter 1 defines *cultural logics* as ways of reasoning common to groups of people who come together for shared beliefs or goals. This chapter focuses on how identifications haunt cultural logics in order to motivate groups of people, first, to believe certain things and, then, to act in certain ways. Analyzing and understanding such motivations can help writers compose their everyday writing tasks.

Let's take as our topic a cartoon featuring an adult penguin standing at the edge of a melting ice floe saying to a child penguin, "Back when I was your age, my folks had to walk for days before reaching open water to find food." The cartoon focuses on climate change to encourage people to protect the environment (#1). As such, the cartoon implies a set of beliefs about the environment, the most important being: *protecting the environment* and *teaching children to appreciate their life's benefits*. By appealing to these beliefs, the cartoon encourages its audiences to identify with the penguins (another popular image associated with climate change). Whether parents or children (or both), audiences are meant to identify with this scene because, chances are, they have experienced a similar lecture from their parents about what their parents had to suffer when they were young (#2).

The beliefs promoted in a text indicate the presence of a cultural logic. Several environmental cultural logics exist (#3). The cultural logic of environmentalism reasons that protecting the environment is a political issue that governments should address with regulatory policies (e.g., The Paris Agreement) (#4). The cultural logic of environmental competition argues that the best way to protect the environment is by inventing new technologies (e.g., machines to delete CO_2 from the atmosphere) that will address the causes of climate change and simultaneously grow the economy (#4). And, finally, the cultural logic of some religious fundamentalists purports that climate change inevitably results from a divine plan and indicates end times; within this logic, people should take no corrective action because that would be interfering with God's plan (#4).

Understanding people's identifications with cultural logics can help listening writers anticipate arguments and counterarguments and then decide how to best address their audiences. In climate change debates, the stakes are incredibly high: if the science is correct, the quality of human life and even human survival are at stake (#5). Those persuaded by scientific research need a significant majority of citizens to alter their food consumption and energy consumption to literally save the planet. To make their case, proponents of science need to convince those functioning in other cultural logics to change their beliefs and cultural scripts. To do so, proponents of science cannot simply dismiss competing cultural logics as "ignorant" or "politically shortsighted"; such insults will only alienate audiences. Instead, proponents of science must listen to and communicate in terms of dissenting cultural logics. For example, when science proponents talk to religious fundamentalists, they cannot simply say that if we do not act, we could cross an irreversible climate threshold, and the safety of people we love is at risk; that message might be heard as evidence of God's revelation. Instead, science proponents might talk about how science and religion are interconnected or about how addressing climate change is means of fulfilling the Biblical charge for men and women to be stewards of the earth (#6).

The goal of this tactic is not to debate which cultural logic is better. Instead, the goal is to increase understanding of multiple perspectives about a debate, its stakes, and possible arguments and counterarguments; to reflect on the multiple perspectives; and to use this understanding to make strategic writing decisions. In this way, listening writers benefit by knowing what different cultural logics exist and determining how identifications appeal to them.

Tactic #3: Analyze How Identifications Form Identities.

1. Select a person to analyze (yourself or someone else).

2. Determine a value or set of values assigned to that person's identity.

3. Analyze why that value or set of values is assigned to the person.

4. List the specific practices, or cultural scripts, identified with that value or set of values.

5. Analyze how those practices, or cultural scripts, create both helpful and harmful consequences in the person's life.

This tactic of identification helps people make sense of others and themselves in terms of values. Often, people are identified by others as having particular properties and, thus, come to know themselves through other people's perspectives. Everyone who has received an unexpected compliment will attest how wonderful a positive identification can be to their sense of self. But people can also assign properties to themselves, too. Take, for example, the cartoon where an elementary school-aged girl and boy are playing on a see-saw and the little girls says, "That was a pretty depressing lesson on the effects of climate change" after which the little boy replies, "I think I have Pre-Traumatic Stress Disorder." The little girl is explaining to her friend that she found the video on climate change *depressing*, thus assigning that property to herself. The little boy responds by claiming that he now believes he has *pre-traumatic stress disorder*, effectively assigning that property to himself (#1).

To explain how this cartoon connects identification to identity, let's focus on its stated values. First, similar to the previous cartoons mentioned, this one promotes the value of environmental awareness (#2). We know this because a common appeal to environmental awareness is to think about our children's future. So, by depicting children who are depressed about their environmental future, this cartoon argues that its audience should think more carefully about increasing climate changes (#3). Second, another value that this cartoon promotes is protecting children against unnecessary exposure to trauma (#2). When the little boy states that he thinks he might have pre-traumatic stress disorder, he could be saying that watching the video was traumatic; in this case, the fault would lie with the teacher or school who showed the children the video without proper preparation. More likely, he is saying that the realities of climate change have caused him to anticipate future trauma when the environment gets worse; in this case, the fault would lie with those who are ignoring climate change (#3). Either way, the important point is that the girl and boy now define their identities in terms of a cultural logic of climate change. By identifying themselves as audience members who are or will soon be affected by climate change, they become marked by that knowledge. Now living in fear of the constant threat of environmental catastrophe, the children understand their selves differently than before they knew about the problem (#3).

Living with depression and trauma is a scary reality. It is difficult to feel self-worth and to form attachments to others. So, claiming that there are benefits to experiencing depression or pre-traumatic stress disorder is, in some ways, insensitive to the reality of these psychological disorders. Still, by recognizing that climate change can affect people's identities and, thus, alter their abilities to form communities, people can, this cartoon suggests, begin taking important steps toward addressing the problem. People can talk with each other about the dangers of climate change, become more active in protecting our children's environmental futures, and even create new texts that call attention to their experiences of climate change (#4). All of these actions have the capacity to help people change the sense of their own identities; instead of defining their identities in terms of a helpless exposure to environmental catastrophe, they could define their identities in terms of working to solve the problem for future generations (#5).

Tactic #4: Analyze Identification and Disidentification.

1. Find a text (image, video, advertisement) that claims an identification is "natural" or "universal."

2. Analyze the situation and reasons for deeming the natural/universal identification as true.

3. Analyze the situation and reasons for deeming the natural/universal identification as not true (disidentification).

4. Pose questions that will help develop a stance, either defending or challenging the "natural" or "universal" identification or somehow bridging them.

Identification and disidentification work in conjunction with one another. Identifications associate things: a person and a property (such as *generous*), two people with each other and a property (*colleagues*), etc. Disidentifications separate two ideas that have been presented as naturally associated (via a previous identification) and, thus, serve as a valuable method for questioning identifications that usually go unquestioned. The easiest way to begin the process of disidentification is to ask a simple question: *"Is the association between two ideas necessarily true?"*

For example, consider a cartoon about climate change where the scales of justice contain, on one side, only one person labelled "climate denier" and, on the other side, a mass of humans labelled "virtually every scientist in the world"; the climate denier side weighs more than the mass of scientists' side, with the caption echoing a scientist's voice saying, "Either he's **that** dense, or he doesn't believe in gravity either." The question haunting this cartoon is: Is climate change true? Given the cartoon's scale of justice, only two answers are possible: the "yes" side is represented as crowded with scientists, and the "no" side is represented by one wide-eyed climate denier. When the caption suggests that the climate denier is "dense," as indicated by the fact that his scale is weighted down lower than the crowded one, the caption is implying that the denier is *really, really* dense, pun intended. (#1).

What is deemed a natural connection is informed by cultural logics of the two sides. For the scientists, the association of science with data about climate change constructs a natural connection, given that they base their conclusions on scientifically designed, data-based modelling, although viewers of the cartoon are not provided the data (#2). For the climate denier, the connection of science with data about climate change does not construct a natural connection, though viewers are not told why the denier disidentifies with science (#3).

For listening writers, this cartoon provides an interesting starting point for researching and defining stated identifications and disidentifi-cations with climate change. For listening writers, this cartoon also im-plies interesting questions: What are scientific data supporting climate change? Are they convincing? Why might someone deny them? And for listening writers, this cartoon might even trigger research about other universal/natural identifications haunting the topic: for example, given that climate change is often represented in popular culture as if it affects all people equally, perhaps writers should question this assumption of universality, researching how the effects of climate change may fall, at least initially, disproportionately on poor and BIPOC communities (#4).

Listening writers may employ the concept and tactics of identifica-tion to understand the formation of personal and collective identities and also to find spaces in competing arguments or unstated assumptions for thinking and acting together. To focus on sites where identifications generate collective identities, the next chapter addresses the rhetorical concept and tactics of myth.

5 Myth

Histories are myths, according to Harvard historian and *New Yorker* staff writer Jill Lepore. In *The Secret History of Wonder Woman*, LePore argues that the US cultural origins of Wonder Woman have gone underground despite the facts that this character "has never been out of print" and that her "fans number in the millions" (xi). Within the narrative world of Wonder Woman, the character's origins begin with her life among the Amazons. But within US cultural history, unlike the creators of X-Men (Stan Lee), Spiderman (Jack Kirby), and Superman (Jerry Siegel and Joe Schuster), the writer who created Wonder Woman has been erased from the popular imagination. Interestingly, Wonder Woman was created in the early twentieth century in the mind of a "scholar, professor, and scientist" named William Moulton Marston who loved and lived with two women who were "suffragists, feminists, and birth control advocates" (xiii), thus prompting LePore to argue that "Wonder Woman began in a protest march, a bedroom, and a birth control clinic" (xiv)—the often invisible, gritty[1] sites of feminist struggle in the early twentieth century.

As illustrated by Wonder Woman, a rhetorical problem that writers encounter when writing histories is how to engage their myths and mythic erasures. For example, writers might ask: What version of a myth is being told—and why?[2] How can the Wonder Woman myth's cultural origins in the sites of feminist struggle hide in plain sight, and what role, if any, does the mythic figure of Wonder Woman herself play in the process of hiding her own origins? Is there something about myth, as a *form of argument*, that is able to produce such complicated outcomes as evidenced by people's identifications with cultural logics of gender (patriarchy, egalitarianism, feminism)? Finally, what is at stake in such mythic identifications—and for whom?

As Lepore demonstrates, not only do myths' origins and complex effects pervade public and private lives, but they also sometimes need to be challenged. The question is: How?

Mythic criticism, a popular analytical method from the late nineteenth-century until the mid-twentieth century,[3] died in academic circles as other critical methods came to the fore, its demise resulting in no small part from its focus on "universal themes" and "savage minds,"[4] both of which invoke sexist and racist assumptions. For example, the idea that myths are universal was challenged in 1972 by science fiction writer Joanna Russ who famously argued that "culture is male" and evidenced it by reframing classic plots with women as heroes, some favorites being "A young girl in Minnesota finds her womanhood by killing a bear" or "Alexandra the Great" (80). Likewise, Claude Lévi-Strauss's famous trope *la pensée sauvage* translated as *savage mind*[5] was challenged in as recently as 2017 by Savannah Martin, a member of the Confederated Tribes of Siletz Indians and a PhD student in biological anthropology, when she argued that *Savage Minds* is an inappropriate title for an anthropology blog whose mission is to bring anthropological knowledge to the general public: "From dictionary definitions to historical texts, to modern day slang,[6] 'savage' denotes a lack of restraint, inherent violence, primitive nature, or particular cruelty. These negative definitions are precisely why the descriptor was used to dehumanize Indigenous peoples in facilitation of a hallucinated 'manifest destiny' in the first place." Clearly, when the study of myth is associated with such troubled assumptions, then methods must change.

To revivify an interest in mythic criticism, Jill LePore and Kenneth Burke offer a different set of assumptions and methods. LePore models how unstated assumptions and erasures surrounding myths must be explored, acknowledging that we learn as much from what is left out of a myth as from what is left in. Burke insists that myths should be imagined and analyzed as a rhetorical concept, an argument outlined in *The War of Words* (20–21, 23), the newly discovered second half of his 1950 *A Rhetoric of Motives*. This new manuscript was published in 2018 thanks to the detective work of Kyle Jensen and Jack Selzer in the Kenneth Burke archives at Penn State University and thanks to the willing collaboration of Burke's son Anthony Burke. These three editors explain in their introduction that Burke spent "considerable time during 1947 thinking through the complexities of myth as they govern and are governed by identification and persuasion" (20). Haunted by fascist myths dictating World War II and by communist myths fueling the impending Cold War, Burke is in *The War of Words* working through ways to define rhetorical dimensions of myths, ways to analyze existing myths and their ideological underpinnings, and ways to construct new myths.

Following LePore's and Burke's leads, rhetorical listening benefits from a consideration of myth as a rhetorical concept and tactic that may be used to define and address rhetorical problems. Because rhetorical listening is invested in figuring out how individual thinking and collective thinking are linked, it profits not just from the study of claims and cultural logics but also from the study of individual beliefs and myth. Given the three elements of a cultural logic (definitions of a dominant trope, associated beliefs, and resulting cultural scripts), rhetorical listening invokes myth as one kind of cultural script that individuals and groups embrace and perform or, when necessary, revise or reject. In this way, rhetorical listening invites listening writers to *identify* myths haunting rhetorical problems and *assess* their effects not just on imagined solutions but on what other solutions may be imagined. Indeed, rhetorical listening encourages listening writers to stand under the discourses of myths in order to understand what different communities value and believe, thus exposing the socializing and normalizing powers of myths as well as the effects of myths on everyday thinking and writing.

To demonstrate connections between myth and a rhetorical education grounded in rhetorical listening, this chapter defines *myth* as a rhetorical concept, discusses why to study myths, and poses sample tactics that may be used for analyzing and employing myths in everyday writing tasks.

WHAT IS MYTH AS A RHETORICAL CONCEPT?

Today a quick internet search for the trope *myth* will render myriad websites defining myth as a false story: "5 Myths about Bodybuilding" or "10 Myths about Introverts." Such websites imply that if readers will simply rid themselves of these myths-as-false-stories and uncover hidden truths, then they will be able to plan effective bodybuilding regimes or successfully negotiate their introverted personalities. But this use of *myth* is short-sighted, for *myth* has (and has historically had) a richer, more complex meaning. Indeed, myths are narratives that rise to a certain status within a culture or across cultures. While all myths are stories, not all stories rise to the level of myths. Myths achieve their elevated status because they 1) underwrite the values and belief systems of cultural groups, 2) explain human motivations for individual and collective actions, and 3) provide lessons about and scripts for ethical and unethical actions. As such, myths help people determine what is typically and often non-consciously accepted as *essentially* true, even if (or especially when) the effects of myths manifest as "empirical grit" (Dyson, "Foreword" ix).

As a rhetorical concept, myth often depicts or echoes the *origins* of cultural values and beliefs and, as such, explains the underlying motivations for individual and collective actions. In this way, myth distinguishes itself from other rhetorical concepts associated with rhetorical listening because it defines rhetorical problems as perennial issues that haunt humans within and across cultures, linking past and present and demanding ethical action. According to Burke, myth invokes origins by appealing to symbolic regression—the idea that if we go back far enough in history, the original catalyst of a conflict may be rooted out, confronted, and revised in order to achieve more equitable outcomes (*A Grammar* 430).

Symbolic regression can inspire equitable outcomes as when myths grant hearings on cultural issues and perspectives that have heretofore been unspoken or relegated to the margins of acceptability. Consider, for example, Octavia Butler's *The Parable of the Sower*, Marlon James's *Black Leopard, Red Wolf,* Ryan Coogler's *Black Panther*, and Robin Coste Lewis's *Voyage of the Sable Venus*, and many other texts. Mythic images such as Coste Lewis's sable Venus help readers confront histories of racial and sexual violence and imagine new narratives that redress the gendered horrors of slavery and systemic racism.

But symbolic regression can also produce inequitable outcomes. Namely, it can enable people to imagine *origins* wrongly as an objective method for thinking about history,[7] to focus purposefully or inadvertently on false origins, to overgeneralize the scope of their insights, to bury unstated assumptions, and even to silence narrative figures that still need a hearing. Imagining myth as a rhetorical concept, then, demands recognizing that humans' drive to create origin stories is driven by symbolic regression, and such imagining also demands being attentive to the limitations of such regressions.

Imagining myth as a rhetorical concept can be challenging, however, because familiarity can discourage critical thinking. As familiar childhood companions, myths are often simply accepted, and the values they represent are simply assumed to be truthful or natural. Think George

Washington. Think Harry Potter. Think Wonder Woman. Someone
created stories about them, and someone believed the stories, so much
so that the stories rose to the level of myth. Thinking critically about
myths becomes easier, interestingly enough, when myth is characterized
as a rhetorical concept that people construct and employ to "make sense"
of the world or to imagine a better one. Imagining myth as a rhetorical
concept transforms mythic values and beliefs in stories *from* unstated
assumptions that are naturalized as truth *into* stated claims that are debatable. This transformation of myth's unstated assumptions into debatable claims, in turn, encourages listening writers to better understand
how myths link individual and collective identities, represent cultural
values, and serve as a metaphoric vehicle for addressing real-life rhetorical problems.

To understand how listening rhetorically to myths helps identify
mythic identities related to a real-life rhetorical problem, consider a Superman cartoon. The scene portrays Superman standing, head bowed,
before a superhero licensing board because he has taken illegal performance-enhancing drugs (PEDs); the caption relays the board's decision,
"I'm sorry, but you're going to have to hand over the cape. Your test came
back positive for anabolic steroids." To make its point about PEDs, the
cartoon assumes an audience whose identity includes knowing something about the mythic identity of Superman. He is an alien from the
planet Krypton who is transported as a baby to rural America and found
by his adoptive parents, Jonathan and Martha Kent. As he grows, his
adoptive parents teach him to use his superpowers so that his actions
embody "Truth, Justice, and the American Way."

To understand how listening rhetorically to identities of characters
and audiences simultaneously identifies cultural values, consider what
makes Superman a superhero. Obviously, no governing body licenses
him. Rather, his own actions credential him because they invoke values (Truth, Justice, and the American Way) associated with the mythic
founding of America. In this way, the Superman myth is a *version* of our
nation's mythological origins, and these underlying values of our nation are always threatened in each Superman comic. To the extent that
Superman acts to save the day and uphold these cultural values, he is
identified as a superhero and an ideal man. To the extent that he fails,
he is considered a fraud or, possibly, a villain. Either way, Superman's
powers do not manifest from illegal substances. For that reason, we can

deduce that there is more at stake in this cartoon than Superman's status as a superhero.

In addition to a focus on identities and values, myths also function as metaphoric vehicles for questioning other topics. In the cartoon, Superman serves as a vehicle for commenting on professional athletes and their use of performance-enhancing drugs. Just as the myth of Superman's strength is exposed as false by the cartoon's licensing board, so too is the myth of professional athletes' abilities exposed as false. Rather than call out specific athletes, the cartoon makes Superman stand trial on their behalf, his mythic status emphasizing the degree to which athletes have violated the cultural values of Truth, Justice, and the American Way. By using Superman, the illustrator argues that there is no such thing as an untainted hero and implicitly questions why those born with seemingly superhuman qualities would be motivated to cheat when they and those who look up to them have so much to lose. By linking the Superman myth to PED usage in professional sports, Superman's position as a mythic hero is questioned, but conversely, and more to the cartoon's point, his presence raises the successes and failures of contemporary athletes to the level of myth. Those who take PEDs become tragic heroes or villains, whose failures violate principles that exceed the governing rules of their sport. Those who did not take PEDs become mythic heroes who uphold the timeless principles that maintain the integrity of the sport and, by extension, their nation.

When listeners use myths as a rhetorical concept in their own writing processes, they may explore how myths haunt arguments, how myths may be reimagined as debatable claims, how myths champion certain cultural values and beliefs; how myths posit stakes and consequences for allowing such cultural values and beliefs to remain invisibly naturalized or to be made visible, how individual and collective action in the present and across time may be linked, how myths may be more equitably reimaged, and how myths may help listening writers generate information that may be used to compose responses to rhetorical problems (such as a cartoonist's deciding how to make a statement against PEDs).

WHY STUDY MYTHS AS RHETORICAL CONCEPTS?

Myth has played only a peripheral role in the twentieth-century's recovery of rhetorical studies. Granted, noted rhetorical philosophers have relied on myth to ground their claims as when Kenneth Burke invokes

Samson in the 1950 *A Rhetoric of Motives* to exemplify multiple types of identifications (3–5) and when George Kennedy plays with the dual role of Corax as "human" and "crow" in the 1992 "A Hoot in the Dark" (5). A few rhetoric scholars have even invoked Burke in their attempts to elevate myth's status in our field. In a 1997 *Poetics Today* article, C. Allen Carter claims that Burke's rhetorical theory includes "a narrative construction of the self" that circles between logic and narrative (343–344) and then argues that this innovative use of narrative necessarily includes a consideration of myth (356). In a 2013 book on Burke and myth, Laurence Coupe argues, first, that Burke "refus[es] to see mythology as a quaint worldview that has been superseded" (3) and, second, that myth inflects Burke's treatments of society, literary criticism, ritual drama, victimage, and ecology. Around the same times, feminist scholars in rhetorical studies also emphasized the import of myth. In a 1997 *Quarterly Journal of Speech* article, Helene Shugart argues for appropriation as a feminist rhetorical strategy, citing myth as a fruitful site for appropriation (212). In a 2003 *Rhetoric and Public Affairs* article, Bonnie Dow argues that the myth of individualism in the US poses "continuing problems" for feminism at the turn of the twenty-first century. And in a 2018 *Rhetoric Society Quarterly* article, we argue for the importance of mythic considerations in feminist renderings of rhetorical history. But the text that has the potential to catapult myth into the center of rhetorical studies is Kenneth Burke's own *The War of Words,* first published in 2018, which underscores the organizing role that myths play in rhetorical philosophies.

The War of Words takes the above arguments one step further by showing how Burke imagines a new mythic image (the War of Words) to create a rhetorical philosophy grounded in identification. As a mythic image, the War of Words explains why linguistic conflict obtains across time irrespective of political system or world culture. As Burke argues in *A Rhetoric of Motives*: "For rhetoric as such is not rooted in any past condition of human society. It is rooted in an essential function of language itself, a function that is wholly realistic, and is continually born anew; the use of a symbolic means of inducing cooperation in beings that by nature respond to symbols" (43). Perhaps there was a time when human beings did not have language and thus were not divided from one another, but that time is not accessible in any narrative form besides myth. The best we can do, according to Burke, is recognize that human societies have created myths and mythic images to explain the linguistic state of division that defines human existence. By analyzing such myths and mythic images, rhetorical critics may explain, for example, why efforts to create communities via identification do not eliminate wars over linguistic and material property assignments. Invoking the War of Words as myth, rhetorical critics may define rhetorical problems as well as the limits or possibilities of rhetorical action in new ways.

As described in the introduction to this chapter, mythic criticism has historically relied on troubled assumptions about universality and primitive minds. But dismissing myth as old-fashioned does not erase its organizational power for naturalizing cultural assumptions, for motivating human actions, and for upholding institutional structures such as political movements, governments, religions, cults, universities, entertainment industries, etc. Given the import and impact of myths, mythic criticism can and should be reimagined within rhetorical studies. It will help listening writers accrue a deeper understanding of what myths are, how myths function, and how myths may be employed in their own writing processes.

Consequently, helping listening writers think critically about myth is important for the following reasons.

First, studying myth as a rhetorical concept helps listening writers understand how myths travel through history and across cultures in order to emphasize "universal" qualities of human experiences. Myths try to rise to the level of the universal, explaining why all humans act as they do, regardless of cultural place or historical moment. The problem with myth's impulse toward universality is twofold: first, mythic stories originate in particular times and places and, thus, are often culturally specific, inflected by these origins whatever the iteration of the myth; second, when mythic stories are reproduced in different times and places, they are inflected, too, by these different times and places. In this way, myths accrue meanings.

So even as individual heroes travel from culture to culture, century to century, they change in the process. This duality of travel and change is important: first, travel allows mythic heroes to reveal something about *what it means to be human* across time and place and, in the process, creates a tradition that people can embrace; second, change allows mythic heroes to reveal something about *what it means to be human* in a specific time and place. Consider, for example, Cinderella. Different versions of her story posit small feet as a sign of women's beauty, beauty as a necessary element of her identity, and magic shoes as a vehicle to her happily ever after. Yet, the versions change across time and from culture to culture. Walt Disney's 1950 US Cinderella differs from the Brothers Grimm's 1812 German Cinderella, who in turn differs from Charles Perrault's 1697 French Cendrillion, or Duan Chengshi's 850 CE Chinese Ye Xian. Consider too, the myth of Odysseus (Ulysses), the cunning Greek warrior king who invented the Trojan horse to sneak Greek soldiers past Trojan barricades. He appears in Homer's *Odyssey* (eighth-century BCE), in Alfred Lord Tennyson's poem "Ulysses" (1833 CE), James Joyce's novel *Ulysses* (1922 CE), and in the Coen Brothers' *O Brother, Where Art Thou* (2000 CE), a film starring George Clooney—to name only a few manifestations.

While achieving mythic universality may be impossible, the impulse toward universality is incredibly strong, hence the danger of misrepresenting a culturally-situated myth as a universal Truth. To resist this impulse, rhetorical critics should analyze each iteration of a myth for what is stated, implied, and denied or omitted. What is stated or implied in multiple versions of the Odysseus myth are the values that Western culture has embraced: a cunning intellect, a brotherhood of warriors, a determination to live life to the fullest, the use of home as the ultimate goal, and the favor of a powerful deity. What changes is how each culture defines *cunning, warrior, fullest, home*, and *deity* and, thus, how each culture operationalizes mythic values. Multiple versions of this myth also reveal common temptations that humans should beware: the lure of adventure over responsibility or playing the field over fidelity. What is often denied or omitted in iterations of Odysseus myths is the backstory of its women characters, something that Edna St. Vincent Millay points out in her poem, "The Ancient Gesture," which reimagines the story of Penelope, the wife of Odysseus, during the years she awaits his return. Also missing in most versions of how this myth travels (including our version above) are non-Western perspectives. For example, how would the Trojans have narrated Odysseus's feats? Also missing is a recognition of how myths often offer gendered cultural scripts for heroes. For example, would the cultural values that are associated with Odysseus-as-hero work for Cinderella-as-hero? Probably not. Traditionally, it would have been difficult to imagine reading a story to young children about a woman who travels around her known world, having affairs with different men and using a tricky intelligence to get out of adventurous situations, before arriving home to reunite with her husband after ten years. It would have been equally difficult to imagine reading a story to young children about a man who is forced to stay at home doing chores and waiting for a princess to save him, finally attracting a princess with his beauty and small feet. Drew Barrymore's film *Ever After* attempts a middle ground, keeping the class and gender identities of characters in *Cinderella* fairly intact but redefining them in ways that allow the prince and Cinderella to save each other. Given the changes in gender identity currently under discussion in the US, it will be interesting to see how this story will evolve. In a 2021 Amazon movie version of *Cinderella*, for example, Billy Porter plays the Fairy Godmother as nonbinary, arguing that "magic has no gender," which is a queering of the character in a way that echoes the impulse toward universality (Reddish).

Second, studying myth as a rhetorical concept helps listening writers identify how myths provide cultural scripts that influence people's thinking and acting. This influence is why myths are imagined as rhetorical. As socializing forces, myths offer people lessons in ways to behave and not behave in order to reaffirm or to question prevailing norms. For example, prevailing gender norms are reinforced by traditional myths that offer girls a cultural script of passivity, such as the one featuring a long-locked Rapunzel high in a tower waiting to be saved. This script encourages girls to believe they are in need of rescue by a valiant prince or a magical fairy godmother who will ensure the young girls' happily-ever-afters.

Contemporary revisions of such myths have attempted to offer cultural scripts with more girl power. For instance, the Disney version of Rapunzel, *Tangled*, represents a young woman yearning to see the world and taking action to make it happen. Yet, she and the other Disney princesses are still valued in large part because of their beauty and their class status as princesses. Other revisions exist, too. A *New Yorker* cartoon features a dad sitting beside his daughter's bed reading a bedtime story; the caption reads, echoing the daughter's voice, "Skip to the part where the princess climbs to the top of the corporate ladder." The phrase "climb to the top of the corporate ladder" is a comic reversal of the common mythic trope where a prince climbs to the top of a tower to rescue the princess. In the little girl's mind, the princess is the agent of her own destiny, which seems to befuddle the little girl's father. With this scene, the cartoon questions a value that a culture has long held (women are not strong enough to act on their own) as well as an associated cultural script (the prince or fairy godmother rescues the princess). It also imagines a new value (women are strong enough to act on their own) as well as a new associated cultural script (a princess can climb a corporate ladder and not hit a glass ceiling). When listening writers generate new cultural scripts by revising existing myths and imagining new ones, they are invoking a powerful writing tool.

But even new myths must be examined for what is denied or omitted because no myth is totalizing. For example, what systemic elements exist in corporate America that will enable this cartoon's new myth to be performed, and what systemic elements need to be redesigned in order to make such performances possible? And the young girl in the *New Yorker* cartoon is clearly middle class and white. Is the myth she invokes available not just to her but to others who do not fit her identity categories?

Third, studying myth as a rhetorical concept helps listening writers map how myths comment on the real world even when the myths are not grounded in real people or events. Obviously, no one thinks that Zeus is a real god, that Katniss Everdeen is a real tribute, that Harry Potter is a real wizard, or that Black Panther is a real king. The good news is that myths do not have to be grounded in real or even plausible events in order to affect how people think and write. Though characters may not be real, the values and beliefs they represent are very real to the people and cultures that celebrate them. Zeus represents powerful hypermasculinity; Katniss and Harry represent underdogs whose truth, justice, and bravery inspire followers to create a better world; and Black Panther represents intelligence, courage, the visibility of a hidden past, and a forward-looking leadership grounded in social justice.

The mythic tension between fictional characters and real values explains the humor in a superhero cartoon: a man standing outside a movie theater is having an emotional breakdown as passersby walk past, clearly not understanding his despair. There is no caption, only a theater marquee that reads "Batman v. Superman." Passersby cannot understand why the distraught man does not get that the movie is just a movie, not real; he, on the other hand, cannot believe how passersby remain unmoved by the film's pitting Batman against Superman, a plot that violates his core beliefs about the world of DC Comics as well as the values of heroic action, loyalty, and brotherhood. A similar tension between fictional characters and real values emerged after the final season of *Game of Thrones*. The internet was rife with calls for fans to sign a petition demanding HBO rewrite, reshoot, and reshow the story's conclusion because the filmed ending violated the fan's core beliefs about the world of Westeros as well as their values about family, romantic love, earning one's place in the world, and even good storytelling. They wanted a different version of this myth.

Yet even fictional myths must be examined for what is denied or omitted. For example, would the pitting of Wonder Woman and Batman cause the distraught man as much anguish as the pitting of Batman and Superman? Or would the pitting of Superman and DC world's non-white heroes such as Ralph Jackson and Jackie Johnson trigger such a breakdown?[8] Why? Why not? And what about other countries' comic heroes? Why are they not adapted for an international audience the way US superheroes are?

Fourth, studying myth as a rhetorical concept helps listening writers map how myths can be rooted in historical facts, which can make them seem more persuasive. Examples include the *300* films that depict the Battle of Thermopylae, which was fought in 480 BCE between King Leonidas of Sparta with his force of three-hundred men and the invading Persians. Celebrated in art, literature, and film, the Battle of Thermopylae has retained mythic status for 2,500 years. This myth appears in Emily Dickinson's nineteenth-century poem "Go Tell It" in which the battle symbolizes a metaphoric "last stand," or a last chance to relate one's feelings to a loved one. In 2006 and 2014 the Hollywood's *300* films celebrate the mythic fight for freedom when a community is threatened by deadly invaders, a theme that resonates in a twenty-first-century US threatened by terrorism.

In our times, other real-life events and places have also entered the realm of the mythic: the Holocaust, the fall of Apartheid, and 9/11. Actual historical figures have also achieved such mythic status: Hua Mulan, Joan of Arc, Sojourner Truth, Abraham Lincoln, Albert Einstein, Billy Jean King, Martin Luther King Jr., and Tupac Shakur. When invoked by writers, such historical events or figures carry a persuasive weight because they, in turn, invoke not just the values associated with them but also the dominant trope of *the real*, with this trope quickly being associated with *the truth*. In this way, listening writers build credibility into their writing, borrowing or leaning on the ethos of the historical event or figure that has risen to mythic status.

But again, questions of what is denied or omitted in such myths must be addressed. Real life events are remembered through histories, and all histories have points of view. So listening writers should ask: What points of view have dominated a particular telling—and why? And because real-life people are human and not perfect, listening writers should also ask: To what extent should human failings affect the mythic status of Albert Einstein or Martin Luther King Jr.? Do their human failings make their mythic status less appreciable? More so?

Fifth, studying myth as a rhetorical concept helps listening writers determine how myths often shape people's perspectives at a non-conscious level. Whether ancient or contemporary, real or not real, myths haunt people's everyday lives, often at a non-conscious level. Non-conscious simply refers to a state of being somewhere between being aware and being totally unaware. Claiming that myths function at a non-conscious level means that people are somewhat aware of the myths they carry in their imaginations but do not fully articulate them and certainly do not think critically about them. People carry myths in their imaginations because they are born into them and socialized to believe they are true or the natural order of things.

Such naturalizations of myths occur in paradoxical ways. For example, when myths are built on historical events and people, their *fictional* elements can come to be viewed as *factual* elements. Consider the myth of George Washington cutting down a cherry tree as a child. The moral of this story is that, from an early age, Washington was committed to telling the truth. By implication, this myth suggests that our country's leaders should follow Washington's lead. But this story is not factually true (Pruitt); it is a fiction that has risen to the level of myth so as to represent the American value of honesty. Of course, it doesn't help that this myth was first circulated in a biography of George Washington, a genre that we assume delivers only facts.

And yet, myths also become naturalized in the exact opposite way. Sometimes, when people assume that myths are *only* fictional, they do not take seriously how the myths can organize their beliefs and value systems, their motivations, and their actions. People will say things such as "That's just a story we tell . . ." and, in doing so, assume that stories have no power over our lives. At the same time, such people will also enact these stories as when people perform cultural scripts such as sitting on Santa's lap to ask for gifts or attending a prom dressed as a prince or princess.

Regardless of how myths are naturalized, listening writers benefit from making non-conscious myths the subject of conscious reflection. Otherwise, unstated values and ideas remain unstated and denied. Often such values and ideas become a matter of conscious public debate only when someone calls a mythic representation into question, as when a presidential candidate offers a particular version of America; when myths are questioned, people often feel either frustrated or supportive of a represented value or idea and, as a result, often dig into an "I'm right, you're wrong" argument. But listening writers need not get stuck in such bickering; indeed, they need not wait on such invitations either. By incorporating the investigation of myths as rhetorical concepts into their writing processes, they continually learn both how myths define the values and beliefs that motivate individuals and groups and also how such myths may be turned into debatable claims that inform everyday writing tasks.

Studying myth as a rhetorical concept benefits listening writers in several ways. It provides opportunities to explore different cultures and cultural logics to find common ground and productive differences. It exposes that a group's myths facilitates communication among members who agree yet hinders communication with non-members who do not agree. It reinforces the power of story, especially when it rises to the level of myth, to influence attitudes and actions. It focuses attention on how language is used to construct and interpret past events, to assess current rhetorical problems, and to envision future change. It fosters choices about what version of a myth to tell and what purpose to select for telling and retelling. As such, studying myth as a rhetorical concept invites listening writers to contemplate the values, motivations, and ethical actions that inflect their everyday rhetorical problems.

WHAT ARE TACTICS FOR RHETORICAL MYTHS?

Tactics for contemplating rhetorical myths are important tools for listening writers. These tactics help such writers envision their critical thinking moves; as a result, these writers better understand the stories they tell in order to explain who people are in relation to other people, to their cultures, and to other cultures. Such understanding enhances listening writers' abilities to define and analyze their rhetorical problems and then compose their responses. To demonstrate how tactics of rhetorical myth work, this section takes as its topic textual adaptations, or how stories migrate from one type of text or genre to another, as in Cinderella's travel from oral traditions to books to films.

Tactic #1: Analyze how myths provide cultural scripts that influence people's thinking and acting.

1. Select a popular text (image, film, book, videogame, song) that incorporates or adapts a myth.

2. Identify the main conflict in the myth.

3. Determine the values and beliefs that motivate the characters' individual and collective actions in relation to this conflict.

4. Identify how the cultural scripts provided by the myth offer moral lessons for everyday life in contemporary society.

The Disney film *Moana* (#1) adapts Polynesian myths to the big screen for a world audience. The conflict in the myth hinges on a looming environmental catastrophe that must be stopped in order to save Moana's island culture (#2). This catastrophe is sparked by the overzealous actions of Maui, who steals the heart of the island goddess Te Fiti, the giver of life. Moana, the Chief's daughter, and Maui, a hero and trickster, must return Te Fiti's heart if they are to save Moana's community from environmental destruction.

One way to unpack the values and beliefs that a myth supports (#3) is to identify conflicting values and beliefs and the different cultural scripts they imply. For example, Moana is motivated by a desire to save her island culture and the people she loves. The conflicting cultural scripts confronting her in the film are that she is expected to stay home, lead her community, and respect her father's guidance, yet her destiny demands she leave the island reef and assert her own agency to save not only her community but also every island culture affected by Maui's theft.

To begin thinking through this set of conflicting values and beliefs and their associated cultural scripts, try using the following tactic: *It is wrong to (x) unless the reason for doing so is (y)*. In Moana's case, it might look something like: It is wrong to *shirk your leadership responsibilities at home and pursue personal desires elsewhere*, unless the reason for doing so *is to achieve a greater good for everyone*, at which point the action of shirking leadership at home is acceptable. In Maui's case, it might look like this: It was wrong to *steal the heart of Te Fiti* because the reason for doing so was *to achieve personal glory*, which is not a greater good.

Understanding values that drive and are encoded in cultural scripts highlights the myth's moral lessons (#4). For example, Maui's selfish ambitions have several negative consequences: he loses his most prized possession (his hook and thus his power to transfigure into any living being); he is stranded on a deserted island; he loses his hard-earned reputation; and, most importantly, he accelerates an environmental catastrophe that will harm everyone. Until he learns to put aside his selfish ambitions, he cannot be redeemed as a character and the land cannot be saved from catastrophe. This myth is an ancient one that explains how human greed and the desire to control the environment can have disastrous consequences for individuals, for cultures, and for the earth.

In the film, Moana is an important character because She serves as a role model for young children watching the film. In that capacity, she serves as the catalyst for redeeming not just Maui, not just her community, not just the land, but also the idea of woman as hero. Her actions are heroic in both traditional and contemporary ways: she is traditional by repeating the age-old pattern of women being the moral compass for men; she is contemporary in that she is a female who strikes out on her own as the hero of her own story yet achieves great things for everyone.

Tactic #2: Analyze how myths travel through history.

1. Select a popular text (image, film, book, videogame, song) that adapts or incorporates a myth.

2. Identify the conflict that drives the action in the story.

3. Determine how the story's conflict is represented in different cultures across time.

4. Analyze how the values associated with this conflict travel and change in each iteration of the myth, considering what is stated and what is denied a hearing.

Wonder Woman has recently resurged in popularity as a mythic hero, thanks to the hugely successful 2017 film (#1) that presented a representation of warrior women not usually seen. Its main conflict, however, questions why civilizations are constantly at war with one another: Wonder Woman, a member of the community of Amazons whose sacred responsibility is to protect humans from ongoing threats of war, must confront Ares, the classical Greek god of war who constantly incites humans to violence (#2).

Although the Wonder Woman myth is a little more than one hundred years old, the Greek myths invoked in the film are ancient, exemplifying how myths may travel through history and function transhistorically. Weaving different historical moments together to explain why humans wage war, the film explicitly connects an ancient conflict (between Zeus and Ares in ancient Greece) with a modern conflict (between Britain and Germany in World War II). By highlighting this ancient-modern connection, the story suggests that the problems in World War II Britain and Germany are a result of problems that an ancient civilization initiated but did not resolve. Consequently, the problem of war repeats as a familiar cultural script whether it is fought with thunderbolts, special swords, bows and arrows, guns, chemical compounds, or nuclear weapons (#3).

Regardless of its origin, a myth is adapted only when it successfully addresses a contemporary problem. In *Wonder Woman*, for example, the Amazonian culture addresses women's desire to have role models who are strong, smart, and heroic. Likewise, Wonder Woman's victory over Ares comforts our contemporary anxiety that terror and war are ever on the horizon. The *Wonder Woman* audience can invest her with their unrealistic expectations (such as her saving the world) so that, for 119 minutes as audiences watch the film, they can feel safe from their anxieties, imagine possibilities of another world, and reinscribe the contemporary values of peace, justice, and heroic action (#4).

But because no myth can offer a totalizing vision, what is not reckoned with in this movie is what happens to those not represented in the film and what happens after "The End"? Does the defeat of Ares signal the end of all war, and what will happen to Wonder Woman? The 2020 sequel answered those questions, though given the problems with the sequel, perhaps these questions should have remained open (#4).

Tactic #3: Analyze why myths do not have to be grounded in real events to be true.

1. Select a popular text (image, film, book, videogame, song) that adapts or incorporates a myth.

2. Identify the elements of the myth that are implausible in the real world.

3. Describe the values and beliefs that these implausible elements are meant to represent in the real world.

4. Determine the moral lessons that are meant to be drawn from the mythic representation of implausible events.

To analyze how *implausible* components of a myth are grounded by an entirely *plausible* system of values and beliefs, a listening writer might complete the following claim: *In the myth of (a), the following component of the story (b) is implausible in our world, but because this component represents the value/belief of (c), it helps me reflect on my life and/or contemporary cultures in the following ways (d).*

Take, for example, J. K. Rowling's beloved *Harry Potter* books and film series (#1), which have become a myth for modern times. Though fictional, the magical world and characters that Rowling built feels real to fans, and the values and beliefs of that world ring true to fans as well. This linkage of Potter myth to reality is captured in a cartoon immediately following the death of Alan Rickman, the actor who played Severus Snape. The scene paints Harry and a regular Joe sitting at a bar toasting Snape, with the caption reading, "Here's to the best damned antagonist a guy could ask for." Yet, no matter how many theme park attractions are built, Harry and Snape's struggle with Voldemort is fictional, and magical wands are just toys (#2).

But the values and beliefs in the story are very real. On the one hand, these values are very desirable to many readers. For example, Harry, Hermione, and Ron's search for the Deathly Hallows represents loyalty, trust, talent, friendship, and love used not for personal gain but for common good. Dumbledore's and Snape's sacrifices via a magical spell that kills Dumbledore represent friendship, loyalty, wisdom, talent, and goodness used not for personal gain but for common good. And Professor McGonagall's caretaking and stepping up when needed represent loyalty, talent, initiative, and love. As these examples show, values are both individual and communal, the latter ones threaded across characters. On the other hand, the values in Harry Potter's world may not be as desirable to other readers who do not identify with the narrowness of the series' vision. After all this fantasy world's conflict is grounded in reinscribed racism (muggles, mudbloods, and pure bloods), the cult of personality (what if Harry hadn't disposed of the Elder Wand at the end?), a narrow sexuality (heteronormative), and a non-diverse community (mostly white) (#3).

The series' values (as evidenced by Harry) or the lack of these values (as evidenced by Voldemort) offer readers and film audiences lessons for how to live and how not to live a moral life. For example, when confronted with an ethical conflict, fans might ask, "What would Harry do?" or "What might Dumbledore or Ron or Hermione, etc., do?" If fans want to figure out what not to do, they might simply ask, "What would Voldemort do?" or "What would Lucius Malfoy do?" But if fans want to figure out how to navigate more conflicted choices, they might ask, "What would Narcissa Malfoy do?" After all, she follows Voldemort but saves Harry and later saves her husband and son by leading them away from the final showdown between Harry and Voldemort. Or fans might even query, "What might J. K. Rowling have imagined differently—and to what end?" With all of these questions, fans would generate a variety of possible responses and a deeper understanding of how myths work rhetorically (#4).

Tactic #4: Analyze how myths gain power from being grounded in real events.

1. Select a popular text (image, film, book, videogame, song) that adapts or incorporates a myth.

2. Analyze the myth to identify

   a. Elements of historical events present in the myth and their accuracy.

   b. Elements of historical events omitted from the myth.

3. Analyze how the values or beliefs in the myth are affected by their links to 2a or 2b.

4. Determine the moral lessons that may be drawn from this mythic adaptation of historical events.

Disney's *Pocahontas* mythologizes a sixteenth-century person for contemporary society (#1). To understand how Disney has mythologized her life, writers might ask: which historical events are prioritized and how accurate are they? (#2a), and which historical events are omitted? (#2b). These moves can be incredibly helpful for imagining the *historical grounds* upon which *mythic stories* are built and the implications of how they are built.

The animated film represents a real person, Pocahontas, but takes liberties with the facts of her life and culture. She was a real person named Amonute, with a private name of Matoaka; her nickname was *Pocahontas*, meaning "playful"; born in 1595 near the place the English called Jamestown, Virginia, she was a member of a collective Algonquin community led by her father (Townsend). The film represents inaccuracies, promoting more what Disney writers/animators imagined about Pocahontas than what they researched about her actual identity and community. For example, Disney's "blue corn moon" symbol from one of the film's popular songs was not a part of Pocahontas's culture (blue corn is a crop associated with the Southwestern US or Mexico, not Virginia) (#2a).

This passing of Disney imagination as historical "fact" pervades the film. Pocahontas is imagined as a young woman who saves and then is attracted to John Smith while she introduces him to her culture and learns about his. But in real life, she met John Smith when he was kidnapped by her uncle, and what is omitted is that, instead of being a handsome blonde hunk with a Mel Gibson voice, Smith was a short, squat dark-haired man. Moreover, Pocahontas actually met Smith when she was eleven years old, so a romance between the pair seems (we hope) unlikely. Later, she was kidnapped by the English, and her father refused to ransom her by fully returning all the weapons and prisoners demanded by the English (#2b). Depending on which version of history is consulted, either Pocahontas wanted to marry the Englishman John Rolfe whom she met during her captivity, or she was forced to marry him in lieu of the remainder of her ransom (a not unimportant difference!). After her marriage to Rolfe, she travelled with him to England where she died young. Important to note: the dominant culture's version of Pocahontas's life comes from other people's writings about her, then and now (#2a and #2b) (Townsend). But "The Pocahontas Project" created by Northwestern University students records how her story has come down through "The Mattaponi Oral Tradition" (Woll).

Once listening writers understand *how* a person or event has been mythologized, they can ask *why?* For example, why was the Pocahontas myth adapted for contemporary times, and why does the Disney film deviate so much from the historical record? Such questions help identify values and beliefs underlying an adapted myth. If writers ask, "Why did Disney deem it important to make a film about an Indigenous princess," they might conclude that Disney thought it would make money, capitalizing on the success of their multicultural princess theming. After all, profit is a fact of life in business. But why did they select Pocahontas in particular? The film was released in 1995, at the height of American multiculturalism, so it could be argued that Disney was attempting to foster knowledge and understanding among different ethnic communities (#3). But if so, why did Disney deviate so much from the historical record? Were they trying to sanitize a troubled national history for a world-wide Disney audience? Or were they unaware of the cultural erasures and genocide suffered by Indigenous peoples? Neither marketing nor ignorance is a good enough answer to the question of historical deviation.

For a myth to have meaning in a particular context, it must tap into the values and beliefs of that context. Disney's 1995 *Pocahontas* attempts to do just that. On the one hand, the film sends the multicultural message that cross-cultural communication and respect of different cultures are important. On the other hand, the plot omits the tragic consequences for the historical Pocahontas, and the acultural use of a blue corn moon reinforces US stereotyping, repeating a pattern of the dominant culture's not respecting differences between Indigenous communities, including their symbols, and not recognizing that Indigenous people inhabit entire American continents, not just the Southwestern United States. In this way, the adapted myth says more about who is representing the myth (Disney) than about the historical events, places, and people represented (Pocahontas) (#4). Grappling with the tensions between these conflicting messages about values and beliefs can be the start of interesting and culturally significant arguments and actions.

Tactic #5: Analyze how myths often function at a non-conscious level.

1. Select a popular text (image, film, book, videogame, song) that adapts or incorporates a myth.

2. Analyze how the myth circulates in public (What types of media does it circulate in? Where does it circulate? Who is the target audience? What must audiences have or do to access the myth?).

3. Explain how the myth becomes naturalized in a culture (At what points of its circulation is a myth perceived as "just the way it is/

was" as opposed to being perceived simply as "one version" of the myth?).

4. Discuss how this naturalization has been/may be/should be/ should not be interrupted.

The best way to understand how myths function at a non-conscious level is to focus on how texts *circulate* (travel through history and across cultures) and become *naturalized* (achieve the status of an unquestioned "normal" or "that's just how it is/was"). With this focus identified, listening writers can reflect on why certain myths such as the first Thanksgiving emerge and re-emerge at certain points in history.[9] Listening writers can also reflect on how the values and beliefs that myths promote can be used to analyze and compose their everyday writing tasks.

The circulation of a myth can be traced in two ways. First, listening writers can identify *particular points of view or cultural logics* from which myths are told. For example, the story of the first Thanksgiving, which occurred at the Plymouth Plantation in 1621, may be represented by different points of view. A contemporary cartoon pictures an Indigenous man saying to a Pilgrim man, "You just show up here illegally and expect us to tell you about corn?" This cartoon raises the questions of how Thanksgiving stories are told (or how they are known but not spoken) and also how the point of view of the telling may affect whether a cultural group desires to celebrate Thanksgiving as a national holiday or not. Indeed, the cartoon questions the dominant narrative of Thanksgiving as a time of peaceful, intercultural sharing and suggests Thanksgiving as a time of white people's gaining an uninvited foothold in the "New World" (#2).

Second, listening writers can identify how *parts* of myths are adapted and circulated in different places. Consider how different parts of the dominant first Thanksgiving myth — attire, food, weapons, postures, people — appear in contemporary grocery ads, greeting cards, school plays, movies, comic strips, etc. Consider a Snoopy cartoon where Snoopy is dressed as a Pilgrim and Woodstock (his small yellow bird friend) is dressed as an Indigenous person and where the banner at the bottom reads "THE BEST THINGS IN LIFE ARE MEANT TO BE SHARED." This cartoon invokes some parts of the Thanksgiving myth: food (corn), clothes (Pilgrim hats and Indigenous headdresses), themes (sharing), and people (Pilgrim and Indigenous) (#2). In terms of people, the cartoon's associating Snoopy with Pilgrims invites readers to identify with Pilgrims more while, at the same time, associating a smaller less prominent character with Indigenous peoples invites readers to feel more distanced from them (#2).

Audiences who view this cartoon and simply smile do so because, for them, the dominant narrative has become naturalized. Naturalization of a myth as a dominant narrative can be traced in a couple ways, too. First, listening writers can identify the audiences who have access to a myth at any given point in history. US citizens have gained access to the first Thanksgiving story since 1621 by oral tradition, journalistic stories, fiction, and poetry throughout US history; by political proclamations at different points in US history (for example, by Sam Adams in 1777, by Abraham Lincoln in 1863, and by Franklin D. Roosevelt in 1941); and by film, TV, and the internet from the twentieth-century to today (#3). Still, such naturalization of a dominant myth can be interrupted (Sherman); for example, the United American Indians of New England hold a day of mourning every November, a day of remembering the genocide of their peoples. Such interruptions can also be done in schools, for example, when students are asked to study the rhetorical nature of myths (#4).

Second, listening writers can trace the naturalization of a myth by exposing the technologies of naturalization. The more widely a myth is distributed, the more pervasive its presence in a culture, and, thus, the more likely it is that the myth influences everyday lives either consciously, non-consciously, or even unconsciously. For example, internet access in 2021 enables the dominant narrative of Thanksgiving to reach many more readers than a political pamphlet in 1777 (#3). Internet access also encourages dissemination of challenges to the dominant narrative as when social media and journalistic pieces question whether schoolchildren should use Indigenous ritual dress as costume or acknowledge that it was Wampanoag's generosity that helped white settlers survive during that first Thanksgiving period (#4) ("What Does").

Once listening writers use this tactic to generate information, they can ask additional questions to deepen their understanding of Thanksgiving. For example, why is the myth of the first Thanksgiving so popular that it circulates as both whole and part across several centuries , across several cultures, and across several media? What is at stake in celebrating a coming together of Indigenous and settler cultures—and for whom? Does the holiday conceal a history of racism in the US? How do the answers to the previous questions affect how a writer interprets a family dinner, Macy's Thanksgiving Day Parade, or even a grade school Thanksgiving play?

This chapter's focus on how myth functions as a rhetorical concept and tactic enhances listening writers' rhetorical education and prepares them to proceed to the next chapter, a study of rhetorical devices.

6 Rhetorical Devices

James Clear's internationally bestselling book, *Atomic Habits* offers simple tactics for transforming bad habits into good ones. Although Clear draws on a wide range of research to inform his recommendations, many of them formalize the findings of contemporary sports analytics and behavioral economics, which argue that human beings have a tendency to overvalue certain attributes that they intuitively align with a desired outcome. This overvaluation, in turn, obscures less obvious, non-intuitive attributes that, when brought to conscious attention, align more successfully with the desired outcome. For example, Clear argues that the British Cycling team went from national embarrassment to perennial champion "by making small adjustments . . . [to] overlooked and unexpected areas" that, when aggregated, paid significant dividends; they stopped focusing on big picture training techniques and began paying attention to seemingly minor variables such as which massage gels facilitated the fastest recovery and how best to wash one's hands to prevent illness (14). By making these small changes, the team produced "what is widely regarded as the most successful run in cycling history" (15). Clear also argues that making small adjustments works for individuals: "Qiana used a little math and a clever visual trick. 'I stopped drinking soda,' she wrote. 'I added up all the sodas I drank for the week and counted how many tablespoons of sugar were in those soda cans and bottles. I began to scoop the amount of sugar into an enormous bowl. The visual did it for me. I had to break that habit'" ("30 One-Sentence").

The most helpful lesson in Clear's book for listening writers is his principle: "motivation is overrated; environment often matters more" (*Atomic* 82). (Notice the function of identification here: Clear ascribes the evaluative properties of *overrated* to motivation and *matters more* to environment). To explain this principle, Clear describes how behavioral psychologists help businesses achieve greater profits by placing certain products in their retail stores either at eye level or at the end of an aisle. "End caps are money making machines for retailers," Clear explains, "because they are obvious locations that encounter a lot of foot traffic . . . the more obviously available a product or service is, the more likely you are to try it" (83). The upshot for listening writers is that "many of the actions we take each day are shaped not by purposeful drive and choice but by the most obvious option" (83). In other words, consumers who purchase paper towels from an end cap (the end of an aisle) do so not because they are motivated at some deep level to use that particular brand but, rather, because they simply find the paper towels in a convenient location as compared to other options and so unwittingly choose to purchase them. This behavior of choosing the most convenient option reflects how people use and respond to rhetorical devices, too.

Rhetorical devices, one could argue, serve as the end caps of argumentative life. As "the most obvious option" for expressing an argument, rhetorical devices invite audiences to identify with the formal rhythms they establish (*Atomic* 83). In the British Cycling team's case, the minor variables (massage gel efficacy, hand-washing protocols) served as rhetorical devices, promoting the argument that they were a team and that small changes made together would build the team's strength. In Qiana's situation, the sugar accruing in the sugar bowl served as a rhetorical device, promoting the argument that this much soda was bad for her and that she should change her drinking habits. Even chapter titles in books serve as rhetorical devices, arguing that a change of topic is occurring from the previous page.

But, you may be wondering: despite these examples, what exactly is a rhetorical device?

Rhetorical devices, according to Kenneth Burke in *The War of Words*, are argumentative moves that through situated, habitual repetitions coalesce into unnoticed argumentative *patterns* that shape perceptions, influence judgments and, in the process, become associated with users' identities (266). As such, rhetorical devices have five important dimensions.

The first dimension of devices is that they haunt every aspect of our daily lives, taking forms appropriate to their situations in order to forward a situated argument. For example, in addition to the rhetorical devices described above that relate to a cycling team's bonding and an individual's overcoming sugar addiction, one common device in the entertainment industry is the "standing ovation," the act of audience members standing to applaud and cheer at the end of a performance. An ovation-as-device forwards the audience's argument that the performance was enjoyable, perhaps stellar.

The second dimension of devices is that they encourage audiences to interpret the world according to prevailing wisdoms that are established, convenient, and situated. For example, because the prevailing wisdom in the US is to show appreciation for stellar public performances via standing ovations, audiences may jump to their feet at the end of an innovative Broadway show, after a basketball player's well-executed drive to the hoop, or after an entertaining drag performance. Ovations are indeed *established* practice; they are *convenient* because they provide immediate feedback and require no further action; and they are *situated* in that while fans in a sports arena might jump to their feet when a player makes a basket, they would probably not do so if listening to the game over earbuds in a university library.

The third dimension of devices is that they are most often performed at the level of the non-conscious, an intermediate space between conscious and unconscious attention. This location enables devices not to call conscious attention to themselves. That is why audiences and fans jump to their feet and applaud without really thinking about it, and that is why this learned device feels intuitive.

The fourth dimension of devices is that they encourage non-conscious consumptions of arguments (very broadly construed). For example, for standing ovations to occur, audiences must be persuaded that a Broadway show is *innovative*, that a basketball drive is *well-executed*, or that a drag performance is *entertaining*. In turn, the audiences' ovations convey these arguments back to performers, production teams, and other audience members. The ovations, though seemingly spontaneous and intuitive, are actually learned behaviors that reflect cultural values.

The fifth dimension of devices is that, given their non-conscious pervasiveness in culture, they and their effects are readily, and sometimes necessarily, available for listening writers to pause and identify, track and analyze, and then reflect on and act on. Standing for a stellar singing performance may be an easy non-conscious response to express appreciation; reflecting on what the profits from a show actually support may be another matter, perhaps requiring subsequent action. Such reflection and action are necessary because, as Burke warns, rhetorical devices are at their most dangerous when they remain at the level of non-conscious consumption. To disrupt their tendency to reside in the non-conscious, Burke recommends bringing rhetorical devices as well as any associated injustices "to *consciousness*" and then making them "a matter of *conscience*" (*War* 143).

To demonstrate how and why the concept of rhetorical devices is important to a rhetorical education grounded in rhetorical listening, this chapter defines rhetorical devices as a rhetorical concept, explores why they should be studied, and offers model tactics for analyzing and composing.

WHAT ARE RHETORICAL DEVICES AS A RHETORICAL CONCEPT?

As defined in the previous section, rhetorical devices are argumentative moves that through situated, habitual repetitions coalesce into unnoticed argumentative *patterns* that shape perceptions, influence judgments and, in the process, become associated with users' identities (again, think standing ovations) (Burke, *War* 266). Through repeated uses in the register of the non-conscious, rhetorical devices naturalize themselves, their arguments, and the cultural logics that haunt them, thus making the devices, their arguments, and their unstated cultural logics appear as natural, familiar, truthful, persuasive, and even intuitive. As such, rhetorical devices drive socialization in two important ways: they train people to accept dominant social norms (such as students' raising their hands before they speak, fans' standing for "The National Anthem," or English-speaking society's classifying people as *women* and *men*) and, perhaps even more importantly, they encourage people to assume that those norms are "just how things are." Such naturalization and socialization are enacted via multiple agencies and sustained via shared identifications with cultural logics. If cultural logics are the infrastructures that give form to competing values and beliefs and their associated actions, then rhetorical devices (with their naturalizing and socializing identifications) are the nails and glue that hold the infrastructure together.

In *The War of Words*, Burke presents a list of rhetorical devices characteristic of modern rhetoric. In creating his list below, he makes clear that rhetorical devices are not peculiar to the modern period. In fact, he goes out of his way in *A Rhetoric of Motives* to list rhetorical devices (which include rhetorical figures) characteristic of the classical Greek and Roman periods, both times when rhetorical devices were consciously learned and deployed for highly scripted social situations such as legal proceedings, political speeches, or public ceremonies. What makes Burke's list of devices modern is, first, the ubiquity, pervasiveness, and complexity of information they engage and, second, their location within the nonconscious, an intermediate area of expression located between the conscious and the unconscious (*Rhetoric*, xiii). Consequently, even though modern rhetorical devices shape perceptions, judgments, and identities, most writers and audiences are not fully cognizant of the devices or their potential implications.

Burke's list of modern rhetorical devices includes (but is not limited to):

1. *The Bland Strategy* is a rhetorical device where you say one thing but imply the opposite. For example, you say an ironic "Perfect" when you spill coffee in your lap. The bland strategy also applies to arguments that conceal dangerous motives by couching them in positive terms: for example, parents offer to "make snacks" for their child's friends during a get-together in order to eavesdrop and discover whether the kids are doing something suspicious (*War* 46–52).

2. *Shrewd Simplicity* is a rhetorical device that identifies either simplicity with lovability or stupidity with innocence. For example, you deliberately "fly under the radar" of your friends' criticisms by acting as if you don't understand the full impact of a bad decision about a movie choice (*War* 51–56).

3. *Undo by Overdoing* is a rhetorical device that questions another person's argument by over-exaggerating its virtues. For example, by giving a political candidate too much praise, you encourage audiences to question whether that candidate is really that trustworthy (*War* 56–63).

4. *Yielding Aggressively* is a rhetorical device for "rolling with the punch" or allowing something to occur while still disagreeing with the outcome. For example, a government accepts criticism for an unfavorable economic outcome today in order to eventually say, "See, I told you so . . ." (*War* 63–68).

5. *Deflection* is a rhetorical device for distracting audiences from an issue by directing their attention toward an adjacent topic that is

more favorable to your position. For example, a political candidate might change the subject from a failure by saying something like, "The *real* issue is . . ." (*War* 68–78).

6. *Spokesman* or, to update it, *Spokesperson* is a rhetorical device for speaking *to* an audience when, in fact, you are speaking *on their behalf.* For example, you might say something like, "If that had just happened to me, I'd be way more angry than you are." The purpose, in this case, is to incite a friend's anger by telling them how they should have reacted (*War* 76–79).

7. *Reversal* is a rhetorical device for turning the tables on an argument by asserting, "You think you know the truth, but the alleged truth is in fact a lie." For example, Mary Daly claims that the structure of patriarchy functions by reversing issues related to women, as in Zeus giving birth to Athena and underwear that restricts women being called *Free Spirit* (*War* 80–88).

8. *Say the Opposite* is a rhetorical device for clearly and deliberately opposing an argument with a competing argument. For example, you might say, "I don't agree with you and here are the reasons why. . . ." Although the previous framing promotes an "I'm right, you're wrong" argument, this device might also be used to lay competing arguments side by side. For example, you might say, "I'm hearing you say this. Here's what I'm thinking. Where does that leave us?" (*War* 90–92).

9. *Spiritualization* is a rhetorical device for assigning deeper meaning to material objects, local experiences, or physical spaces. For example, although a toy may be a lump of plastic, it can represent the innocence of childhood; although a concert is a commercial enterprise, the performance can reveal the beauty of the human soul; and although a quiet trail in the mountains is simply a nature site, it can represent peacefulness. In effect, this device takes a specific object, experience, or space and makes a general claim that appears to apply to everyone (*War* 90–99).

10. *Making the Connection* is a rhetorical device for subtly suggesting that two things are related, not making the connection explicitly but allowing an audience to draw the conclusion for themselves. For example, by placing headlines and pictures in close proxim-

ity to one another, a news media outlet implies (and its readers infer) that the picture and headline are connected (*War* 109).

11. *Say Anything* is a rhetorical device used for "hit-and-run purposes"; it is concerned not with disseminating facts to an audience but, instead, with giving an audience what it wants to hear to earn its agreement. For example, a politician might attack an opponent's family instead of the opponent's record. This device is often used to level the playing field when the user of the device is at an argumentative disadvantage; it is most commonly associated with leaks, rumors, and slander (*War* 119–20).

As this partial list of Burke's devices demonstrates, rhetorical devices possess formal purposes via discursive agency; they invoke cultural logics via cultural agency; they potentially produce material consequences via material agency; and they are repeatable via personal agency unless, of course, the repetitions are non-consciously automatic. If listening writers learn to identify each of these devices, then they may become more conscious not only of how others use rhetorical devices but also of how they may use rhetorical devices in their own everyday writing tasks.

Burke's list of devices, however, is not exclusive. Listening writers may find or generate and then employ devices *other than* the ones in Burke lists; in such cases, writers may name the devices in ways that explain how the specific devices function within particular situations.

Consider as a case in point Robert Lorenz's 2012 baseball film, *Trouble with the Curve* starring Clint Eastwood, Amy Adams, and Justin Timberlake. The film dramatizes the competition between two cultural logics associated with managing baseball teams, and these competing cultural logics become visible to viewers via two sets of rhetorical devices. Let's name these two sets of rhetorical devices the old school "feel for the game" devices and the new school "dispassionate facts/stats" devices. One "feel for the game" device is the casting of Eastwood as the film's lead. Using casting as a device, the film trades on Eastwood's status as an aging but mythic embodiment of the Western hero who preserves justice and integrity in the face of a new threat, which, in this movie's case, includes computers and the businessmen who use baseball data to predict players' and teams' successes. Eastwood's casting as a rhetorical device argues that "a feel for the game" management tactic maintains the integrity of the game while the "dispassionate facts/stats" management tactic compromises it. Casting Adams as Eastwood's daughter, is another "feel for the game" rhetorical device, making an argument to audiences that her reconciliation with her father as well as her younger age assures that *their* view of the game will continue, even after the Eastwood character retires or dies.

Rhetorical devices, though grounded in particular rhetorical situations, may travel from situation to situation. For example, the "feel for the game" or the "dispassionate facts/stats" casting devices have emerged in other films such as in Bennett Miller's *Moneyball* starring Brad Pitt and Jonah Hill who play, respectively, the manager and the economics graduate who led the real-life Oakland A's to a successful 2002 season by pioneering sabermetrics, the statistical model for managing baseball that the Red Sox later used to win the 2004 World Series. Within the world of *Moneyball*, the "dispassionate facts/stats" device is a main character in the film, a hero in fact, though the film is also haunted by a wistfulness for the passing of an era. But baseball films are not the only places from which rhetorical devices travel.

Other examples of rhetorical devices travelling beyond film and TV include *Happy Days'* "Jump the shark," which forwards the argument that a bid for publicity has gone too far; *The Godfather's* "Go to the mattress," which forwards the argument that a person's action may be so out of control that the person may have to go into hiding; and *Buffy the Vampire Slayer's* "I mean, did we not put the 'grr' in 'girl?,'" which forwards the argument that girl power should be celebrated. Each catchphrase has been used by many different people in many different contexts to forward an argument specific to their own contexts, as when, for example, two women who have created a successful business together quote Buffy to one another. In the women's case, no more needs to be said because their rhetorical device of choice functions as an enthymeme, making their argument via unstated assumptions.

As noted in this section's introduction, rhetorical devices often reinforce a culture's prevailing wisdoms that have become so naturalized as to seem "just the way things are," but rhetorical devices may also interrupt and attempt to redefine a culture's prevailing wisdoms. For example, consider how the rhetorical device of "undo by overdoing" (Burke, *War* 56–63) is employed by drag performers, both queens and kings. When using exaggerated gender markers such as wigs, makeup, clothing, or gestures in their performances,[1] drag performers rearticulate the "undo by overdoing" device for their own ends; that is, they perform gender scripts so as to satirize, interrupt, and redefine gender norms that have become naturalized within a culture. As Judith Butler argues, the repetition of such a device produces "a string of performances that constitute and contest the coherence of" the gendered "I" that is naturalized by prevailing gender discourses and socialized by their norms ("Imitation" 311).

Because rhetorical devices have the capacity to both affirm and interrupt prevailing wisdoms, the same device may be used for competing purposes. For example, after observing the "undo by overdoing" device in drag performances, listening writers might also observe this same device in the hypermasculinity argued for and performed by men's rights' groups. Though such groups are unlikely to frame their tactics in terms of rhetorical devices, they nevertheless use them. That is, they attempt to undo weaknesses that they perceive in other views of masculinity by performing their own versions of hypermasculinity, in short, undoing perceived attacks on masculinity by overdoing masculinity.[2] The irony, of course, as Butler points out, is that such "corrective" hypermasculine performances underscore the precarity of masculinity as a gender category ("Imitation" 314).

When confronted with competing uses of the same rhetorical device (such as "undo by overdoing" in drag performances and men's rights group performances), listening writers can lay these competing uses side by side to understand the competing cultural logics haunting them. On one hand, the celebratory, interruptive queer performances in some drag communities can feel to some men's rights groups like a direct threat to their value systems. On the other hand, the non-conscious hypermasculine performances of the men's rights groups can feel to drag communities like an overt act of emotional, and even physical, violence.[3] Once listening writers have mapped these devices and their cultural logics, they may reflect on them and decide what actions to take based on their reflections, both in writing and in daily life.

As sites that encourage reflection and potential action, rhetorical devices have tremendous transformational potential. If made the subject of conscious reflection, rhetorical devices can help listening writers recalibrate public attention toward justice and equity. For example, Chris Jordan's "Whale" from his online art collection, *Running the Numbers II: Portraits of Global Mass Culture* uses the device "making the connection" to expose how the habitual use of plastic bags affects oceans' ecosystems. Zooming in on "Whale," audiences will notice that it consists of images of "50,000 plastic bags, equal to the estimated number of pieces of floating plastic in every square mile in the world's oceans." Jordan did not create "Whale" to call out consumers for consciously overcrowding oceans with plastic. Just the opposite, he is drawing attention to how the unconscious and non-conscious consumption of plastic produces dangerous consequences. As Jordan explains in his artist statement, "we are stuck with trying to comprehend the gravity of these phenomena through the anaesthetizing and emotionally barren language of statistics. Sociologists tell us that the human mind cannot meaningfully grasp numbers higher than a few thousand; yet every day we read of mass phenomena characterized by numbers in the millions, billions, even trillions." By rendering such practices visually comprehensible to popular audiences, Jordan renders unconscious and non-conscious habits into conscious knowledge and then, to echo Burke, into "a matter of *conscience*" (Burke, *War* 143).

Once available to people's conscious attention and consciences, rhetorical devices may be tracked. Tracking rhetorical devices across different media can happen in one of two ways: (1) devices can be tracked as repetitions about a specific topic or (2) devices can be tracked as repetitions across different topics. In either case, repeated devices may focus on images, terms or phrases, ideas, performances, cultural logics, etc. Interestingly, tracking rhetorical devices often exposes larger patterns of argument such as cultural logics, all of which influence the way people feel, think, and act—with the devices' influence increasing with their number of repetitions.

WHY STUDY RHETORICAL DEVICES?

Studying rhetorical devices from a listening stance helps listening writers identify, analyze, and explain how situated and habitual argumentative moves (devices) shape perception, judgment, and identity at a non-conscious level. Such study helps listening writers understand how rhetorical devices invoke and buttress familiar cultural logics with the goal of motivating audiences' feelings, thoughts, and actions. As the subject of conscious attention and as a matter of conscience, rhetorical devices help listening writers, first, assess the benefits and dangers of cultural logics and their devices; second, determine whether and to what degree cultural logics and their devices make ethical action possible or impossible; and third, decide what actions to take. With this reflective awareness, writers have an easier time selecting which rhetorical devices can help them address their rhetorical problems while not inadvertently causing violence. In the process, writers become more attentive to form and formal patterns.

Helping listening writers think critically about rhetorical devices, then, is important for the following reasons.

First, studying rhetorical devices offers listening writers knowledge of an argument's formal patterns at a granular scale. As "Chapter 1: Rhetorical Listening" demonstrates, breaking a cultural logic into a syllogistic if/then/therefore structure helps listening writers track the logic's organizing term, its associated beliefs, and its resulting actions. Yet arguments involve more than these logical moves. Save when writing sitcom scripts for nerdy teenage-boy characters (e.g., *Young Sheldon*), writers do not typically rely on the formalized structure of a syllogism to make arguments in real time. More often, writers within specific rhetorical situations write arguments with enthymemes, leaving assumptions unstated or unknown and relying on rhetorical devices (or unnoticed moves within cultural logics) that are intuitively familiar because of their repetitions and, thus, seem to fit the situation.

While this distinction between syllogistic and enthymemic arguments originates with Aristotle's classical rhetoric (*Rhetoric* 4; I.2.8), it manifests differently in the modern world, at least according to Burke. In *The War of Words*, he captures this modern experience well: "But we are not greatly concerned with rhetoric as argument. Argument usually involves sustained attack; but the characteristic rhetoric of today is done in quick raids, as with Indian warfare, guerilla tactics, commando operations. It is neither good argument nor bad argument; it is not argument at all. For argument it substitutes *identification* and *dramatization*" (134). Twitter's formal pattern of only 280 characters is a good example of this modern experience; thus, a "tweet" is a good example of a modern rhetorical device.

When Burke claims in the above quotation that modern rhetoric is not concerned with argument, he is making a distinction between formal and informal argument. While modern rhetoric has indeed expanded beyond classical rhetoric's focus on formally structured arguments, it has not left argument behind. For rhetorical devices, even tweets, do actually forward informal arguments. Consider, for example, the following devices: the standing ovation argues for appreciation; the casting of Eastwood argues for an old school ethos and management style; the performing of hypermasculinity argues for traditional gender norms; and the six-character "@Me1oo" tweet argues for an end to sexual harassment and violence.

Second, studying rhetorical devices provides listening writers an important concept, collaborative expectancy, for understanding how formal patterns work at a granular scale. Burke introduces this concept in *A Rhetoric of Motives*:

> Many formal patterns can readily awaken an attitude of collaborative expectancy in us. For instance, imagine a passage built about a set of oppositions ("*we* do *this*, but *they* on the other hand do *that* . . ."). Once you grasp the trend of the form, it invites participation regardless of the subject matter. Formally, you will find yourself swinging along with the succession of antitheses, even though you may not agree with the proposition that is being presented in this form. (58)

Burke's use of the term "awakening" to characterize this formal process does not signify a person's conscious realization. Rather, it signifies a person's intuitive or non-conscious recognition of the *direction* an argument is taking.

As implied by Burke's concept of collaborative expectancy, rhetorical devices *as formal patterns* (that is, as patterns of form) both precede and exceed people's immediate experiences of them. If, for example, a writer experiences a situation where the "yielding aggressively" device is used positively, that is, where someone manages to assert an argumentative stance without coming across as domineering, then that writer might identify future uses of that device as positive without thinking about its content. This non-conscious acceptance of a formal pattern without thinking about its content is what Burke means in the above quotation by "swinging along with the succession of antitheses" (*Rhetoric* 58). Given this agency of formal patterns (as a type of discursive agency), rhetorical devices have the potential to authorize and even authenticate whatever content they present. This swinging-along process can happen with texts (as when a W-9 form invites taxpayers to write down information such as social security numbers that they might not otherwise share); this swinging-along process can also happen with people (as when the US military follows orders of the President, regardless of who inhabits the office of President). The danger, as Burke explains, is that we may non-consciously swing along with the formal pattern of a rhetorical device even though we might otherwise consciously disagree with the content of its argument. That is why bringing rhetorical devices to conscious attention and conscience is so important.

Third, studying rhetorical devices also offers listening writers places for intervening into arguments. As Burke's observations about formal patterns imply, listening writers may feel ill-prepared to intervene in many rhetorical situations because the argument moves so quickly and, in some cases, so indiscriminately that it is hard to keep up. And yet, in Burke's affirmation, listening writers may discover a key tactic for slowing down rhetorical situations that threaten to spin out of control: that is, instead of immediately evaluating an argument to determine if it is good or bad, listen for the rhetorical devices in order to find places for intervening.

For example, in May of 2021 the Texas legislature passed an act entitled Senate Bill 8 (SB8) that, effective September 1, 2021, made it illegal in Texas for anyone to perform an abortion or for anyone to assist a woman in getting an abortion after a fetal heartbeat is detected (around six weeks). The catch is that this law is not to be enforced through local, state or federal law enforcement agencies but, rather, "exclusively through the private civil actions" of private citizens who may sue anyone involved in this medical procedure (except the woman herself) for "not less than $10,000," the only exception being a "medical emergency" ("Texas").

Although the Supreme Court of the United States, when consulted, allowed the law to go into practice, Justice Sonia Sotomayor wrote a blistering dissent. To intervene in the "private civil actions" section of the bill for her audiences, she employed a rhetorical device of reframing these "private civil actions" with the term *bounty hunters*:

> In effect, the Texas legislature has deputized the state's citizens as bounty hunters, offering them cash prizes for civilly prosecuting their neighbors' medical procedures. . . . By prohibiting state officers from enforcing the act directly and relying instead on citizen bounty hunters, the legislature sought to make it more complicated for federal courts to enjoin the act on a state-wide basis.

By invoking this commonly-known term to reframe the role of citizens, Justice Sotomayor, instead of debating the morality or the legality of abortion, intervenes into this debate on the grounds of the bill's enforcement process. Her reframing "state's citizens as bounty hunters" invokes a hunting metaphor that elicits fear of being hunted, a bounty metaphor that elicits fear of being ruined financially, and a citizen enforcement metaphor that elicits fear of vigilantes. The term *bounty hunters* echoes historically with Western films and contemporarily with bail bond companies, and in all these cases, bounty hunters are imagined as having a single-minded purpose, to track down those wanted by the law whether guilty or not. Though well-worn by the time Justice Sotomayor employed it, the term *bounty hunters* has travelled subsequently through the news cycles and remains attached to discussions of Texas SB8.

As evidenced by this example, pausing and assuming a listening stance to find rhetorical devices puts writers such as Justice Sotomayor in a place that may be generative and productive, helping them to reframe an issue so that it can be presented from multiple perspectives. As Burke explains, "you have been realistic enough. You have not been cynical. Even in time you may be just. And you have moved Stoically in the direction of order, solace, and placement" (*War* 160). Moving in that direction signals that listening writers have brought rhetorical devices to conscious attention and made them available for private reflection and public debate; this process is particularly important given the power of rhetorical devices to sweep people off their discursive feet.

Fourth, studying rhetorical devices helps listening writers become more mindful about the persuasive capacity of rhetorical devices and of form more generally. Such study helps these writers decide where to pause and determine whether or not the content of an argument actually aligns with their consciously held values. Such study prepares listening writers to more effectively choose which devices best support the arguments they value, and obviously, the ultimate goal of such study is to create the best alignment between form and content so as to increase the possibility of equity, justice, and understanding.

For example, during the 2021 Summer Olympics, Simone Biles stepped away from the gymnastics competition, citing "mental health issues" (Ingle). This move of "stepping away" is a rhetorical device of removing one's body from a situation, in the process making the argument that it is being done for one's own good. Biles's stepping away immediately made the argument that it was for her own good because she felt that she could no longer focus and, thus, compete safely. Biles's rhetorical device and its argument went viral and responses to it were telling: USA Gymnastics tweeted its support of her decision to step away (Ingle); former Olympian Michael Phelps hoped that her stepping away "would 'blow the doors open' over athlete mental health" (Ingle); and former gymnast and first to accuse publicly the former USA gymnastics coach Larry Nassar of sexual abuse, Rachael Denhollander tweeted, "You all who are railing at Simone's choice will never know the incredible sacrifice and effort it took for her to HAVE a choice. Much respect" (@R_Denhollander).[4]

As Phelps and Denhollander each note, Biles's stepping away signifies more than just one individual's decision for a particular situation. It has been repeatedly invoked by the media to call attention to systemic problems associated with Olympic athletes' mental health (Leong) and with the sexual abuse of young gymnasts by Larry Nassar (Shabad). In the contexts of the 2021 Summer Olympics and the fall 2021 trial of Nassar, Biles's stepping away has functioned as a rhetorical device that writers in the media have used to question just how well the International Olympics Committee and USA Gymnastics have aligned their values of discipline, training, and winning with the values of respect and care for athletes' physical, mental, and emotional well-being. Media's repeating this device of Biles's stepping away has reinforced the on-going work of athletes, former athletes, parents, administrators, coaches, trainers, sportswriters, associated organizations, etc., to convert the dominant cultural logic associated with "stepping away" from its being perceived as "failure" to its being perceived as "necessary and deserved care."

Given all the above reasons for studying rhetorical devices as a rhetorical concept, the next section turns to how to put this concept into practice. Indeed, the tactics below help listening writers become more conscious about the roles that rhetorical devices play in daily life and also about how to use such devices to create greater alignment between the form and content of their own arguments.

WHAT ARE TACTICS OF RHETORICAL DEVICES?

The tactics presented below are models for employing rhetorical devices. To exemplify how rhetorical devices work, these tactics use the on-going rhetorical problem of internet privacy. These tactics of rhetorical devices are not the only ones available. Listening writers may develop their own tactics (as well as develop their own devices); indeed, writers are encouraged to do so to make their situated arguments as effective as possible.

Tactic #1: Identify and name a rhetorical device.

1. Find a rhetorical device in a topic of your choosing (image, word, trope, idea, cultural logic, performance, etc.).

2. Determine the primary purpose of the device (what outcome is it designed to accomplish?).

3. Name the device based on its function (e.g., it *undoes by overdoing* or it *deflects attention*), either invoking devices in Burke's list or constructing new ones.

Identifying rhetorical devices can be tricky because they are usually designed for non-conscious, uncritical consumption. But writers can use the characteristics of rhetorical devices to get started. For example, writers know that rhetorical devices are, by definition, repeated, which allows them to look for argumentative patterns in different types of texts. By identifying the pattern and its function first, writers are then in a position to name the device based on its function.

To understand how this tactic works, consider the cartoon that shows an intact egg labelled "This is your privacy" and a fried egg in a pan labelled "This is your privacy online." The cartoon uses familiar images of an egg in a shell and an egg in a frying pan to help audiences conceptualize a complex topic, the dangers of online privacy (#1). Echoing a 1980s ad that compared a fried egg to a person's brain on drugs, this cartoon depicts an equally scary scenario about privacy online (irreversible damage to one's reputation), a scenario whose purpose is to discourage a concerning trend of behavior surrounding privacy (freely sharing private information online) (#2).

This cartoon exemplifies Burke's "shrewd simplicity" device (#3). Comparing a fried egg to exposed online data *simplifies* the problem of online privacy, yet this simplification is *shrewd* because audiences, if they identify their privacy as the egg, will intuitively want to avoid its being broken open, placed under heat, and eventually consumed by others. Once listening writers understand how "shrewd simplicity" works in this cartoon, they may begin to see this device elsewhere. Though not all examples of this device will use images of eggs and frying pans, they will employ simple words, images, styles, genres, performances, etc., to convert complicated ideas into simple ones in order to make a shrewd point.

Tactic #2: Track repetitions of a rhetorical device across different media.

1. Identify an image, term, idea, cultural logic, performance, etc., that is repeated across different media.

2. Track the repetitions to determine how they function as a rhetorical device across different media.

3. Analyze whether the feelings, thoughts, or actions that this device encourages are the same in every instance of its repetition.

4. Name the device based on its function, either invoking an established device or naming new one.

To demonstrate how this tactic works, consider the Cookie Monster cartoons described below. Regularly featured on the television show *Sesame Street* as well as in all of its marketing offshoots, Cookie Monster already counts as a repeated image across different media—TV, film, clothing, stuffed animals, etc. (#1).

Consider this cartoon scenario. In panel one, an innocent-looking person is using a computer; in panel two, the innocent user receives a message asking if he/she/they will share cookies; in panel three, the innocent user agrees to share cookies; and in panel four Cookie Monster appears sitting at his desk in the dark, calling the innocent user "Fool." Cookies, of course, are bits of data that a website sends to a computer to record the user's browsing history. By sharing cookies with Cookie Monster, the innocent user has turned over access to his/her/their browsing history, thus obliterating any online privacy. In the second cartoon, Cookie Monster is sitting alone at his desk in front of a computer, having an extremely panicked reaction to the computer's instructions about cookies, thinking to himself, "DELETE COOKIES?!" (#2). As a cookie lover, he can think of no more egregious action.

In both cartoons, Cookie Monster serves as a rhetorical device for commenting about online privacy, with the play on the word *cookies* making him an irresistible device for cartoonists who question online privacy. In the first cartoon Cookie Monster is the bad guy who tricks an innocent user into sharing cookies; thus, the cartoonist is using Cookie Monster as a device to argue against invasions of online privacy. In the second, Cookie Monster is the innocent user showing a resistance to deleting cookies (and thus a resistance to protecting himself as a computer user); in this way, the cartoonist is using Cooking Monster as a device to argue that people should take actions to protect their online privacy. Although Cookie Monster seemingly takes opposing roles in these two cartoons (first villain and then victim), the both cartoonists are using him as a "cookie-addicted" character to question issues of online privacy. Audiences are invited not so much to approve or disapprove of Cookie Monster's roles but, rather, to heed the cartoonists' warnings about dangers of online data collection via cookies. By using Cookie Monster to draw attention to the role that cookies play in online browsing, both cartoonists implicitly argue that audiences need to understand the very basics, the A-B-Cs if you will, of online privacy (#3).

As for naming this device, the Cookie Monster cartoons represent Burke's "shrewd simplicity," or using simple images and words to explain a complicated matter. What becomes apparent after analyzing the egg and pan cartoon from Tactic #1 as well as the Cookie Monster cartoons here is that "shrewd simplicity" is a dominant device for cartoons in general. But the particular use of Cookie Monster to question online privacy questions related to cookies could easily be named the "Cookie Monster" device, which, if it becomes a category in listening writers' minds, would alert them about what to expect when in the future they run across cartoons containing images of Cookie Monster and a computer.

Tactic #3: Analyze how rhetorical devices invoke cultural logics.

1. Identify and name a rhetorical device.

2. Determine how it invokes one or more cultural logics.

3. Determine how the formal quality of the rhetorical devices, when presented in the context of the cultural logic, is designed to make us feel, think, and act.

4. Evaluate the benefits and dangers of reinforcing this cultural logic with this rhetorical device.

To understand how this tactic functions, consider a Facebook cartoon. It represents a middle-aged male computer user looking at Facebook on a computer screen while unaware that a giant eyeball labelled "Facebook privacy policy" hovers behind him collecting data about his usage; as such, the cartoon and the eyeball in particular employs the "making the connection" device (#1).

This device asks audiences to make a connection between Facebook's privacy policy[5] (as represented by the eyeball) and the cultural logics about surveillance that haunt our daily lives. One cultural logic of surveillance is "beneficial surveillance," which reasons that if people know someone is always watching their public and even private behaviors, then everyone will live in a safer, more responsible environment. An unstated assumption in this cultural logic is that the data collected by surveillance technologies will necessarily be used to benefit the public good. A second cultural logic of surveillance is "dangerous surveillance," which reasons that if people know someone is always watching their public and even private behaviors, then everyone will be living in a more dangerous environment, stripped of their privacy and vulnerable to the collecting system's whim. An unstated assumption here is that the data collected by surveillance technologies will necessarily be used for profit, not the public's benefit, and will ultimately end up erasing people's rights to privacy (#2).

Because the computer user on Facebook does not seem to sense the presence of the hovering eyeball, this cartoon suggests that "the dangerous surveillance" cultural logic is in play. The eye's size relative to the computer user and its strained blood vessels indicate that Facebook is big, powerful, and looking too hard at the user's browsing habits. Viewers of the cartoon will identify with the computer user, but because they can see the eyeball, they will feel more threatened than this user appears and perhaps think twice about their Facebook and other online usage (#3). Through this "making the connection" device, the cartoon invites audiences to question whether the benefits of online usage outweigh the dangers of losing one's personal privacy (#4). Of course, writers could also name this device "the Facebook eyeball" device and then be alert to such surveillance every time they use social media.

Tactic #4: Analyze how rhetorical devices produce material consequences.

1. Identify a rhetorical device in images, terms, ideas, cultural logics, performances, etc.

2. Describe how audiences are meant to feel, think, and act in response to it.

3. Describe the material consequences (both small scale and large scale) that could occur if audiences find the device persuasive.

Burke's "undo by overdoing" device is evident in a cartoon featuring a sidewalk newspaper vendor (older, overweight, white male) sitting in a kiosk whose sign indicates that he is selling not "News" but, rather, "Data Collection Lists . . . Cheap!" His kiosk shelves are filled not with newspapers and magazines but, rather, with lists of data such as social security numbers, driver's license numbers, medical histories, etc. (#1). Because the man does not look particularly friendly or concerned with the safety of the data, audiences are expected to be afraid of the possibility that information such as bank records, marital status, and internet habits could be easily gathered and put on sale at a cheap price for public consumption. In short, by *overdoing* the sale of personal data, the cartoonist hopes to *undo* the audience's casual acceptance of existing methods for collecting and disseminating such data (#2).

The "undo by overdoing" device in this cartoon suggests myriad material consequences. On a smaller scale, if one viewer casually glances at the cartoon and then glances away, a material consequence is that nothing will change either in the individual's life or in the institutions collecting and selling data. If one viewer takes the issue seriously and drops, say, his Facebook membership, then the material consequences are that the man's daily habits will change and that the data collected by Facebook will be slightly altered. Similarly, another viewer who takes this cartoon seriously might buy better encryption services to protect her information.

Of course, one cartoon will not tip the scale in a major public issue such as internet privacy. But if enough people become aware of the problem through tactical uses of rhetorical devices, actual change could occur. On a broader scale, if this cartoon works in conjunction with other warnings, material consequences could be that public groups will form to support internet privacy reform. Legislators could take up the issue of internet privacy and enact privacy laws. Businesses might even reform their own practices, echoing Tim Cook of Apple who in a recent interview claimed that the one question every leader should ask is not "What can I get away with?" but rather "What are the consequences?" (Aten) (#3).

Tim Cook's question is an appropriate one on which to end a chapter on rhetorical devices because simply identifying them is not enough. As a matter of conscience, we must all also ask: what *are* their consequences? And then act accordingly.

Appendix A: Rhetoric, Language, Discourse, Argument

WHAT IS RHETORIC AND WHY STUDY IT?

Classical rhetoric, as defined by Aristotle, is the faculty of discovering in any particular case all the available means of persuasion (*Rhetoric* I.2.1). As such, the study of classical rhetoric promotes critical thinking (the faculty of discovering evidence and generating proofs) to compose persuasive arguments for law, politics, and civic events. Extending this classical focus, *modern rhetoric* in its broadest sense is the study of how people use signifying systems and how signifying systems use people. Signifying systems are what people use to make meaning: examples include language and discourse, body language, mathematics, colors, musical notes, images. People use signifying systems for a variety of ends. Novelists and speechwriters use language and discourse to imagine new worlds. Cosmologists use mathematics to map parts of our universe that lie beyond what our eyes or telescopes can observe. Pop stars and classical composers use musical notes to express their feelings in just a few bars. But signifying systems also use people for a variety of ends: they socialize us to think, believe, and act in certain ways—even when we are unaware of it. Voters are persuaded (or not) by speechwriters' words and by candidates' delivery to vote for certain candidates. Cosmologists are persuaded (or not) by other cosmologists' theories to work with those theories. And music lovers are persuaded (or not) by musicians to feel upbeat after hearing the opening notes of a song like the Temptations' "My Girl." Because a broad history of rhetoric is beyond the scope of this book, *Rhetorical Listening in Action* focuses on writing from a listening stance in ways that may inform learning in academic, workplace, public, and personal communications. As such, this book takes the signifying systems of language and discourse as its primary objects of study.

Language is a signifying system comprised of words. Language helps people, first, to conceptualize their own and others' ideas, emotions, values, beliefs, and actions and, second, to communicate with others. Even though a language may be associated with a country or community,[1] the analysis of language (whether French, Swahili, Navajo, or English) is often done at the level of structure. For example, language may be categorized into specific elements (phonemes, morphemes) and logical patterns (grammar) so that its users can create meaning together. In this way, the study of language within the field of linguistics is a content area of academic research much like biology, business, or art. On the other hand, fields like applied linguistics, anthropology, and rhetoric and composition studies often focus on how language functions within particular contexts as discourse.

Discourse describes how language functions within specific contexts about specific topics.[2] When babies are born in the US, they are immediately immersed into and labelled by existing cultural discourses of health, gender, race, nationality, family, ethnic heritage, socioeconomic status, beauty, etc. Likewise, as they grow, they might use the English language to read, write, speak, and listen to existing discourses of health, religion, beauty, gender, politics, sports, careers, relationships, etc. Whenever discourses (e.g., religion) are analyzed, they need to be considered contextually not just in terms of how they are connected to cultural groups (e.g., Baptists, Catholics, Muslims) and their institutions (e.g., Southern Baptist Convention, the Vatican, American Muslim Institution) but also in terms of how these cultural groups and institutions employ discourses and rituals to shape people's perspectives (via sacred texts, worship services, conventions, etc.). This book focuses on how to analyze discourses and how to use them in everyday writing tasks. Analyzing discourses helps writers to develop critical thinking skills and generate ideas for composing.

Consider the following example. Imagine that a young woman feels sick and is having a conversation with friends about whether or not she needs to see a doctor. The way she talks about *health* or *sickness* is not specific only to her personal experiences; her talk connects to broader cultural discourses of health that are generated and perpetuated by hospitals, doctors, scientists, patients, pharmaceutical companies, insurance companies, religions, TV, websites, etc. These discourses are on-going and ever-changing. If her dominant discourse includes a scientific definition of health and her experiences reinforce that discourse, then she might decide to visit a doctor. But if her dominant discourse includes a religious definition of her illness as sin, then she might succumb to shame and avoid a doctor. Analyzing multiple discourses of health (and their intersections) can help the young woman locate where definitions of *health* and *sickness* originate, intersect, and affect her decision-making. Indeed, by questioning these discourses, the young woman may realize that her taken-for-granted "personal opinions" about health are actually shared cultural ideas that have complex histories, practices, discursive affiliations, and institutional associations, all of which influence how the young woman understands her relationship to herself, to other people, and to institutions. Such studies of discourses, then, help writers locate the places where they stand to think critically and figure out what they and their audiences each think, feel, value and believe.[3] This understanding helps writers decide how to act, including when, where, and how to write. And it helps them decide whether or not to perpetuate discourses, revise them, or reject them altogether.

With a discussion of ideas, feelings, values and beliefs, and actions, we circle back to where we began: the study of rhetoric. As we tell students when we teach rhetoric, the first principle of rhetoric is this: reasonable people may disagree. An important corollary, however, is to be attentive to who gets to define *reasonable*. The point, of course, is that actions in academic, public, workplace, and personal spheres do not depend on one hundred percent consensus; instead, reasonable people may disagree but still work together for pragmatic action while being aware of power differentials. The study of rhetoric from a listening stance provides writers with concepts and tactics for analyzing language and discourses and also for writing about their ideas, emotions, values and beliefs, and actions in ways that their audiences can actually hear them and give their writings a fair hearing, all while attending to power differentials. By encouraging rhetorical analysis and effective writing for audiences, the study of rhetoric prepares listening writers for everyday writing tasks.

WHAT DO WRITERS STUDY WHEN THEY STUDY RHETORIC?

Studying rhetorical concepts and tactics of rhetorical listening, agency, rhetorical situation, identification, myth, and rhetorical devices helps writers learn how to analyze and compose effectively. But *what exactly do writers study when they study rhetoric more broadly?* One answer is: they study 1) context, 2) purpose, 3) audience, 4) textual choices, and 5) elements of argument—all of which are related to everyday thinking and writing tasks.

First, *context* is an important feature in the study of rhetoric. It refers to the places, times, scenes, and situations that affect every-day thinking and writing tasks. Writers consider contextual questions, such as "Where do their writing tasks originate?" and "How are the final writing products delivered?" As the chapter on rhetorical situation explains, every context or situation both encourages and constrains what can be said or written (Bitzer 6). Bitzer's exigences and constraints may function in two ways. Sometimes they are explicit: when writers publish an editorial in a newspaper, for example, there is a situation encouraging them to speak out and a word limit that determines how much they can write. At other times, exigences and constraints are implicit: when customers go to a restaurant, other customers' behaviors can model how to behave so that customers realize that having a shouting match in a restaurant is socially discouraged even though there are no signs that explicitly read, "Shouting matches prohibited here."

Second, *purpose* is a key feature in the study of rhetoric. It obviously refers to a writer's reasons for writing, and it is important to note that there are usually multiple purposes for everyday writing tasks. For example, if a student writes a paper in a composition class, his purposes may be to pass the class, to learn to write more effectively, perhaps even to earn an "A." If another student writes an email to a parent asking for money, her purposes may be to convince that parent that her request is legitimate but not to anger her parent. And if yet another student writes a resume, her purpose may be to persuade a potential employer that she has the appropriate knowledge, skills, experience, and character to be a valuable employee. Purposes, though, are complex. Each writer's purposes are closely tied to a particular context, to a particular audience with specific decision-making power, and to a genre appropriate to the context and audience, which demands certain specific textual choices. Moreover, a writer's purposes cannot not control all the ways that a text and its discourses will be interpreted. Often texts and discourses assume lives of their own, accruing meanings with audiences beyond anything an individual writer might intend.

Third, *audience* is an important feature of rhetorical study, too, according to both classical and modern rhetorical theorists (Aristotle I.2;

Ede and Lunsford 155–156; Bitzer 7–8). If writers want to be persuasive, they need to know something about the people whom they hope to persuade, particularly their audience's values and beliefs. But the point of writers knowing their audiences is *not* to tell their audience what they want to hear (that's pandering). Rather, the point of writers knowing their audiences is to find enough common ground with them so that writers can find effective ways to communicate about their own ideas, feelings, values and beliefs, and actions in ways that their audience can actually hear and reflect.

Fourth, *textual choices* about genre, about reasons and evidence, and about sentence style (diction, length, punctuations, transitions, etc.) feature prominently in the study of rhetoric. In everyday writing tasks, the probability of making effective textual choices increases when writers consider how context, purpose, and audience inform one another. Sounds simple, right? It's not. Part of learning how to analyze and to write everyday writing tasks is recognizing that making textual choices based on audience analysis is simply an educated guess. Sometimes writers' educated guesses about their audiences will be right. But at other times, they may be wrong. What writers thought would be a homerun set of textual choices, given their context and audience, becomes a reason to revise in light of evolving conditions and understanding. Effective writers, though, use context, purpose, audience, and textual choices as part of their writing processes to compose texts that are adaptable to changing conditions. Quintilian names this writerly adaptability *facilitas* (Murphy and Wiese xxxi). The movement from concept to tactic in pursuit of *facilitas* assumes the interanimation of theory and practice, with examples of practice being teachers' teaching, students' learning, administrators managing programs and people, preachers' preaching, political groups, negotiating, etc.

Fifth, in addition to studying context, purpose, audience, and textual choices, students of rhetoric study *argument*, broadly conceived. Argument is too often reduced to a static, formulaic genre (think five-paragraph themes or three-point speeches). But in everyday life, arguments exist in multiple situations and in multiple genres such as films, Congressional bills, novels, tax form instructions, relationship discussions, etc. All are arguments. No matter what situation, purpose, audience, or genre an argument takes (whether academic essay, business report, or email to friends), it is often associated with the following six fundamental concepts of classical and modern rhetoric.

Persuasion, for classical and modern rhetoricians alike, represents an important purpose of any oral speech or written text, the goal being to persuade an audience to think or to act in ways that the speaker or writer directs. Politicians argue to persuade their colleagues to pass a bill; lawyers argue to persuade judges to decide in favor of their clients; and citizens argue to persuade fellow citizens to embrace and perform civic values and beliefs. As teachers of rhetoric, Aristotle and Quintilian catalogued the elements of persuasive speeches and written texts to identify rhetorical concepts and tactics that would help their students analyze and compose persuasive arguments.

Main claims are a writer's or a speaker's stance about a topic or rhetorical problem. Whether in academic arguments, billboards, or Twitter feeds, the primary job of a main claim is to present a focused argument. In academic papers, main claims are called *thesis statements*; they answer an implied question, are arguable, and often acknowledge the tension in an argument. As such, main claims are strongest when derived from a writer's critical thinking, not from an unexamined opinion. The type of main claim needed differs depending on the context, purpose, and audience. For example, a magazine with limited space might publish a film review sporting the main claim, *"Wonder Woman* challenges Hollywood heroes." But a student writing a critical essay for a film history class might write a slightly more complicated version, *"Wonder Woman* challenges traditional Hollywood hero movies not simply by flipping genders of the movie hero (and all that entails) but more importantly by interrupting the token woman syndrome and providing a tradition of strong women."

Reasons explain *why* a main claim, or a thesis statement, is true or reasonable. Reasons complete *because* statements, either stated or implied, associated with your main claim. To build an effective academic argument, students need to develop several reasons or *because* statements and, just as importantly, to link the reasons together to form a chain of reasoning. In the *Wonder Woman* example, a student might write, *"Wonder Woman* challenges the traditional Hollywood hero movie *because* she is a woman and *because* this gender reversal redefines the characters of hero and sidekick." Sometimes, especially in non-academic settings, one reason is sufficient to persuade an audience, as when a parent tells children that they cannot play in the street *because* they might get hit by a car or that they cannot leave the house *because* I say so.

Evidence is details that support reasons by deeming them valid or true. Evidence comes in different versions: 1) writer's reasoning, 2) empirical evidence, 3) statistics, 4) textual details, 5) scientific observations and results, 6) historical facts, 7) explanations by authorities on your topic, 8) eyewitness testimony, 9) personal experience (biography, autobiography), etc. A good writer knows not just what kinds of evidence exist but also what kinds of evidence are available, what kinds of evidence "count" in particular situations, what kinds of evidence most appeals to audience(s), or even when no evidence is needed because a reason is obvious.

Appeals are tactics that writers use to persuade audiences. According to Aristotle, there are three appeals (I.2.2–6). *Logos* is the appeal to reason; it involves tactics used to construct reasoned arguments intended to persuade an audience by logic. It is important to note, again, that the situation or context will determine what counts as a reasoned argument, due to the influence of competing cultural logics. For example, a reasoned argument in law is different from a reasoned argument in physics or even in a marriage proposal. *Pathos* is the appeal to emotion; it involves tactics used to render audiences emotionally receptive to an argument. This appeal, too, is dependent on situational appropriateness. For example, pictures of starving children are used in pleas to increase donations for nonprofit organizations but not in fashion ads. *Ethos* is the appeal to authority. Writers invoke authority by establishing their own credibility via either their character (ethical, kind) or the position they hold (parent or President) or by citing credible experts. Aristotle implies that *ethos* can be the most persuasive type of appeal because when people in authority tell someone to do something, those in power need not provide reasons or evidence (I.2.4). Power persuades. But any argument can invoke one, two, or even all three of these appeals and in different ways.

Unstated assumptions are ideas, feelings, power dynamics, or cultural logics that haunt a text by exerting influence over a writer's production or an audience's reception of that text. As Cheryl Glenn has argued, "silence and silencing deliver meaning" (*Unspoken* xi). Thus, unstated assumptions are important to identify and analyze. They may reflect assumed cultural norms or values that speakers/writers and their audiences may agree upon, and, as such, they can be a place where common ground is found. But they may also reflect challenges to assumed cultural norms or values. More on this concept is discussed in Chapter 1.

As evident by this short definition, *rhetoric* is not the study of all style and no substance. Rather, the study of rhetoric offers listening writers a deeper understanding of how people are socialized by the languages they inhabit (whether that socialization is conscious or not); the study of rhetoric also offers listening writers a deeper understanding of how people may use language to express themselves, communicate with others and, when necessary, reimagine their worlds.

Appendix B: Writing Processes

The term *writing process* refers to a set of tactics each writer uses when completing a writing task—from initial brainstorming to final written product. Writing processes are different for different writers, and these processes can also vary for a single writer, depending on the writing task, situation, purpose, and audience. Considerable scholarship has been written since the 1960s about the concepts of writing process,[1] post-process,[2] and even beyond post-process.[3] For writers, making their own writing processes the subject of conscious reflection can be an incredibly helpful activity. To help listening writers map their writing processes, below are six key elements associated with writing processes: 1) reading, 2) inventing, 3) drafting and revising, 4) collaborating, 5) editing, and 6) reflecting.

Although the six key elements of a writing process are numbered sequentially, they rarely follow a neat, linear progression. Indeed, people's writing processes are recursive (Sommers 379).[4] For one writing task, a writer might need to *read* more toward the end of his process to *revise* effectively. Or *inventing ideas* might involve simultaneous *reading* and *collaborating* with peers. The reason writing is not a paint-by-number process is that each writing task requires listening writers to figure out how the six key elements need to be performed, both singly in relation to one another. This figuring out is achieved through listening writers' practice and study, which results in their developing a literacy about which steps are most needed in particular writing situations.

Reading is a process of a writer's gathering information about a topic so as to develop the topic into a rhetorical problem.[5] But reading involves more than simply gathering information that agrees with a writer's initial perspective; that's confirmation bias. Rather, reading involves consulting writings that agree with, disagree with, or complicate a writer's existing perspective. If writers learn how to read and listen so as to engage perspectives different from their own, then they will increase the persuasiveness of their argument by demonstrating that they are open-minded, that they are respectful of those who think differently, and that they have thought carefully about the issue. When writers read and listen to different perspectives, they are better able to anticipate potential counterarguments to their claims. What's more, they learn to see just how complex problems in everyday life can be, thus mapping more territory for discussion. No deep understanding or effective solution can be developed without reading. So, listening writers should plan on making this a prominent step in their writing processes.

Inventing is the process of generating information.[6] In all likelihood, most writers have already learned brainstorming tactics to get their writing processes started. In academia, student writers have often been taught these tactics to produce a thesis statement. Invention can be imagined more broadly, especially if tied to a concept-tactic approach to writing. Identifying rhetorical concepts and especially their associated tactics helps listening writers to generate information about their everyday writing tasks, information that is informed by listening to competing perspectives. Rather than encourage writers to brainstorm about a general topic that they are disinterestedly studying, rhetorical invention asks writers to use what they have learned about the concepts in this book to identify rhetorical problems that affect their and others' everyday lives and then decide what arguments to make and how to deliver them. Of course, the invention process will involve considerations of context (where is the writer submitting the writing), purpose (why is the writer writing), audience (to whom is the writer writing), and textual choices (what genre, organization, evidence, diction, etc., are effective for a task) as well as what is at stake for the writer and the audience.

Drafting and Revising are processes of writing and rewriting with an ear toward listening to improve a writer's understanding and final written product. *Drafting* is the process of writing and rewriting to clarify ideas. Research shows that all writers, no matter how experienced, benefit from drafting and revision.[7] In fact, a case can be made that the more a writer drafts, the more he increases the clarity and, thus, the effectiveness of his writing. While drafting, a writer may discover that her purposes change, that her understanding of her audiences' needs change, or that her contextual details change. Such changes invite a writer not just to rewrite but to revise a draft. *Revising* is the process of a writer's re-seeing writing from different perspectives, listening to these perspectives, and then incorporating them into their text.[8] Sometimes, different perspectives will come from books or essays. Other times, they will come from a teacher or a peer. A writer can even develop a different perspective by stepping away from their arguments for a time, listening to their own words, and going back to them later, once they have had time to reflect. Regardless, the act of revision is always substantive, indicating a change in meaning that adds dimension or complexity to an argument. Although drafting and revision take time and effort, they can be worth that time and effort. Learning to draft and revise is a bit like learning to eat healthy foods. Initially, the process does not seem to be worth the trouble. But over time, the work is easier and the benefits obvious.

Collaborating is a process of sharing one's brainstorming and writing to test one's ideas and writing tactics.[9] First, collaboration may be done at any stage of the writing process. Because this book is co-authored, we obviously value collaboration. We can produce writing on our own. But when we collaborate, we enrich our writing in a manner that cannot be attained if we work alone. Does collaboration always lead to enrichment? No, of course not. But even seemingly ineffective collaborations may be valuable because they help identify where writings might be confusing or underdeveloped, especially for audiences who disagree with us. Second, collaboration can be productive in the classroom at certain drafting stages of a students' writing process. For example, students' peer review sessions of full drafts, when effectively implemented, benefit student writers because they can test run their written products by an audience so as to determine what is done well and what needs to be revised. Students' peer review sessions also benefit reviewers by providing them with models and challenging them to determine if they have internalized the terms of the assignment and the criteria for success well enough to make suggestions to their peers and to revise their own writing. Thus, if we listen to all review comments not just for specific advice but for places in texts that attract attention and thus may need work, then every collaboration can pave the way for rich revision.

Editing is the process of making changes to sentences or paragraphs — specifically changing punctuation, wording, or organization. Editing is not simply about fixing errors to ensure correctness; rather, it involves making changes to sentences to ensure *effectiveness*. The study of sentence-level choices is, according to classical rhetoricians, the study of style. Sentence choices are an important part of everyday writing — whether academic, workplace, public, or personal — because writers must write sentences differently for different situations. Good writers develop *different styles*, among which they may code-switch (again, what Quintilian calls *facilitas*), so as to be able to employ an effective style in different situations. After all, effective sentence style in an email to a friend is not effective sentence style in a job application letter; likewise, sentence style in a philosophy essay may not be effective sentence style in a chemistry lab report. Such stylistic code-switching is a key to writing effectively, and editing is the step in the writing process where attention to style may take center stage. In addition, editing may entail clarifying ideas for audiences or changing paragraphs so as to create more logical links between ideas for audiences. Editing can also involve deciding what to leave in and what to delete, based on listening and discerning what the audience needs to know and what they already know.

Reflecting is the process of writers' looking back at what they have written and evaluating both their written texts and their writing processes. To grow as a writer while studying rhetoric, listening writers need to reflect on the quality of their analyses, their composing processes, and their written texts. Maybe a student writer identifies that her essay's thesis statement was actually stated most clearly in her conclusion, not in her introduction (a very common rhetorical device); reflecting on this fact lets a writer become aware of her pattern so that she can be alert for it next time she writes an essay. Or maybe, after barely meeting a few deadlines, a writer on a business team discovers that he and his team need to begin drafting earlier in order to give themselves enough time to collaborate effectively. By reflecting on the strengths and limits of writing processes and written products, writers create opportunities to make conscious improvements to them, and as research indicates, reflection fosters the retention of such learning (Yancey 6–8).[10]

Appendix C: Research

Research is an invention strategy that informs all kinds of everyday decisions, whether a person is buying a car, selecting a college, choosing a movie, or picking a restaurant. At its most fundamental level, research deepens people's understanding of issues and helps them take ownership of their decision-making and their subsequent actions. For everyday writers in the twenty-first century, research becomes more important than ever because knowledge is expanding exponentially in all areas of life even as the shelf-life of that knowledge is growing shorter. Because writers simply cannot keep all that information in their heads, research made available through technology becomes even more important for providing information at writers' fingertips.

But access to information is only the first step to performing effective research because not all information is equal. Good writers need to determine what information is valid and why, what sources are valid and why, and to recognize that information does not exist in a vacuum but must be framed as knowledge. In short, writers need to become information literate. According to the American Library Association (ALA), "To be information literate, a person must be able to recognize when information is needed and have the ability to locate, evaluate, and use effectively the needed information. . . . Ultimately, information literate people are those who have learned how to learn" ("Evaluating Information: Information Literacy").

To foster information literacy, the ALA offers the following tips:

1. Consider the source. Click away from the story to investigate the site, its mission, and its contact info.

2. Read past the headline. Headlines can be outrageous in effort to get clicks. Go beyond headlines.

3. Assess the credibility of the author. Do a quick Google search on the author. What is their expertise? What organization do they represent?

4. Look at the links and sources supporting the article. Click those links. Determine if the subsequent information supports the story. Consider the reliability of the sources.

5. Check the date.

6. Consider that the item might be satire. If it seems too outlandish, it might be satire. Do some quick research on the site and author to find out.

7. Consider that it might be promotional. Is the purpose of the site to sell a product?

8. Check your biases. Search other news outlets to see if the news is widely reported. ("Evaluating Information: Home")

Even beyond these eight important tips, a listening writer should develop a rhetorical mindset for conducting research. A rhetorical mindset inflected by rhetorical listening is useful for research because different writing tasks engage different rhetorical problems, purposes, audiences, and situations.[1] This mindset is useful, too, given that research includes not just finding information but also figuring out how to evaluate and employ the information originating from competing cultural logics. To demonstrate how research may be performed via a rhetorical mindset inflected by rhetorical listening, this appendix offers a brief summary of how research is classified and then a series of research tactics that writers may employ. The purpose of this appendix, then, is to help listening writers expand their repertoires of research options for everyday writing tasks, whether in the academy, workplace, public sphere, or private life.

Tactic #1: Analyze a writing task as a rhetorical research problem.

To determine what research is necessary for any writing task, writers must develop methods for thinking rhetorically about information. To do so, writers may ask themselves the following questions:

1. What is my purpose   that is, what is my task and who gave it to me?

2. How may my writing task be imagined as a rhetorical problem—that is, as a problem that invites a written response?

3. What sources will help me develop a fuller understanding of the rhetorical problem?

4. What sources will help me situate myself among competing perspectives?

5. What sources will offer me reliable information about my rhetorical problem?

6. What sources will be credible for my audience, given my situation and genre?

7. What is at stake in my using this research?

8. What is at stake for audiences?

Tactic #2: Decide on an appropriate ratio of primary and secondary sources.

Research sources are generally classified as primary and secondary in ways that assign value to the types of information. *Primary* refers to sources that are the direct focus of study. When students write an academic essay about a novel, the primary source is the novel itself. When workers write a corporate history for an employer, some primary sources are the company's documents and employees' testimonies. *Secondary* refers to sources that are expert, second-hand accounts. For students writing that essay on a novel, a secondary source is an article on narrative criticism written by a scholar about the novel, and for employees writing a corporate history, secondary sources may be experts in business as well as newspaper accounts and history textbooks.

While knowing how to identify differences between *primary* and *secondary* sources is important, knowing how to evaluate and employ them is even more important. Sometimes primary sources are most effective; sometimes secondary ones are. For example, if a writing task is to explain what it was like to work with Steve Jobs at Apple or Bill Gates at Microsoft, then the most persuasive information is probably garnered from primary sources such as employees' testimonies or other eyewitness accounts. If the purpose of a writing task is to describe how the Digital Revolution redefined ways that people understand information, then a writer's most persuasive information will likely be secondary sources from a variety of different types of experts, such as cultural critics who could provide longitudinal studies of technology users, software engineers who could explain their particular contributions to the development of technology, or historians who could offer historical accounts of how digital technologies evolved over time.

To figure out what types of sources needed for a writing task, writers may make the following moves:

1. Analyze the rhetorical situation of the writing task to determine what would be considered a primary source.

2. Analyze the rhetorical situation of the writing task to determine what would be considered a secondary source.

3. Evaluate how the value system implicit in #1 and #2 helps or hinders the writing task.

4. Decide which type of sources will be most effective for this writing task, given the purpose, audience, and situation.

Tactic #3: Decide on research methods appropriate to a rhetorical problem, writing task, and rhetorical situation.

While primary and secondary refer to types of research sources, a different classification refers to types of research methods: *quantitative* and *qualitative*. Quantitative research methods are typically ways of collecting numerical data that are employed to find patterns, make predictions, and make decisions. For example, tracking a university's enrollment patterns in course enrollments enables administrators to make predictions and schedule courses effectively. Qualitative research methods are typically ways of collecting non-numerical data, such as interviews, ethnographic studies, focus groups, etc. One example is observing women's preaching, finding patterns in their sermons and their interactions with parishioners, and drawing conclusions as Roxanne Mountford did in *The Gendered Pulpit*.

Research methods are associated with certain locations and situations. In universities, research methods are traditionally disciplinary: English majors learn methods for reading a text closely to determine the quality of its literary and cultural elements; accounting majors learn methods for compiling financial documents and reading them closely to determine the financial health of businesses; environmental chemistry majors learn methods for analyzing the chemical properties of groundwater, food, etc., to determine the safety of our surroundings; political science majors learn methods for surveying voters and interpreting data to determine voting patterns and project election results. More recently, university research methods have become interdisciplinary. An example is when professors of engineering, sociology, language, and literature combine their knowledge and research methods to address real-world problems, such as how to build a well in an underdeveloped country, a project that will increase water quality and lessen the workload on women. Engineers alone can build the well, but if they do not interview people in their own language and understand the cultural practices of the local area, the well may stand unused. In non-university contexts, research methods differ as well. For example, conducting research on potential donors at a non-profit organization will entail using different research methods than tracking climate change research at NASA, which is different from doing research on which family car to purchase.

The point to keep in mind is this: *research methods dictate the kinds of information gathered and, thus, the conclusions drawn and recommendations offered.* For these reasons, to successfully complete the writing task at hand, writers need to understand their research situations, the kinds of information needed (primary and secondary), and the best methods (qualitative or quantitative) to use for gathering needed information that will be used, in turn, as evidence. To define the best methods for particular rhetorical situations associated with writing tasks, writer may make the following moves.:

1. Identify the kinds of information that, given the situation, will make the best kinds of evidence.

2. Identify research methods typically associated with the site and rhetorical situation.

3. Analyze what information that traditional research methods will offer — and what information it will not offer.

4. Analyze the writing task to determine if other types of methods might generate useful data/information that may be used as evidence.

Tactic #4: Research multiple perspectives on a rhetorical problem by attending to competing claims about it.

Rhetorical problems are often more complicated than two-sided right-wrong debates, so researching several competing claims enables writers to define rhetorical problems more broadly and understand them more deeply. Researching multiple perspectives generates a plenitude of ideas (or what Desiderius Erasmus called *copia* in 1512). Even if writers do not use all the discovered information in their written products, the information generated will map the rhetorical problems broadly so that their written claims, conclusions, and counter-arguments may be more readily imagined. To that end, writers may:

1. Locate multiple competing claims about a rhetorical problem.

2. Identify and analyze the main points in the competing claims about a rhetorical problem.

3. Identify and analyze erasures, or what is missing, from each of the competing claims.

4. Analyze the stakes, or consequences, of the competing claims and the erasures for the writers of the competing perspectives and for the audience of the writer's writing task.

Tactic #5: Research unstated reasons and assumptions haunting competing claims.

All comments or claims have unstated assumptions haunting them. These assumptions may be an unstated purpose, unstated assumptions about audiences, unstated assumptions about what is appropriate or not in any given situation, etc. For example, tactics associated with enthymemes (or rhetorical syllogisms) discussed in Chapter 1 may be used to research unstated premises. The purpose of studying the unstated is for writers to achieve a greater understanding of rhetorical situations and problems as well as, possibly, to find common ground with audiences. To those ends, writers may:

1. Focus on a part or whole of a written text and analyze it for what is assumed about its writer.

2. Focus on a part or whole of a written text and analyze it for what is assumed about its audiences.

3. Focus on a part or whole of a written text and analyze it for what is assumed about its topic or rhetorical problem.

4. Focus on a part or whole of a written text and analyze it for what is assumed about its rhetorical situation.

5. Compare the assumptions noted in 1–4 against your understanding of the following and research additional information as needed:

   a. Writer's purpose

   b. Audience's needs

   c. Rhetorical problem

   d. Rhetorical situation

Tactic #6: Research cultural logics haunting the competing claims

Once competing claims and unstated assumptions have been analyzed to determine what additional research information may be needed to complete a writing task, another research possibility is to research information about cultural logics haunting the competing claims. Chapter 1 outlines ways to build cultural logics. Once the cultural logics surrounding a rhetorical problem are identified, then writers can determine what additional information might strengthen their cases. The purpose is for writers to achieve a greater understanding of their rhetorical problems and situations as well as to possibly find more common ground with their audiences. To achieve these goals, writers may:

1. Locate the dominant tropes in a rhetorical problem.

2. Build multiple cultural logics surrounding that trope.

3. Determine which ones do, or should, inform the rhetorical problem.

4. Research information about the cultural logics.

5. Decide which cultural logics will resonate most with the audience and which ones will need more explanation.

6. Choose accordingly, which ones to make visible and invoke.

Tactic #7: Locate a writerly stance among competing claims and cultural logics.

Once a writer has researched information about competing claims, unstated assumptions, and cultural logics, it is time to take a stance on the topic. For listening writers, taking a stance does not mean hammering the "right" answer at an audience. It means demonstrating knowledge and an understanding of the rhetorical problem being written about as well as demonstrating a respect for those with competing views. Some moves to make include the following:

1. Ask: is there any way to reconcile the competing claims, assumptions, cultural logics?

    a. If so, how — and what additional research might help support this idea?

    b. If not, why not?

2. Ask: where do I locate myself amidst all this information?

    a. Why?

    b. What are the stakes of this location, given the rhetorical problem and writing task at hand?

3. Ask: how might competing viewpoints be inserted into the writing task?

    a. To demonstrate knowledge of other perspectives.

    b. To show respect for audiences with other perspectives.

Tactic #8: Reflect on What You Have Learned.

Writers should reflect on what research and careful consideration of a rhetorical problem has uncovered. Writers learn from laying competing perspectives side by side. Not only do they learn about the rhetorical problem, claims, assumptions, and cultural logics. They also learn about themselves—their stances (including their own claims, assumptions and cultural logics), their critical thinking processes, and possibilities and limits of their information literacy. To achieve these ends, writers may:

1. Reflect on the claims written.

2. Reflect on unstated assumptions of the written text.

3. Reflect on the cultural logics haunting the text.

4. Reflect on their own critical thinking about sources, i.e., their own information literacy.

In a world of ever-expanding cries of "fake news" and embraces of conspiracy theories, the need for people to be information literate is at an all-time high. Only by using personal agency to evaluate the plethora of available sources can listening writers provide credibility for themselves and useful information for their audiences.

Appendix D: Style

For classical Greek and Roman rhetoricians, style was deemed an important concept for study and practice. As an element of rhetorical education, style was conceptualized as the third of five canons of rhetoric, which include invention, arrangement, style, memory, and delivery. Style follows invention (ways of generating ideas) and arrangement (ways of organizing ideas, which connotes both logic and genre) but precedes memory (ways of retaining and storing ideas) and delivery (ways of disseminating ideas).[1] According to Edward P. J. Corbett and Robert Connors, style focuses on "an integral and reciprocal relationship between matter and form" (2).[2] In other words, style is not simply the polish laid on content; style is content. It speaks. And people should listen, both to others' styles and to their own as well as to the reactions to both. Located at the level of word and sentence, style results from the choices that speakers and writers make, choices that are lexical (vocabulary), grammatical (sentence structures), and syntactical (arrangement of words in sentences).

For students of rhetoric, stylistic choices are best evaluated in terms of their *effectiveness*, not correctness. Stylistic effectiveness attends to what the Greeks called *kairos* (appropriate to the moment), meaning that writers must match their styles to their situations, purposes, and audiences. Sometimes effective style entails performing a standard of correctness fostered by lists of rules in style handbooks and embraced by institutions (schools, judicial systems, business offices, etc.). More often, however, effective style depends on a speaker/writer's ability to code-switch to particular conventions of any given situation, purpose, and audience. For example, you don't write a report for your boss in the same style that you text a friend.

It is important to note, however, that scholars have called into question how, and whether, to promote code-switching from style to style as a path to rhetorical effectiveness. Specifically, what is questioned—in terms of the production and reception of student texts—is whether students actually need to conform to existing stylistic conventions of standard English in institutions of education, business, or government, given that these standard conventions have traditionally reinscribed a racialized whiteness in language use. In terms of students' production of texts, while arguing in *Linguistic Justice* for an "Antiracist Black Language Pedagogy," April Baker-Bell warns that a code-switching pedagogy has significant limitations unless it is carefully and critically contextualized to foreground "racial realities" of students (x; 30). She defines a code-switching pedagogy as "a color-evasive approach that teaches students to use language to fit the time, place, audience, and communicative purpose, which is usually only with friends and at home in the case of Black Language" (23). Too often, Baker-Bell argues, such a pedagogy, generates an "Anti-Black Linguistic Racism [that] occurs when Black students are uncritically taught to code-switch without learning the social-cultural factors that inform the social positioning of Black Language and White Mainstream English" (23). Baker-Bell further questions why code-switching is celebrated as a means to success and survival if its use denies the richness of Black culture and cannot save Black lives, as in the cases of Michael Brown or George Floyd (29–31). In terms of teachers' reception and evaluation of students' written texts, Asao Inoue argues in *Antiracist Writing Assessment Ecologies* for what he deems socially just ways of grading. The assessment ecology he advocates is grounded in student-teacher negotiated labor contracts, not in students' written texts meeting stylistic conventions of standard English. Given the intersectionality of people's identities, such stylistic concerns about production and reception also haunt other identity categories such as region, class, etc.

The complexity of stylistic choice is best understood when style is imagined as having both individual and collective signatures. For example, a sentence written by Toni Morrison indicates her personal style, rather like a fingerprint, but her style also indicates a literary style, reflecting the times (late-twentieth-century), places (US), and communities in which she wrote. As a member of the African American literary tradition, she first worked at Random House as an editor in her early career, contributing to the tradition by recruiting now-noted Black authors such as Toni Cade Bambera; later, as an author herself, Morrison wrote to imagine stories about African American lives whose details and perspectives had not been recorded in US history books, an example being the story of the Middle Passage in *Beloved*. As a member of a women's literary tradition, she wrote to imagine women characters as protagonists and definers of their own stories. And as a student of an Anglo-American literary tradition, she negotiated tensions between, first, modernism with its psychological interiority of characters demanding free associative sentences that supersede plots and, second, postmodernism with its textual play of calling attention to gaps in personal, cultural, and historical narratives by experimenting with perspectives and form. Though not every writer rises to the level of Morrison's genius or negotiates multiple literary traditions, all writers produce texts marked by personal styles underlaid with echoing traces of different communities that they inhabit.

The complexity of stylistic choice is also best understood when style is imagined as having both aesthetic and political effects, not simply one or the other. To understand how aesthetics (a sense of beauty) and politics (a sense of cultural purpose) combine in a sentence, consider this famous sentence from Virginia Woolf's *A Room of One's Own*: "Let me imagine, since facts are so hard to come by, what would have happened had Shakespeare had a wonderfully gifted sister, called Judith, let us say" (46). Aesthetically, Woolf's stylistic form of free association in this sentence mimics the way a person's mind works, a hallmark of British modernism, which was a literary style forwarded by a group of early twentieth-century mostly white British writers who tried to capture in writing how the mind consciously and unconsciously processes life via observations, flashbacks, associations, collapsing of time, etc. Politically, Woolf's invocation of the "wonderfully gifted" Judith Shakespeare echoes the politics of early twentieth-century British feminism, which concerned itself with incommensurate opportunities available to British men and women. For another example of how aesthetics (a sense of beauty) and politics (a sense of cultural purpose) merge, consider Queen Latifah's sentence style in a lyric from her celebrated 1993 song "U.N.I.T.Y": "Instinct leads me to another flow / Every time I hear a brother call a girl a bitch or a ho / Tryna make a sister feel low / You know all of that gots to go." Aesthetically, the lyric echoes 1990s hip hop music with its parallel structure, end rhymes, and lack of punctuation creating a flow that generates a rhythm to fit the beats of the song. Politically, Queen Latifah's call out is hailed both as a feminist anthem for questioning the disrespect and mistreatment of Black women and as a hip hop anthem for follow-ing in the tradition of keeping it real about what she knows to be true, in this case that Black men and women must pull together in unity.

Any rhetorical listening approach to teaching style in terms of *effec-tiveness* would need to recognize and attend to concerns such as the ones voiced by Baker-Bell and Inoue and to the dimensions of style that are personal/collective, aesthetic/political. For instance, a rhetorical listen-ing approach to style would invite teachers and students to foreground cultural logics that drive different pedagogical approaches and language use more generally. A rhetorical listening approach would also invite questions about unstated assumptions haunting rhetorical situations in terms of how situations discipline style. (And all situations discipline style—though to different degrees and with different effects for differ-ent people). In such a pedagogy, *effectiveness* could remain a dominant trope by foregrounding (not just implying) that in some situations code-switching might be deemed effective but that in other situations refusing to code-switch might be the more effective choice. The determination depends, in part, on how writers define *effectiveness* for themselves in different situations and also on how well their definitions and purposes align, or purposely do not align, with the cultural norms of *effective-ness* assumed in each situation. A rhetorical listening approach to style would recognize that, in any stylistic choice, there are always stakes and always consequences—ranging from slight to grave. What is important to ask in every rhetorical situation, then, is: What are the stakes, the consequences, and the ethics of stylistic choices? How do stylistic choices function? Whom do they benefit, or not benefit—and why? And how may they be interrupted when necessary?

Given the long history of rhetoric that locates style at the levels of word and sentence and given the same history that emphasizes a sen-tence's form as well as its content, the study and practice of rhetorical style offers to writers today myriad choices (again, what in 1512 Erasmus called *copia*) so that they may write effective sentences and reflect on their sentences' stakes, consequences, and ethics. To help listening writ-ers put such study into practice, what follows are examples of six "Style Tactics," each linked to one of the six rhetorical concepts discussed in this book.

RHETORICAL LISTENING: STYLE TACTICS
RELATED TO PARALLEL STRUCTURE

As a rhetorical concept, rhetorical listening asks writers to lay competing ideas side by side in sentences and analyze them in conjunction with one another. Rhetorical listening may inform sentence style when the effectiveness of sentences is analyzed in terms of parallel structure, a stylistic tactic that puts comparable ideas in comparable grammatical positions, thus foregrounding the relationships between the words and between content and form.

Style Tactic #1: Put parallel ideas in parallel grammatical form.

Parallelism has four important benefits:

1. Parallelism gives equal ideas in a sentence equal *grammatical weight*.

    a. *Non-Parallel:* I like to ride bikes. I like to find hiking trails as well as going skiing with friends.

    b. *Parallel:* I like to ride bikes, to hike, and to ski with friends.

2. Parallelism makes sentences *concise* (each word counts).

    a. *Non-Parallel:* Writing makes me nervous yet fills me with feelings of excitement.

    b. *Parallel:* Writing unnerves yet excites me.

3. Parallelism makes sentence meanings *clear*.

    a. *Non-Parallel:* The government that the people have created so that they may govern themselves shall not perish from the earth.

    b. *Parallel:* ". . . the government of the people, for the people, by the people, shall not perish from the earth." — Abraham Lincoln

4. Parallelism creates sentence cadences and rhythms that make important sentences *memorable* and easily *quotable*.

    a. *Parallel Dependent and Independent Clauses:* "If you do not tell the truth about yourself, you cannot tell the truth about other people." — Virginia Woolf

b. *Parallel Sentences:* "Something is happening in Memphis; something is happening in our world." — Dr. Martin Luther King

c. *Parallel relative clauses* (introduced by *that*) *and parallel modifiers:*[3] "There is a way <u>that nature speaks, that land speaks</u>. Most of the time we are simply not <u>patient enough, quiet enough</u>, to pay attention to the story." — Linda Hogan

These three sentences are more than merely memorable and quotable because of their parallel form; they resonate with the importance of their writer's stakes and consequences. Virginia Woolf's sentence comes from her living a life in which she could not be completely open about her sexuality or about her mental health issues, the latter eventually triggering her suicide. Dr. Martin Luther King Jr.'s sentence comes from his living a life of non-violent protest that threatened the white power structure by championing Civil Rights and anti-war movements in the 1950s and 1960s; the sentence is from his speech "I've Been to the Mountaintop," which he delivered in Memphis the day before he was assassinated by forces trying to quell the influence of his words and actions. Finally, Linda Hogan's sentence comes from living a life attuned to the earth; it appears in an interview in which she reflects on Barbara McClintock's winning a Nobel Prize for discovering gene transposition in corn plants: "the way she did her research was by listening to the corn. It turned the scientific community on its 'ear' when it found she did research by, in her own words, intimately getting to know each plant of corn, the 'story,' she called it, of each plant. She found what the other members of the scientific community wanted to know but couldn't discover through their learned methodologies" (D. Jensen 124).

Style Tactic #2: Make the form and the content of a sentence parallel, each reinforcing the other.

Literary writers use this tactic all the time, but it is useful for *all* writers because it also makes sentences clear, concise, and memorable. For example, consider these two sentences:

Example A

<u>Jack stopped.</u>

Example B

<u>Jack</u>, while contemplating the right action for all people involved, walked slower and slower and slower and then eventually <u>stopped</u>.

Both sentences convey the idea that Jack stopped. But their shapes are very different. They both are grammatically correct. But a good writer focuses not just on correctness but effectiveness. Which sentence is more effective? It depends, in part, on the writer's intent. The first sentence is short and quick; if the writer is trying to communicate that Jack stopped quickly, then this form is the better choice. The second sentence is longer and meanders a bit; if the writer is trying to communicate that Jack took a while to stop, then this second sentence is the better choice. In both cases, the parallelism between form and content may not only represent a writer's intent but also inscribes meanings for audiences.

And speaking of form reinforcing content, let's return to the parallel structure example from Style Tactic #1: "I like to ride bikes, to hike, and to ski." This sentence form indicates that all three activities are equally liked. But what if skiing is preferred? To make the form and content reinforce one another, the sentence might be revised to read: "Although I like to ride bikes and to hike, I really love to ski." See the difference? "To ski" is in the main sentence, and "to ride" and "to hike" are relegated to an introductory dependent clause.

Parallel Structure Style Exercise

Select a page from your own writing and mark sentences that you think need work. Then proceed sentence by sentence according to the following steps:

1. Find parallel ideas in each sentence.

2. Underline them.

3. Ask yourself:

   a. Are the parallel ideas in parallel form?

   b. Do the form and content reinforce one another?

4. If not, revise your sentence accordingly.

AGENCY: STYLE TACTICS RELATED TO
SUBJECT AND VERB POSITIONS

As a rhetorical concept, agency (whether personal, discursive, cultural, or material) asks listening writers to consider who or what has the capacity or power to act on their writing processes. Agency informs style when the effectiveness of sentences is analyzed in terms of 1) how well the subject position in a sentence names *the agent* of action; and 2) how well the main verb position in a sentence names *the actions* of agents. Too often subject and verb positions are taught in a rhetorical vacuum, with a focus only on identifying them, not on how to use them. In elementary and junior high school, for example, did you ever complete worksheets that asked you to read other people's sentences and then underline subjects and circle main verbs? Did you ever wonder why you were doing that exercise? Well, that's an excellent question.

While identifying a sentence's subject and main verb is important, *knowing how to use those sentence positions effectively* is even more important. Building on the parallel structure idea that form and content should reinforce one another, the following two Style Tactics encourage writers not just to identify but also to analyze subject and verb positions so that the most important sentence content is reinforced by the most important grammatical positions in a sentence.

Style Tactic #3. Put the logical subject (or main idea) of your sentence in the grammatical subject position of your sentence.

To better understand this style tactic, look at the following examples of two grammatically correct sentences.

Example A

Edmonia Lewis sculpted *Minnehaha* in 1868.

Example B

Minnehaha was sculpted by Edmonia Lewis in 1868.

Many style handbooks would advise that the first sentence is better than the second because sentences with active voice verbs are better than sentences with passive voice verbs. Example A is active voice because the grammatical subject (*Edmonia Lewis,* whom the Smithsonian hails as the first professional African-American sculptor but who was also part

Haitian and Ojibwa) actively performs the verb's action (*sculpted*). Example B is passive voice because the grammatical subject (*Minnehaha, her sculpture*) does not perform an action but rather receives the action (it *was sculpted by* Lewis). The problem with such handbook rules about style is that they ignore context: put another way, such general rules of *correctness* rarely consider contextual *effectiveness*.

Given that rhetoric focuses on effectiveness, consider the following style suggestions. If you are writing about the sculptor Edmonia Lewis (that is, if she is the logical subject of your sentence), then Example A is probably the better choice because the words *Edmonia Lewis* are in the grammatical subject position of the sentence. If, however, you are writing about the sculpture *Minnehaha* (that is, if the sculpture is the logical subject of your sentence), then Example B is probably the better choice because *Minnehaha* is in the grammatical subject position of that sentence. And for the record, this paragraph's suggestions are just that— suggested guidelines, not hard and fast rules.

Style Tactic #4: Put the logical action of your sentence in the grammatical main verb position in your sentence.

To understand this style tactic, examine the following grammatically correct sentences.

Example A

The soccer team <u>won</u> the Olympic gold medal, which earned them an invitation to the White House.

Example B

The soccer team <u>was invited</u> to the White House because they won the Olympic gold medal.

To determine which sentence is more effective for your purposes, consider the following. If you are writing about the action of winning an Olympic medal, Example A is probably the better choice because the main verb is *won*. If, however, you are writing about the action of being invited to the White House, then Example B is probably the better choice because the main verb is *was invited*.

Subject and Verb Positions Style Exercise

Select a page from one of your drafts and mark sentences that you think need some work Then proceed sentence by sentence according to the following steps:

1. Bracket the main point, or logical subject, of your sentence.

2. Underline your grammatical subject once.

3. Ask yourself: Do #1 and #2 match? If not, revise your sentence accordingly.

4. Bracket the main action of your sentence.

5. Underline your main verb of the sentence twice.

6. Ask yourself: do #3 and #4 match? If not, revise your sentence accordingly.

RHETORICAL SITUATIONS: STYLE
TACTICS RELATED TO DICTION

As a rhetorical concept, rhetorical situation asks writers to consider contextual factors that influence a particular writing task. Rhetorical situations may inform discussions of sentence style when the effectiveness of sentences is analyzed in terms of diction, or word choice. Writers choose particular words for particular effects, both for expressing their own ideas, values, and beliefs and also for inviting audiences to understand the words and to take them seriously. In short, word choice matters because different words evoke different images, ideas, and values. Consider, for example, what is evoked by the words *Catwoman* and *cat lady*.

Effective writers learn to code-switch the diction of their writing so that their words fit their different situations, including different purposes, genres (forms), and audiences. In other words, effective writers learn to adapt to different lexicons (sets of words) appropriate for different discourse communities; for example, applying for an administrative position within a professional basketball franchise might require a different set of words than talking to your best friend about last Saturday's big game.

Style Tactic #5: Select words that express the writer's meaning clearly.

To understand this Style Tactic, consider the following sentences:

Example A

"When, in disgrace with fortune and men's eyes, / I all alone beweep my outcast state . . ." —William Shakespeare

Example B

When I reflect on my bad luck and bad reputation, I get upset about my resulting loneliness.

To determine which sentence is more effective, consider the context. If the expression of aesthetic beauty, rhythm, and a particular feeling is privileged, then Example A wins hands down. But Shakespeare's sonnet employs an early modern language that is not always easily accessible at first glance to contemporary readers. If accessibility of ideas is privileged, then Example B might be the better choice. But in Example B, the *experience* of reading Shakespeare's "Sonnet 29" is missing. This important distinction is why reading a *Cliff's Notes* summary of a literary text is never, ever, ever, *ever* the equivalent of reading that text itself. A written text is not just the summary of its content; it is the experience of its interrelated form and content. The same could be said about a mother's hug: to a child, the idea of it is not the same as experiencing its form and content.

Style Tactic #6: Select words that clarify meanings for audiences.

To understand this Style Tactic, consider the following sentences, the first of which uses legal discourse about wills:

Example A

A testator determines beneficiaries (usually but not always issues), bequests, and directions for the residuary estate.

Example B

A person making a will decides who will inherit (usually but not always children and grandchildren), what gifts will be given, and what will be done with the remaining assets after all the bequests are honored.

Obviously, lawyers and others who work with wills would understand Example A, but most non-lawyers will have to pay lawyers to interpret it. Conversely, non-lawyers would understand Example B, but its diction probably would not be used in legal documents. Different professionals such as lawyers, accountants, photographers, or hip hop musicians have their own lexicons (sets of words) as well as their own discourse conventions ("rules" or guidelines) for using these words. This fact is also true for all communities, whether work, social, cultural, governmental, familial, etc.

Diction Style Exercise

Select a page from your writing and mark words that seem not appropriate for the situation. Then proceed through your circled words, according to the following steps:

1. Analyze whether the word expresses your idea clearly. If so, great. If not, change it.

2. Analyze whether the word is clear and appropriate for your audiences and situation. If so, great. If not, change it.

IDENTIFICATION: STYLE TACTICS RELATED
TO CLAUSES AND PUNCTUATION

As a rhetorical concept, identification asks writers to consider what properties they assign to people, objects, spaces, events, etc., in order to identify or disidentify with them. For example, you assign the property of kindness to a person and then wish to be friends with them because you identify with kindness. Such identification may inform sentence style, too, as when the effectiveness of sentences is analyzed in terms of properties assigned to clauses (independent or subordinate) and to sentence punctuation (period, semicolon, comma plus coordinating conjunction).
    Common definitions of types of clauses are as follows:

- A *clause* is a group of words with a subject and a verb.

- An *independent clause* contains both a subject and a verb and stands alone; it is a sentence. An example is: "Jane walked."

- A *subordinate (or dependent) clause* contains a subject and a verb but cannot stand alone; it is introduced by a subordinating conjunction, such as *after, although, because, if, since, when, while,* etc. An example is "While Jane ran, …." Here *Jane* is the subject; *ran,* the verb; and *while,* the subordinating conjunction. Say it out loud. It will feel incomplete, as if you are compelled to finish the sentence, because a dependent clause *depends* on being linked to an independent clause in order for it to make sense, as in "While Jane ran, Jim walked."

When taught in schools, these definitions are often reinforced by exercises that require the independent clauses to be underlined and the dependent clause to be bracketed, as in the example below:

Example A

The dog sat on command. His trainer rewarded him.

Example B

[Because the dog sat on command,] his trainer rewarded him.

Example C

The dog sat on command [because his trainer rewarded him].

But simply identifying types of clauses does not automatically translate into knowing either how to use them effectively or how to punctuate them. What is important is how a clause's form affects its *meaning.* For example, given that readers often non-consciously assign independent clauses more weight than subordinate ones, Example A suggests that both the dog's sitting and the trainer's rewarding him are equal actions. Example B suggests that the trainer's rewarding the dog is the more important action. Example C suggests the dog's sitting on command is the more important action. Writers should select which of the three sentences would most effectively express their meanings.

What is also important in studying clauses is how their punctuation reinforces meaning. Consider the following options for punctuating two main clauses that show various degrees of separation between the ideas.

Example A. Most separation

The dog sat on command. His trainer rewarded him.

Example B. Less separation

The dog sat on command; his trainer rewarded him.

Example C. Least separation

The dog sat on c ommand, and his trainer rewarded him.

In Example A, the period reinforces the idea that the two main clauses are separate but equal ideas; Example C shows the closest relationship between two clauses, running them together in one sentence. Too often punctuation is presented in textbooks via rules for correct usage (one of us remembers a high school pop quiz that required students to list twenty-one rules for correct usages of commas). Reflecting on how punctuation informs meaning is important to effective style.

The following Style Tactics emphasize how clauses and punctuation may assign *meaning* for readers, often at non-conscious levels.

Style Tactic #7: Combine two related sentences into one sentence using a dependent and an independent clause: Put the most important idea in the independent clause and the less important idea in the dependent clause, thus making clear the association between these two clauses.

To better understand this style tactic, look at the following:

Example A. Two independent clauses

Jane ran. John walked.

Example B. Dependent + independent clauses

While Jane ran, John walked.

Example C. Independent + dependent clauses

Jane ran while John walked.

To determine which sentence pattern is more effective for your purposes, consider the following: If you want to emphasize equally Jane and John, then keeping the two related sentences in A is a better choice because their names are both in subject positions in independent clauses. If your sentence is primarily about John, however, then B is probably the better choice because John is in the subject position of the independent clause.

If your sentence is primarily about Jane, then C is probably the better choice because Jane is the subject of the independent clause.

Style Tactic #8: When punctuating two sentences, select the punctuation that best represents your intent about the relationship between the two sentences.

Basically, there are four ways to punctuate two sentences. While all four examples below are correct, they generate different sentence shapes and have different effects on meaning.

1. Period

   • A period implies a distinct distance between 2 sentences.

   • Example: Jane ran. John walked

2. Semicolon

   • A semicolon implies a closer link between 2 sentences than a period.

   • Example: Jane ran; John walked.

3. Comma + Coordinating Conjunction (*and, but, or, nor, for, so, yet*)

   • A comma and coordinating conjunction implies an even closer link between 2 sentences than a period or a semicolon.

   • Example: Jane ran, but John walked.

   • Exceptions: If two sentences are really short, the following punctuation is conventional:

     1) only a comma: Jane ran, John walked

     2) only a coordinating conjunction: Jane ran but John walked.

4. Colon

   • A colon indicates that the first sentence is general & the second is a particular example of the first.

   • Example: People fled the scene: Jane ran, but John walked.

Clauses and Punctuation Style Exercise

Select a page from your writing and circle sentences that seem related Then proceed according to the following steps:

1. Are the circled sentences equal in meaning?

2. If so, check the punctuation of the two sentences to determine if you have signaled the distance you wish to signal between them.

3. If not, revise the punctuation or make the less important sentence a subordinate clause.

MYTH: STYLE TACTICS RELATED TO CONCISENESS

As a rhetorical concept, myth asks writers to reflect on the stories we tell each other that reflect the values and beliefs of a culture. Myth may inform sentence style when the effectiveness of sentences is analyzed in terms of *the stories we tell each other about what a sentence should be.* (For examples of such stories, see all the Style Tactics above.)

Myths about sentence style abound. Some US myths define style via the negative, invoking commandments of what not to do: don't use passive voice, don't split an infinitive, don't end a sentence with a preposition, don't begin a sentence with *And*, etc. In certain situations, these myths of the negative could be effective. But sometimes they are not: for example, government reports regularly use passive voice intentionally, stating "money was lost" (rarely do they say *who* lost it!), and, frankly, if the logical subject of the sentence is money, then having *money* in the grammatical subject position helps form and content reinforce one another.

Another myth about sentences features wordiness and conciseness. Wordiness entails using too many words to make a point. Imagined as a solution to wordiness, conciseness is then imagined as short sentences. Granted, making wordy sentences more concise often renders sentences shorter. But in fact, concise sentences are simply sentences in which *every word counts,* regardless of sentence length. So yes, a very long sentence could be concise: think Virginia Woolf, Gabriel García Márquez, William Faulkner or Toni Morrison.

Style Tactic 9: Make every word count, regardless of length of a sentence.

1. Use *There is and It is* sparingly as sentence openers . . . only for emphasis.

   a. There are many people who are eligible to apply for the job.

   b. Many people are eligible to apply for the job.

   c. It is important that writers develop effective sentence styles.

   d. Writers should develop effective sentence styles.

2. Convert linking verbs (is, am, are, was, were, be, being, been, has, have, had, seem, feel, appear) to active verbs when the action has been implied rather than stated.

   a. Nimbus clouds *are* indicative of rain. (The action of *indicate* is implied.)

   b. Nimbus clouds *indicate* rain. (The action is stated)

3. Cut unnecessary words (keeping in mind subject and verb positions).

   a. Many different objections about the attempt by the large corporation to take over the small company were made by the corporation's stockholders; its workers also had objections.

   b. Objections to the takeover attempt were made by the corporation's stockholders and workers.

   c. Stockholders and workers objected to the corporation's takeover attempt.

Conciseness Style Exercise

Select a page from your draft and mark sentences that you think need work. Then proceed sentence by sentence following these steps:

1. Mark any *There is* or *It is*: reword unless you have used them sparingly for emphasis.

2. Underline your main verbs in sentences: convert any linking verb (*is, am, are, was, were,* etc.) to an action verb, when appropriate.

3. Examine your sentences word by word to determine if *every word counts*—that is, whether each word adds meaning; if not, cut it.

RHETORICAL DEVICES: STYLE TACTICS RELATED RHETORICAL FIGURES AND IMITATION

As a rhetorical concept, rhetorical devices ask writers to identify patterns of argumentative moves that are effective given different topics, purposes, audiences, and situations. When imagined in terms of effective sentence style, rhetorical devices may inform sentence style via rhetorical figures. In classical Greek and Roman rhetoric, rhetorical figures include, first, schemes that affect shapes and sounds of sentences (such as onomatopoeia with words like *boo, hiss, buzz*), and second, tropes that affect meaning (such as metaphor—*love is a battlefield, love is a rose*). Modern rhetoric remains interested in figures in terms of how they structure thinking and affect meaning in texts, although modern and postmodern rhetorics tend to view *all* figures as contributing to meaning. Modern rhetoric is also interested in the situatedness of certain figures such as the figure of signifyin' within Black communities (which, according to Henry Louis Gates Jr. is the Black trope of tropes that itself contains multiple figures[4]) as well as the figures of playing the dozens, call-and-response, etc. (Gates 84–85; Bell-Baker 78–79).

Rhetorical figures make visible how content and form interconnect to determine a sentence's shape and meaning. Take for example the following sentences from Virginia Woolf's 1929 *A Room of One's Own*. The narrator has been invited to give a talk on Women and Fiction, and she is mulling over what she will say as she sits by the riverside:

> Thought—to call it by a prouder name than it deserved—had let its line down into the stream. It swayed, minute after minute, hither and thither among the reflections and the weeds, letting the water lift it and sink it until—you know the little tug—the sudden conglomeration of an idea at the end of one's line: and then the cautious hauling of it in and the careful laying of it out? (6)

In the first sentence, a fishing line and hook's being lowered into a stream in hopes of catching a big fish is being compared to a woman's thinking in hopes of catching a great idea. The second much longer, yet still concise, sentence imitates the process of that fishing and thinking, capturing not just content details but also the rhythm and feel of fishing and thinking. In these sentences, the narrator uses fishing as a metaphor, not just to compare women's thinking to fishing (and thus illustrating the problems women face by not having access to university training) but also to structure the shape of the sentences.

Knowledge of rhetorical figures helps writers identify and imitate sentence shapes. While metaphor is a commonly known rhetorical figure, many other rhetorical figures exist. Here is a very partial list of figures studied as part of the classical Greek and Roman tradition:

Alliteration — repetition of consonant sounds

Anadiplosis — the last word(s) of one clause becomes the first of the next

Anaphora — the same word beginning a sequence of clauses

Anastrophe — the natural word order is changed

Antimetabole — two or more words repeated in reverse order

Antithesis — posing opposites

Aposiopesis — breaking off of thought in middle of sentence

Assonance — repetition of vowel sounds

Asyndeton — words or phrases piled up without intervening conjunctions

Epanalepsis — same word at the beginning and end of a line/clause

Ellipses – the use of three periods or white space to show the omission of words

Isocolon — repetition of phrases or clauses of equal length

Irony — saying one thing but meaning its opposite

Metaphor — comparison without *like* or *as*

Metonymy — association

Parison — corresponding structure in a sequence of clauses/phrases (i.e., parallel structure)

Parallelism — putting like ideas in like grammatical forms

Polyptoton — repetition of the same root word with different endings

Simile — comparison with *like* or *as*

Syllepsis — using one word while suggesting two senses of it (puns)

Synecdoche — part stands for the whole

Although metaphor is the dominant rhetorical figure in Woolf's fishing passage, other rhetorical figures are in play, too: the second sentence proceeds via 1) asyndeton, or words or phrases piled up without intervening conjunctions, which creates the rhythm of fishing and thinking; 2) assonance, or repetition of vowel sounds in "minute by minute, hither and thither," which provides a sense of flow to the rhythm; and 3) antithesis, or posing opposite actions such as "lift it" and "sink it," which interrupts the flow and reinforces the idea that thinking doesn't always flow smoothly. Is memorizing all these figures necessary? Probably not. Recognizing patterns in how sentences are structured, however, is useful, whether the sentences invoke a style of standard white English, Black English, Spanglish, etc.

A time-honored tactic in rhetorical education, recognizing patterns in sentences is associated not just with rhetorical figures but also with imitation. Imitation entails selecting a written passage from an author you admire as well as a topic of your own and then writing about your own topic by using sentence patterns from the selected passage. An imitation of Woolf's first sentence above might be: "Friendship—to call it by a better name than it deserves—had let its ball bounce off the rim." While imitation at first appears to be simply a paint-by-number proposition applied to writing, it quickly moves beyond that metaphor. Indeed, imitation offers writers a conscious awareness of not just *what* sentences say but *how* they are structured. It also offers a repertoire of style tactics that writers may choose from when writing their own texts. Finally, imitation challenges writers to revise their imitated sentences, to reconstruct sentences into forms that better reflect their contents, their intents.

Style Tactic 10. Identify rhetorical figures (patterns) and discuss how these figures affect sentence structure and meaning.

1. Select a passage from a writer you admire or use one from your own draft.

2. Identify rhetorical figures (patterns) in the passage.

3. Reflect on how the figures (patterns) shape the form and the meaning of the sentence.

Consider the following passage from Nikki Giovanni's *Racism 101*:

There is a photograph that I hung in my son's room. It shows a Black man, clearly emancipated . . . not a slave, standing behind a mule. In his right hand he is holding the plow; in his left he has a McGuffey Reader. I wanted that picture in my son's room because I wanted him to know, viscerally, who he is and where he comes from. I don't know that the picture made all that much difference to Tom. He would probably have preferred some busty woman in some lewd or obscene pose, but since I am grown and he wasn't, I won the first battle of the walls. (95)

This passage may be analyzed for how rhetorical figures reinforce Giovanni's message. Her use of three periods (ellipses) between the words *emancipated* and *not a slave* reinforces, via form, the point that there exists a vast difference between those two states of being and that there exists a lot that has not been said about the distance between those two states. Her repetition of the word *I* at the beginning of her sentences (anaphora) reinforces that this story is told from her perspective, not her son's. Her selection of the poster for its metaphors (a free Black man holding a plow, a metaphor for work, and a McGuffey Reader, a metaphor for education) represents the values and the cultural history that she is trying to impart to her son.

Style Tactic #11. Imitate other writers' sentence patterns to write your own.

1. Select a passage of 2–3 sentences from a writer you admire.

2. Circle some prominent figures (patterns) that you see in the sentences.

3. Select a topic of your own.

4. Using your own topic, write sentences that imitate the form of the 2–3 sentences from the writer you admire.

5. Analyze the sentences you wrote to evaluate how well the forms of the sentences you imitated fit your topic.

6. If the sentence forms fit your topic, no further action is needed. But if the sentence forms do not fit your topic, then play with the form to see what sentence shapes might better fit your topic.

Below is our imitation of Nikki Giovanni's passage. For our topic, we replaced Giovani's "poster" with this "book":

> There is a book that we wrote during the pandemic. It offers a rhetorical concept, clearly performed, . . . not an abstraction, hiding behind abstract words. In one chapter it defines rhetorical listening; in other chapters it defines other rhetorical concepts. We wanted this book in our students' hands because we wanted them to know, consciously, who they are and where they stand as language users. We don't know that this book will make all that much difference to students. They would probably prefer it be a graphic novel with some superheroic or apocalyptic plot, but since we are teachers and they aren't, we offer this story of rhetorical listening.

Notice that our sentence forms mirror Giovanni's pretty closely. Imitating her sentence forms helped us articulate one purpose for this book fairly clearly and in a style we might not have imagined on our own. Our topic, however, does not have the deep resonance of Giovanni's. And our imitating her tone for talking about her son while we talk about students does not work either: much as we admire our students, we don't have the same loving familial relationship with students as Giovanni has with her son, so our presuming to know what they would prefer comes across as a bit dismissive and condescending. And, finally, imitating one of Giovanni's sentences forced us to write something we do not exactly believe: that we don't know that this book will make much difference to students. We hope that it will.

Through these exercises in rhetorical figures and imitation, we learned or relearned important lessons about writing. One, making visible what is usually omitted is important. Two, perspective is important, too, and can be reinforced by the metaphors we invoke. Three, purposes and audiences related to a topic can be clarified through figures and imitation. But, four, not all topics are commensurate; indeed, a writer's relationship to an audience makes a difference in what, and how, something can be written. And, five, form possesses power: when it is the only consideration, it can lead writers into inadvertently saying something that they do not believe. Given these important lessons, imagine what other lessons might be learned when studying other passages to analyze rhetorical figures or to imitate their sentence forms.

Rhetorical Figures & Imitation Style Exercise

1. Select a topic to write about.

2. Select a passage from a favorite author (or use Giovanni's passage).

3. Identify rhetorical figures (patterns, even if you can't name them) in the passage.

4. Reflect on how the figures reinforce meaning.

5. Imitate the passage in terms of its sentence structures, using your own topic.

6. Reflect on how your imitation reinforces—or does not reinforce—meanings related to your topic.

7. Summarize the lessons you learned about writing by doing these exercises.

In sum, our hope for this appendix is that listening writers will contemplate *style* and, more importantly, play and have fun with their own sentences as well as with the sentences of others, even as they are also listening for cultural logics and unstated assumptions haunting all styles.

Notes

INTRODUCTION

1. For a discussion of the situatedness of cultural discourses in which people navigate competing hypotheses, see Flower.

2. Though all wars are violent, they are not equal in how and why they are fought; see Moseley, "Just War Theory."

3. Kohrs Campbell argues for an expansive concept of rhetoric grounded in ontology (the study of being) that allows for epistemology (the study of knowing): an "advantage of the symbolic interpretation of the ontological presumption of human persuadability is that it can encompass the most significant insights of rationalistic and behavioristic theory without incurring their limitations" ("The Ontological" 105).

4. For a discussion of the evolution of Hartsock's standpoint theory, see Welton. It is important to note that standpoint theory grows out of Marxist theory. When society is imagined as a circle with centers of power and margins of marginalized groups, then Marx put the bourgeoisie at the center and the proletariat at the margins; ethnic theorists in the US put whites at the center and BIPOC on the margins; feminist theorists, in early standpoint theory, put men in the center and women on the margins. Crenshaw's intersectionality theory complicates standpoint theory in productive ways.

5. For an interview with Crenshaw about the origins and implications of intersectionality as a concept and theory, see Coaston.

6. In his *Grammar*, Burke differentiates between inextricably intertwined first-nature and second-nature substances that construct identity, with first-nature substance being the material body and physical environment within which we live and second-nature substance being the language through which people mediate our thinking and feeling and experiences within the former (33).

7. April Baker-Bell later invokes this metaphor of war and specifies its function in terms of race when discussing the "Language War" that results from Anti-Black Linguistic Racism, which she unpacks in the second chapter of *Linguistic Justice* (4, 11–38).

8. In his *Rhetoric*, Aristotle notes a similar problem: "[s]peech based on knowledge is teaching but teaching is impossible [with some audiences]" (I.1.12). This impossibility of teaching may occur when an audience does not value experts' assertions of facts. Because one thread of US pragmatism is an anti-intellectual suspicion of experts and expertise, this suspicion lay the groundwork for one side perpetuating conspiracy theories and rejecting science.

9. For extensions and critiques of rhetorical listening, see Glenn and Ratcliffe, Hinshaw, Jordan, Middleton, and Oleksiak.

10. For an overview of classical stasis theory, see Heath.

11. For definitions and descriptions of rhetorical educations associated with rhetorical traditions, see Charney and Secor's *Constructing Rhetorical Education*; Corbett and Connors's *Classical Rhetoric for the Modern Student*; Enoch's *Refiguring Rhetorical Education*; Glenn et al.'s *Rhetorical Education*; Logan's *Liberating Language*; and Walker's *The Genuine Teachers of This Art*.

12. For noted research on the history of rhetoric, see Ballif, Bizzell, Borchers, Glenn et al, Killingsworth, Vitanza.

13. For extended definitions of rhetoric, see Appendix A.

14. While *Rhetorical Listening in Action* invokes traditional definitions of *tactics* as specific moves and *strategies* as overall plans composed of a strategic combination of tactics, Michel de Certeau in *The Practices of Everyday Life* posits alternative definitions. He defines *strategy* as "the calculus of force-relationships" and links it to established places, such as institutions and other cultural forces that produce and execute power (xix). He defines *tactic* as "a calculus which cannot count on a 'proper'" or established place but must instead employ the transitory place of the other, depending on "time . . . always on the watch for opportunities that must be taken 'on the wing,'" and then he links tactics to everyday practices, claiming that "(talking, reading, moving about, shopping, cooking, etc.) are tactical in character" (xix).

15. In "Book Two" of his *Rhetoric*, Aristotle defines "topics" as habits of mind that speakers and writers may use to invent ideas and cultivate critical thinking. He lists four common topics (possible/impossible, past fact, future fact, and degree) as well as twenty-eight others that in subsequent centuries were reconfigured as modes of discourse, which in their best-case usage function as heuristics and which in their worst-case usages are reduced to five-paragraph theme formulas (174–78, 190–204). The shift from generative heuristic to formulaic essay may be seen in the following topics: Define terms (definition essay); Consider the opposite thing in question (compare/contrast essay); Take separately the parts of a subject (classification essay); Consider both good and bad consequences of a subject (cause/effect essay); and Induction/example (argument essay).

CHAPTER 1: RHETORICAL LISTENING

1. The earth-centered theory known as the Ptolemaic model was first theorized in 150 BCE, and the sun-centered theory known as the Copernican model was first published in 1543 CE. For more information, see Matt Williams's article on *Phys.org.*

2. For context about this song and group, see Carlile and Tongson.

3. For an extended definition of *discourse*, see Appendix A.

4. Thanks to Cheryl Glenn's Fall 2021 seminar students for helping to clarify the definition of *accountability.* They questioned whether online apologies for racism that try to pass as accountability somehow affect how this term is received, and I responded that I think the term, when defined as a combined analysis and action, is important enough to recover from that usage.

5. For discussions of how emotions/affect may intersect with rhetorical listening, see Blankenship, Frey, Lindquist, and Oleksiak, "A Fullness."

6. For discussions of how affect complicates theories of critical race studies, see Eduardo Bonilla-Silva's discussion of "feeling race" in his "Reply to Professor Fenelon and Adding Emotion to My Materialist RSS Theory."

7. Tonn explains the gendering of science and nature: "During the scientific revolution, constructions of nature as a feminized object open to domination by masculine science formed the foundation of a new working language for empiricism.[19] For instance, as Sir Francis Bacon described the practice of science in *The Masculine Birth of Time*: 'I am come in very truth leading to you Nature with all her children to bind her to your service and make her your slave. . . .'[20] This masculinist mode of thought can be found in Baconian metaphors for nature as well as in early modern medical cultures which unveiled the secretive, feminine body through the practice of dissection."[21]

8. For discussions of the functions of Aristotle's enthymeme, see Rapp and Walker; for the use of the enthymeme as an antiracist tactic, see Kennedy and Jackson.

9. These four cultural logics are mentioned in Ratcliffe's *Rhetorical Listening* but are not developed as fully there as here.

10. For a rhetorical analysis of white supremacy, see Bonilla-Silva (*White*) C. Crenshaw and Roskos-Ewoldsen; for pedagogical resources to confront it, see "Teaching Tolerance."

11. For a history of how science has been informed by socially constructed concepts of race (locating the beginnings of the use of this term in the 1500s) and for a summary of how human genome research in 2003 disproved these concepts of race even as they continue to haunt science, see the *Yale Journal of Biological Medicine* article (Mohsen).

12. A person's invoking colorblindness as an ideal (i.e., being blind to "color" and its effects) often has the real effect of blinding people to racism and thus absolving them of responsibility for it. For discussions of colorblindness

as the new racism, see Alexander, Bonilla-Silva (*Racism*), Boule, Scruggs, Morrison, Monica Williams, and Wise. For a discussion of interrupting colorblindness, see Milton Reynolds.

13. *Tolerance* is a trope with a conflicted, storied history. As the opposite of *intolerance*, it is viewed as a moral virtue, as when used in the title of the Southern Poverty Law Center's magazine *Teaching Tolerance* or when invoked as "zero tolerance" for bad behavior. From the perspective of those *tolerated*, it may be viewed as condescending or insulting. For critiques by the political left, right, and center in Britain of the term's use, see Bunting.

14. Although critical races studies first gained attention in legal studies, its analytic lens now spans many different disciplines and political institutions associated with anthropology, art, education, film, law, literature, sociology, etc. (Delgado 2–3). In literary/cultural studies, for example, Ayanna Thompson has demonstrated with "RaceB4Race," that pre-sixteenth-century representations of race exist ("Ayanna Thompson"). For a critique of critical race studies, see Subotnik.

15. For an extended discussion of eavesdropping as a rhetorical listening tactic, see "Chapter Four" in Ratcliffe's *Rhetorical Listening* (101–32).

16. For an extended discussion of listening metonymically, see "Chapter Three" of *Rhetorical Listening* (Ratcliffe 78–100).

17. See Kimberlé Crenshaw for her initial definition of intersectionality, which she offered as a means to challenge Black liberationist politics and feminist theory to include Black women ("Demarginalizing" 166) as well as for her discussion of how this concept has travelled since 1989:

> Some people look to intersectionality as a grand theory of everything, but that's not my intention. If someone is trying to think about how to explain to the courts why they should not dismiss a case made by black women, just because the employer did hire blacks who were men and women who were white, well, that's what the tool was designed to do. If it works, great. If it doesn't work, it's not like you have to use this concept. ("On Intersectionality")

18. For an extended discussion of this tactic, see "Chapter Five" of *Rhetorical Listening* (Ratcliffe 133–73).

19. For a similar argument calling for changes to practices surrounding the assessment of student writing, both individually and programmatically, see Inoue (*Antiracist Writing Assessment Ecologies*).

20. For a counterargument, see Kopelson who invokes "*metis* or 'cunning,'" which enables "the marginalized listener-subject" to negotiate listener resistance by performing "the very neutrality that people expect of listeners" (115).

Chapter 2: Agency

1. For a discussion of agency as "capacity," see Schlosser. For an overview of agency within feminist theory, see McNay.

2. Although classical Greek and Roman rhetorical theories posit only reading, writing, speaking, and listening, in *Silence and Listening as Rhetorical Arts* Cheryl Glenn makes a case for silence being included in the list.

3. Rhetoric and composition studies has theorized agency in multiple ways. In 1945, agency appeared as one of five key terms in Kenneth Burke's dramatistic pentad (*Grammar* xv). During the poststructuralist turn in the late twentieth century, agency was imagined as having been defined along a continuum, with one endpoint denoting a fully present modern human exercising an inherent human agency and the other endpoint denoting a postmodern subject totally interpellated by ideology, with *ideological interpellation* being a term offered by Louis Althusser to describe how regimes of state provide scripts that appear natural to citizens in order to maintain the power of the state (105). In the twenty-first century, Michael Leff also interrupted the idealizing of the fully present self with the idea of collective identities that suggests cultural agencies, noting that earlier rhetorics worried that rhetors were too influenced by crowds and arguing that "tradition can mediate between individual and collective identities," and thus tradition "emerges as the primary resource for rhetorical invention" given that tradition is shared (135). The seminal article in the scholarly conversation about agency within rhetoric and composition studies, however, is Marilyn Cooper's "Rhetorical Agency as Emergent and Enacted," which recommends shifting terms from *subjects* to *agents* and viewing agency as "an emergent property of embodied individuals" (421); her concept of agency is grounded in neurophenomenology and posited as a product of a person's lived experience within multiple networks and as a space where ethics and personal responsibility may be imagined (420). In her book on agency, she also addresses "The Agency of Writing," arguing for "[p]utting the agent back into agency" with agents being "individuating entities who act and make a difference, but whose actions are not consciously intended and do not determine the differences they make" and with agency being "a relation [that] has effects" (*The Animal Who Writes* 129, 131). Building on Cooper, Laurie Gries worries that "ontological privileging of human agency reinforces unnecessary hierarchies between culture and nature and human and nonhuman entities" and also that "situating agency as an individual embodied process fails to account for the spatio-temporality of agency as it emerges from and unfolds between a network of complex associations" (pp. 69). Raul Sanchez discusses how discussions of agency have a special emphasis on linking definitions of terms (*humans, subjects,* and *agents*) to possibilities for agency (28–31).

4. In the field of psychology, personal agency has been conceptualized as "cognitive agency." For a discussion of multiple types of cognitive agency and

different methods for studying them, see David et al. For an argument that personal agency is a myth because "cognitive processing is mostly an automatic, non-agentive process and that personal-level cognition is an exception rather than the rule," see Metzinger.

5. For an historical overview of research on socialization via language, see Ochs and Schieffelin

6. For an applied linguistic analytic of *discursive agency*, see Leipold and Winkel.

7. For a social science discussion of two contrasting definitions of cultural agency, see Ratner. For a discussion of social agency and a critique of the assimilationist model, see Treitler.

8. For a theoretical framework of material agency, see Kirchhoff. For discussions of "the many ways that things both occasion rhetorical action and act as suasive rhetorical forces," see chapters in Barnett and Boyle (2); for a discussion of material culture that suggests material agency, see Alexis (83–95).

9. Marilyn Cooper writes that people as agents "intra-act with other agents and agencies" on a daily basis (*The Animal* 131).

10. Feminist studies and critical race studies have taken up the question of agency. Feminists have consistently insisted on the necessity of agency for rhetoric, conceptualizing it as a relational resilience (Flynn, Sotrin, and Brady 2, 7–8), as *"partial," "collective," "pragmatic," "spontaneous,"* and *"disruptive or deceptive"* (Flynn et al 171), as interruption (Nedra Reynolds 58–59; Rhodes 86–87), as resistance (Enoch 26), as dependent on materials conditions (Royster and Kirsch 143), as contradiction within third wave feminism (Renegar and Sowards 2), and as improvisation within social spaces (Chang 55–56). For a history of how the concept agency is invoked in multiple feminist theories and projects, see Bowden and Mummery.

11. For discussions within critical race studies of racialized agency based on "erasures " that "inflate white agency and deny people of color and other marginalized groups their own," see Milton Reynolds (355). To explore agency within intersectionality theory, see Hill Collins and Bilge for discussions of both identity and agency (125) and global networks and agency (206).

12. Intersections of agency and writing pedagogy are available in Vieregge et al.'s discussion of peer production and in Williams's claim that "perceptions" of agency are key to listeners' writing effectively. When rhetorical listening imagines choice, accountability, and change as tropes of agency within rhetorical education, it includes students' and teachers' agencies both within and outside the classroom. Jessica Enoch traces a teacherly agency of women's pedagogical practices from 1865 to 1911 and deems these agential practices "resistance" (26). Although these historical practices may be sites of learning for contemporary teachers, Enoch cautions that these practices of resistance cannot simply be lifted from their own historical contexts and employed within ours. The challenge for contemporary listeners who are students of history, then, is

to adapt past practices to current, local conditions, with an awareness of agency as a rhetorical concept.

13. In Aristotle's *Rhetoric, ethos* "means 'character,' esp. 'moral character' and except in 2.21.16 [a discussion of maxims] is regarded as an attribute of a person, not of a speech" (37.Fn 40). In Cicero's *De Oratore, ethos* is imagined as both "'character (of the speaker)' . . . [and] 'style and its effect on the audience'" (118). For a history of ethos from Aristotle to Cicero, see Wisse.

14. For classification of discourses into primary and secondary, see Gee who defines *primary discourses* as "initial" ones acquired at home and with peer groups and *secondary discourses* as those associated with "non-home-based social institutions—institutions in the public sphere, beyond the family and immediate kin and peer group" (7–8).

15. For conclusions about how discursive agency may enhance students' personal agencies, see Davies.

16. For an example of how sociologists examine the relationship between agency and structure, see Martin and Dennis.

17. For extended definitions of *discourse community* and *conventions*, see Swales.

18. For one scholarly definition in linguistics of the term *code-switching*, see Mabule. For a discussion of how code-switching occurs in daily life, see Thompson's *NPR* report. For a *Harvard Business Review* article about the psychological costs of code-switching, see McCluney et al.

19. Gee calls discourses "'identity kits'" that come "complete with the appropriate costume and instructions on how to act, talk, and often write, so as to take on a particular role that others will recognize" (7).

20. Cooper draws from work by Brooke and Rickert, Coole and Frost, Latour, and Barnet and Boyle to trace her definition of materiality (5).

CHAPTER 3: RHETORICAL SITUATIONS

1. Bryan Stevenson is a lawyer and executive director of the Equal Justice Initiative. His autobiography, *Just Mercy*, has been adapted into a Hollywood film starring Michael B. Jordan and Jamie Foxx.

2. Mamie Till Mobley along with her son is memorialized for her actions on the webpage for the Emmett Till Legacy Foundation, which was started by their cousin.

3. Till's death, like all major historical events, made an impact in the moment and affected the country's direction on racial politics for the immediate future, but, despite the US's popular but mistaken notion about the ever-upward arc of history, Till's death did not solve the problem of US racism for all time. For a discussion of a mode of historiography that counters the ever-upward arc mode and "demonstrates not just how we may eavesdrop on history, circling through time in order to expose the circling of time" but also

how "rememory [Toni Morrison's term] has an agency all its own" see Ratcliffe (107–08, 109).

4. The National Archives has a blog series dedicated to rediscovering the history of Black women who were lynched (Chestnut).

5. An effective pedagogical tactic is to pair Powell's CCCC address, "Stories Take Place," with Natalie Diaz's poem, "The Fact of Art," about white highway builders in Indigenous lands.

6. A popular usage that demonstrates how the concept of rhetorical situation emerges in modern times is journalists' questions: who, what, when, where, why, and how. Although these questions are generative, situations are often more multi-layered than these questions imply.

7. In 1968 Bitzer made the modern concept of rhetorical situation famous with the publication of "The Rhetorical Situation," which advocates analyzing a rhetorical situation by attending to a) its exigences, or "that which strongly invites utterance" (5), b) its audiences, or ("only . . . those persons who are capable of being influenced by discourse and . . . being mediators of change" (8), and c) its constraints, or that which has "the power to constrain decision and action needed to modify the exigence" (8).

8. In 1973, Richard Vatz countered Bitzer's method by arguing that "The world is not a plot of discrete events. The world is a scene of inexhaustible events which all compete to impinge on what Kenneth Burke calls our 'sliver of reality'" (156), which renders the "very choice of what facts or events are relevant . . . a matter of pure arbitration" (157) and offers the conclusion that "rhetoric is a *cause* not an *effect* of meaning. It is antecedent, not subsequent, to a situation's impact" (160).

9. For a rhetorical study of the history of lynching as well as the trope of lynching, see Ore.

10. It is worth noting that Tell at no time invokes the term rhetorical situation.

11. The term *lynching* is an example of how a trope accrues meaning over time and place as situations are invoked and addressed via persuasive speaking and writing. Even as the trope *lynching* maintains the same meaning that Ida B Wells wrote about, it has accrued additional meanings since that time. In 1991, Supreme Court Justice Clarence Thomas called his Senate confirmation hearing, which included questions about whether he sexually harassed Professor Anita Hill, a *high-tech lynching*. In 2020, the Black Lives Matters groups called George Floyd's death by a knee on his neck a *lynching*, and in response Senators Booker and Harris proposed anti-lynching legislation.

12. Exigence is one of three elements (along with audience and constraint) that Bitzer assigns to rhetorical situations (5).

13. Audience is one of three elements (along with exigence and constraint) that Btizer associates with rhetorical situations; he stipulates his definition of audience to only those who have the power to be "mediators of change" (8).

14. Constraint is one of three elements (along with exigence and audience) that Bitzer associates with rhetorical situations, defining it as that which has "the power to constrain decision and action needed to modify the exigence" (8).

15. The study of rhetorical situations has emerged in contemporary rhetorical scholarship in terms of a variety of foci, for example, audiences (Ede and Lunsford), comparative rhetorics (Garrett, Wu), genre (Jamieson, Miller), story (Powell, "Blood") and relation to myth (Burke, *Rhetoric* 203–208).

16. For discussions of this coercive function of common ground, see C. West and Fanon.

17. For an NPR discussion of different hate groups that joined the Capitol rioters, see Thompson and Fischer. For a *The Hill* discussion of differences between legislators, see Wilson.

18. An example of charges levied against those arrested for Capitol riots include "Knowingly Entering or Remaining in any Restricted Building or Grounds without Lawful Authority; Violent Entry and Disorderly Conduct on Capitol Grounds; Assault on a Federal Officer; Certain Acts During a Civil Disorder" (Harrington, et al).

CHAPTER 4: IDENTIFICATION

1. For Freud's discussions of identification as an individual and social function, see his complete works (vol. 1, 248–50; vol. 13, 80–82, 142; vol. 18, 108–09, 113–14, 133–35; vol. 23, 193).

2. For a history of identification, see Fuss (1–19).

3. For Kimberlé Crenshaw's writings on intersectionality through the years, see her *On Intersectionality.*

4. For a discussion of how disidentification informs rhetorical listening, see Ratcliffe (62–64).

5. For comparisons of how identification is employed in Burke and Freud, see Davis, "Identification" and Wright, "Burkean and Freudian"

6. For a discussion of non-identification as a place of metonymic juxtaposition, where you can lay two "things" side by side without collapsing them into common ground, see Ratcliffe (71–77).

CHAPTER 5: MYTH

1. For a discussion of the grittiness of myths, see Dyson's discussion of race as a myth: He describes the effects of the race myth as "empirical grit" ("Foreword" ix) even as he also offers his "theological captivity to hope" (*Long Time Coming* ???)

2. This question is the central organizing question in Papillon's "Rhetoric, Art, and Myth: Isocrates and Busiris" (74).

3. For a genealogy of scholars whose work on myth influenced one another, see Mircea Eliade's "Myth in the Nineteenth and Twentieth Centuries." For specific mid-twentieth-century myth theories about and the "primitive" or "savage" mind, see Joseph Campbell's *Primitive Mythology* and Claude Levi-Strauss's *The Savage Mind*, which argue that all people have an equal capacity for mythmaking. For other influential mid-twentieth-century scholars of myth, see Ernst Cassirer's *Myth and Language* and Suzanne K. Langer's *Philosophy in a New Key*.

4. Some scholars argued that universal themes permeate the study of comparative myths, with the problem being that scholars too frequently define universal through a Western, male gaze. Some scholars also argued that myths reveal fundamental features of the primitive human mind; thus, they investigated Indigenous peoples of South America or hierarchical arrangements of a Proto-Indo-European society, denying the racism that haunts many of these projects even as they argued that all humans have the capacity for mythmaking.

5. Written in 1962, *La Pensée sauvage* was initially translated into English in 1966 as *Savage Minds* (losing in translation the title's French pun of "wild pansies," with pansies serving as a floriography metaphor for *thought*); more recently in 2021, the book was reissued with the title translated as *Wild Thought*. As a founder of structural anthropology, Claude Levi-Strauss wrote *La Pensée sauvage* to argue that all humans' minds possess the same capacity for mythmaking as a way of knowing and being in the world. His argument challenged the idea that the modern Western scientific mind was superior; however, it is haunted by the problem of people being described as civilized or as wild, primitive, savage, or exotic (232).

6. Martin cites different dictionaries to make her point that, regardless of intent, the effect of the term *savage* is dehumanizing. As evidence, she cites a definition of *savage* from dictionary.com: "*Offensive*. (in historical use) relating to or being a preliterate people or society regarded as uncivilized or primitive." And she cites a definition of *savage* from urbandictionary.com: "A savage is some[one] who does not care about the Consequences of his or her actions. Usually the savage will do things that make other people say, 'What the fuck are you crazy?'"

7. *Rhetorical Listening* describes the "origins mode" for thinking about history as a narrative that "begins at the beginning (which is assumed to be obvious but rarely is) and moves in a linear, evolutionary progression"; then *RL* argues that such a narrative, though prevalent, is a false one. *RL* suggests, instead, a "usage mode" for thinking about history, defining it as "shifting the focus from origins to usage" (Ratcliffe 107) and as circling through time in order to expose the circling of time (108), always recognizing the presence of the past in the present or the "*then-that-is-now*" (107). Studying myth as a rhetorical concept enables us to expose the origins mode as a myth of its own and to engage the usage mode.

8. DC comics created "13 Black DC Heroes Before Black Lightning" (Jaffe), though none rose to the popularity level of Batman or Superman or Marvel's Black Panther.

9. For another challenge to a US national holiday, see Frederick Douglass's speech, "The Meaning of July Fourth for the Negro."

CHAPTER 6: RHETORICAL DEVICES

1. For a general discussion of drag, see "Understanding Drag" on the National Center for Transgender Equality website. For scholarship discussing intersections of rhetoric and drag, see Carroll, Heller, and Patterson & Spencer.

2. For a discussion of online performances of such masculinity, see Schmitz and Kazyk (7–8). For an editorial about toxic masculinity and the 2019 American Psychological Association (APA) guidelines, see de Boise. For a popular culture example, consider U.S, Senators Josh Hawley's 2021 claim that the radical left is responsible for undermining manhood and, thus, promoting men's usage of video games and porn (Edwards).

3. For Human Rights Campaign info, see "Fatal Violence." For a National Institute of Health (NIH) "systematic review" of violence surrounding sexual orientations and gender identities, see Blondeel, et al.

4. For other athletes' comments about Biles' having a choice to withdraw, see Svokos.

5. Although all Facebook users should read the company's entire "Data Policy," here is an excerpt from it:

> **Your usage.** We collect information about how you use our Products, such as the types of content you view or engage with; the features you use; the actions you take; the people or accounts you interact with; and the time, frequency and duration of your activities. For example, we log when you're using and have last used our Products, and what posts, videos and other content you view on our Products. We also collect information about how you use features like our camera.

> **Information about transactions made on our Products.** If you use our Products for purchases or other financial transactions (such as when you make a purchase in a game or make a donation), we collect information about the purchase or transaction. This includes payment information, such as your credit or debit card number and other card information; other account and authentication information; and billing, shipping and contact details.

APPENDIX A: RHETORIC, LANGUAGE, AND DISCOURSE

1. According to the OED, *language* is defined as "[t]he system of spoken or written communication used by a particular country, people, community, etc., typically consisting of words used within a regular grammatical and syntactic structure; (also) a formal system of communication by gesture, esp. as used by the deaf."

2. The term *discourse* has a complicated history within academic disciplines, as outlined in Teun A. Van Dijk's two-volume history of the term.

3. Because, as Judith Butler tells us, identifications are an assumption of places, these places are identifications that a listening writer makes (*Bodies* 99). More on identification may be found in Chapter 4.

APPENDIX B: WRITING PROCESSES FOR LISTENING WRITERS

1. In 1971 Janet Emig's *The Composing Processes of Twelfth Graders* helped cement the term process as a dominant trope with myriad pedagogical methods within rhetoric and composition studies; although the history of this term is beyond the scope of this book, for a bibliography, see the bibliography in Jensen's *Reimagining Process*.

2. For discussions of the limits and possibilities of post-process theory for rhetoric and composition studies, see Kent.

3. For discussion of the limits and possibilities of moving beyond post-process for rhetoric and composition studies, see Dobrin, Rice, and Vastola.

4. While Nancy Sommers famous research study indicates that students' revision processes are recursive while writing, David Bruce's research study (which also traces a brief history of research on revision and recursivity) indicates that students' processes are also recursive while creating video compositions (437).

5. The role that reading plays in composition classes has a fraught history in rhetoric and composition studies. In 1983 Winifred Bryan Horner invited prominent scholars to articulate the debate within her edited collection *Composition and Literature: Bridging the Gap*, which offered competing stances; by 1992 James Berlin's discussion of the poststructuralist turn put the debate to rest for some by merging reading and writing as signifying processes.

6. As the first of five canons in classical rhetoric (invention, arrangement, style, memory, and delivery), invention has informed the teaching of writing for 2,600 years. As Janice Lauer writes, classical invention tends toward the systematic or using a set of prompts, such as stasis theory, to generate information via structured association. From the Renaissance forward, invention tends toward less structure and more free association of the imagination, which culminated in twentieth-century composition tactics such as freewriting.

7. For a review of revision from the mid-1960s to 1987, see Fitzgerald; for 2019 research about revision, see MacArthur.

8. For an important historical text that posits revision as a crucial element of writing processes, see Sommers.

9. For a historical overview of collaboration and best practices in rhetoric and composition studies, see Fontaine and Hunter (2005); for an example of the more recent turn to collaborative, public and project-based pedagogy, see Holmes.

10. Yancey's "Introduction" offers a useful history of how *reflection* has been conceptualized in academic endeavors, with a special focus on the teaching of writing.

APPENDIX C: RESEARCH TACTICS FOR LISTENING WRITERS

1. Scholarship about research as rhetorical activity includes McKee and Porter and also Morris.

APPENDIX D: STYLE TACTICS FOR LISTENING WRITERS

1. Classical rhetoricians conceptualized five canons of rhetoric—invention, arrangement, style, memory and delivery—to describe the processes that speakers and writers enact to compose their speeches or written texts. Quintilian's *Institutio Oratoria* is often considered the classical text where many different ideas about these five canons as well as the tactics associated with them were synthesized.

2. Corbett and Connors define Corbett's method of stylistic analysis in chapter four of *Classical Rhetoric for the Modern Student*.

3. Although knowledge of grammatical elements (such as relative clauses or types of modifiers) is helpful in recognizing parallel structure, it is not necessary. A writer may identify repetitive structural elements without being able to name them.

4. In *The Signifying Monkey and the Language of Signifyin(g)*, Gates lists all the figures that are "subsumed within the trope of signifyin(g): *talking shit, woofing, spouting, muckty muck, boogerbang, beating your gums, talking smart, putting down, putting on, playing, sounding, telling lies, shag-lag, marking, shucking, jiving, jitterbugging, bugging, mounting, charging, cracking, harping, rapping, bookooing, low-rating, hoorawing, sweet-talking, smart-talking*, and no doubt a few others that I have omitted" (85).

Works Cited

Adesina, Precious. "How a Photographer, a Group of Models and a Fashion Show in Harlem Kick-Started a Cultural and Political Movement That Still Inspires Today." *BBC*, 3 Aug. 2020, www.bbc.com/culture/article/20200730-the-birth-of-the-black-is-beautiful-movement. Accessed 22 Oct. 2021.

Alexander, Michelle. *The New Jim Crow: Mass Incarceration in the Age of Colorblindness.* The New Press, 2012.

Alexis, Cydney. "The Material Culture of Writing: Objects, Habitats, and Identities in Practice." Barnett and Boyle, pp. 83–95.

Althusser, Louis. "Ideology and Ideological State Apparatuses (Notes towards an Investigation)." *The Anthropology of the State: A Reader*, edited by Aradhana Sharma and Anil Gupta, 1970, Blackwell, 2006, pp. 86–111.

American Library Association. "Evaluating Information; Home." *ALA* 18 Mar. 2019, libguides.ala.org/InformationEvaluation. Accessed 22 Jan. 2021.

—. "Evaluating Information: Information Literacy." *ALA*, 18 Mar. 2019, libguides.ala.org/InformationEvaluation/Infolit. Accessed 22 Jan. 2021.

Anzaldúa, Gloria. *The Gloria Anzaldúa Reader,* edited by AnaLouise Keating. Duke UP, 2009.

Aristotle. *On Rhetoric: A Theory of Civic Discourse.* Translated by George A. Kennedy, Oxford UP, 1991.

Arkowitz, Hal, and Scott O Lilienfeld. "Why Science Tells Us Not to Rely on Eyewitness Accounts. *Scientific American,* 1 Jan. 2010, www.scientificamerican.com/article/do-the-eyes-have-it/. Accessed 9 June 2020.

Aten, Jason. "Tim Cook Says This Is the 1 Question Every Leader Should Ask: It Isn't 'What can I get away with?'" *Inc.com,* www.inc.com/jason-aten/tim-cook-says-this-is-1-question-every-leader-should-ask.html. Accessed 10 Feb. 2021.

Baker-Bell, April. Linguistic Justice: Black Language, Literacy, Identity, and Pedagogy. NCTE Routledge, 2020.

Baldwin, James. *Notes of a Native Son.* 1955. Beacon, 2012.

Ballif, Michelle, ed. *Theorizing Histories of Rhetoric.* Southern Illinois UP, 2013.

Banks, William P., Matthew B. Cox, and Caroline Dadas, eds. *Re/Orienting Writing Studies: Queer Methods, Queer Projects*. Utah State UP, 2019.

Bannister, Linda. "Rhetorical Listening in the Diverse Classroom: Understanding the Sound of Not Understanding." *ERIC*, 15 Mar. 2001, pp. 1–12, files. eric.ed.gov/fulltext/ED450435.pdf. Accessed 25 May 2020.

Barnett, Scot, and Casey Boyle, eds. *Rhetoric, Through Everyday Things*. U of Alabama P, 2016.

Berlin, James A. "Poststructuralism, Cultural Studies, and the Composition Classroom: Postmodern Theory in Practice," *Rhetoric Review*, vol. 11, no.1, 1992, pp. 16–33.

Biden, Joseph. "Inaugural Address." *The White House Briefing Room,* 20 Jan. 2021, *www.whitehouse.gov/briefing-room/speeches-remarks/2021/01/20/inaugural-address-by-president-joseph-r-biden-jr/*. Accessed 8 Oct. 2021.

Biesecker, Barbara A. "Rethinking the Rhetorical Situation from within the Thematic of Différance." *Philosophy & Rhetoric*, vol. 22, no. 2, 1989, pp. 110–30, static1.squarespace.com/static/53713bf0e4b0297decd1ab8b/t/5c3 37683898583b52ee84d47/1546876548474/biesecker_rethinking_the_rhetorical_situation.pdf. Accessed 31 Jan. 2021.

Bitzer, Lloyd. "The Rhetorical Situation." *Philosophy and Rhetoric*, vol. 1, 1968, pp. 1–14, www.arts.uwaterloo.ca/~raha/309CWeb/Bitzer(1968).pdf. Accessed 20 May 2020.

Bizzell, Patricia, and Bruce Herzberg, et al. *The Rhetorical Tradition: Readings from Classical Times to the Present*. 3rd ed., Bedford/St. Martins, 2020.

Blankenship, Lisa. *Changing the Subject: A Theory of Rhetorical Empathy*. UP Colorado, 2019.

Blondeel, Karel, et al. "Violence Motivated by Perception of Sexual Orientation and Gender Identity: A Systematic Review." *Bull World Health Organ*, vol. 96, no. 1, 2018, www.who.int/bulletin/volumes/96/1/17–197251.pdf. Accessed 9 Nov. 2021.

The Body of Emmett Till. Produced by Ian Orefice and Kira Pollack, Red Border Films, 100photos.time.com/photos/emmett-till-david-jackson. Accessed 2 Nov. 2020.

Bonilla-Silva, Eduardo. *Racism without Racists: Color-Blind Racism and the Persistence of Inequality in America*. 3rd ed., Rowman and Littlefield, 2009.

—. "Reply to Professor Fenelon and Adding Emotion to My Materialist RSS Theory." *Sociology of Race and Ethnicity*, vol. 2, no. 2, 23 Jan. 2026, pp. 243–47, doi.org/10.1177/2332649216628300. Accessed 11 Jan. 2021.

—. *White Supremacy and Racism in the Post-Civil Rights Era*. Lynne Rienner, 2001.

Borchers, Timothy, and Heather Hundley. *Rhetorical Theory: An Introduction*. Waveland P, 2018.

Bowden, Peta, and Jane Mummery. "Agency." *Understanding Feminism*, edited by Peta Bowden and Jane Mummery, Routledge, 2009, pp. 123–50.

Bowden, Sean. "Human and Nonhuman Agency in Deleuze." *Deleuze and the Non/Human*, edited by Jon Roffe and Hannah Stark, Palgrave, 2015, pp. 60–80.

Boyer, Dave. "Obama Defends Black Lives Matters Protests at Police Memorial in Dallas." *Washington Times*, 22 July 2016, www.washingtontimes.com/news/2016/jul/12/obama-defends-black-lives-matter-protests-police-m/. Accessed 8 Oct. 2017.

Brooke, Colin, and Thomas Rickert. "Being Delicious: Materialities of Research in a Web 2.0 Application." *Dobrin et al*, pp. 163–79.

Bruce, David. "Writing with Visual Images: Examining the Video Composition Processes of High School Students." *Research in the Teaching of English*, vol. 43, no. 4, 2009, pp. 426–50.

Bule, Jamelle. "Why Do Millennials Not Understand Racism?" *Slate*, 16 May 2014, www.slate.com/articles/news_and_politics/politics/2014/05/millennials_racism_and_mtv_poll_young_people_are_confused_about_bias_prejudice.html. Accessed 2 Oct. 2017.

Bunting, Madeleine. "The Problem with Tolerance." *The Guardian*, 5 Sept. 2011, www.theguardian.com/commentisfree/belief/2011/sep/05/tolerance-frank-fured. Accessed 8 Oct. 2021.

Burke, Anthony, Kyle Jensen, and Jack Selzer. "Editors' Introduction." *The War of Words*, by Kenneth Burke, U of California P, 2018, pp. 1–40.

Burke, Kenneth. *Attitudes Towards History*. 1937. 3rd ed., U of California P, 1984.

—. *A Grammar of Motives*. 1945. U of California P, 1969.

—. Language as Symbolic Action: Essays on Life, Literature, and Method. U of California P, 1966.

—. *A Rhetoric of Motives*. 1950. U of California P, 1969.

—. "The Rhetoric of Hitler's 'Battle.'" *The Philosophy of Literary Form: Studies in Symbolic Action*. 1941. 1967. U of California P, 1974, pp. 191–220.

—. *The War of Words*, edited by Anthony Burke, Kyle Jensen, and Jack Selzer, U of California P, 2018.

Butler, Judith. *Bodies That Matter: On the Discursive Limits of "Sex."* Routledge, 1993.

Butler, Judith. "Imitation and Gender Insubordination." *The Lesbian and Gay Studies Reader*, edited by H. Abelove, M. A, Barler, and D. M. Halperin, Routledge, 1993, p. 307–21.

Campbell, Joseph. *Primitive Mythology*. Penguin. 1959.

Carlile, Brandi. "Brandi Carlile on Indigo Girls: 'They've Never Asked for Credit, But They Deserve It.'" *Rolling Stone*, 17 Feb. 2021, www.rollingstone.com/music/music-features/brandi-carlile-indigo-girls-tribute-1126305/. Accessed 8 Oct. 2021.

Carter, C. Allen. "Kenneth Burke and the Bicameral Power of Myth." *Poetics Today*, vol. 18, no. 3, 1997, pp. 343–73.

Carroll, Lorrayne. *Rhetorical Drag: Gender Impersonation, Captivity, and the Writing of History*. Kent State UP, 2007.

Cassirer, Ernst. *Myth and Language*. Translated by Suzanne K. Langer, Harper and Brothers, 1946.

Certeau, Michel de. *The Practices of Everyday Life*. Translated and edited by Stephen F. Randall, U of California P, 1998.

Chang, Aurora. *The Struggles of Identity, Education, and Agency in the Lives of Undocumented Listeners: The Burden of Hyperdocumentation*. Palgrave Macmillan, 2017.

Charney, Davida, and Marie Secor. *Constructing Rhetorical Education*. Southern Illinois UP, 1991.

Chavez, Karma. *Queer Migration Politics: Activist Rhetoric and Coalitional Possibilities*. U of Illinois P, 2013.

Chestnut, Trichita M. "Lynching of Women in United States Blog Series: The Lynching of Mr., Mary Turner and Her Family" *Rediscovering Black History, National Archives*, 16 Mar. 2018, rediscovering-black-history.blogs. archives.gov/2018/05/16/lynching-of-women-in-united-states-blog-series-the-lynching-of-mrs-mary-turner-and-her-family/. Accessed 29 Jan. 2021.

Chew, Stephen L. "Myth: Eyewitness Testimony Is the Best Kind of Evidence." *Association for Psychological Science*, 20 Aug. 2018, www.psychologicalscience. org/teaching/myth-eyewitness-testimony-is-the-best-kind-of-evidence. html. Accessed 8 June 2020.

Cicero. *De Oratore: Book III*, edited by David Mankin, Cambridge UP, 2011.

Clark, Gregory. *Civic Jazz: American Music and Kenneth Burke on the Art of Getting Along*. U of Chicago P, 2015.

Clear, James. *Atomic Habits: An Easy and Proven Way to Build Good Habits and Break Bad Ones*. Random House, 2018.

—. "30 One-Sentence Stories From People Who Have Built Better Habits." *jamesclear.com*, jamesclear.com/one-sentence-habits. Accessed 9 Nov. 2021.

Coaston, Jane. "The Intersectionality Wars." *Vox*, 28 May 2019, www.vox. com/the-highlight/2019/5/20/18542843/intersectionality-conservatism-law-race-gender-discrimination. Accessed 27 Sept. 2021.

Condon, Frankie, and Vershawn Ashanti Young, eds. *Performing Antiracist Pedagogy in Rhetoric, Writing, and Communication*. UP of Colorado, 2017.

Coole, Diana, and Samantha Frost. "Introducing the New Materialism." *New Materialisms, Ontology, Agency, and Politics*, edited by Diana Coole and Samantha Frost, Duke UP, 2010, pp. 1–43.

Cooper, Marilyn. *The Animal Who Writes: A Posthumanist Composition*. U of Pittsburgh P, 2018.

—. "Rhetorical Agency as Emergent and Enacted." *College Composition and Communication*, vol. 62, no. 3, 2011, pp. 420–49.

Corbett, Edward P. J., and Robert J. Connors. *Classical Rhetoric for the Modern Student*. 4th ed. Oxford UP. 1998.

—. *Style and Statement*. Oxford UP, 1999.

Coupe, Laurence. *Kenneth Burke: From Myth to Ecology*. Parlor P, 2013.

Cowell, Alan. "After 350 Years, Vatican Says Galileo Was Right: It Moves." *New York Times*, 31 Oct., 1992, www.nytimes.com/1992/10/31/world/after-350-years-vatican-says-galileo-was-right-it-moves.html. Accessed 10 Oct. 2021.

Crenshaw, Carrie, and David. R. Roskos-Ewoldsen. "Rhetoric, Racist Ideology, and Intellectual Leadership." *Rhetoric and Public Affairs*, vol. 2, no. 2, 1999, pp. 275–302

Crenshaw, Kimberlé. "Demarginalizing the Intersection of Race and Sex: A Black Feminist Critique of Antidiscrimination Doctrine, Feminist Theory and Antiracist Politics." *University of Chicago Legal Forum*, vol. 1989, no. 1, 1989, pp. 139–67.

—. "Mapping the Margins: Intersectionality, Identity Politics, and Violence against Women of Color." *Stanford Law Review*, vol. 43, no. 6, 1991, pp. 1241–299, dc.msvu.ca/xmlui/bitstream/handle/10587/942/Crenshaw_article.pdf?sequence=1&isAllowed=y. Accessed 26 Nov. 2020.

—. "On Intersectionality, More than Two Decades Later." *Columbia Law School*, 8 June 2017, www.law.columbia.edu/news/archive/kimberle-crenshaw-intersectionality-more-two-decades-later, Accessed 15 Oct. 2020.

—. *On Intersectionality: Essential Writings*. The New Press, 2017.

Cushman, Ellen, Damián Baca, and Romeo Garcia. "Delinking: Toward Pluriversal Rhetorics." *College English*, vol. 84, no.1, 2021, pp. 7–32, library.ncte.org/journals/CE/issues/v84-1/31449. Accessed 23 Oct. 2021.

David, Nicole, Albert Newen, and Kai Vogeley. "The 'Sense of Agency' and Its Underlying Cognitive and Neural Mechanisms." *Consciousness and Cognition*, vol. 17, no. 2, 2008, pp. 523–34.

Davies, Bronwyn. "Agency as a Form of Discursive Practice. A Classroom Scene Observed." *British Journal of Sociology of Education*, vol. 11, no. 3, 1990, pp. 341–61.

Davis, D. Diane. "Identification: Burke and Freud on Who You Are." *Rhetoric Society Quarterly*, vol. 38, no. 2, 2008, pp. 123–47, doi.org/10.1080/02773940701779785. Accessed 4 Nov. 2021.

—. *Inessential Solidarity: Rhetoric and Foreigner Relations*. U of Pittsburgh P, 2010.

De Boise, Sam. "Editorial: Is Masculinity Toxic?" *NORMA*, vol. 14, no. 3, 2019, pp. 147–51, Doi.org/10.1080/18902138.2019.1654742. Accessed 12 Feb. 2021.

Delgado, Richard, and Jean Stefancic. "Introduction." *Critical Race Studies: An Introduction*. New York UP, 2001.

Diaz, Natalie. "The Fact of Art. *The Poetry Foundation*, www.poetryfoundation.org/poems/56354/the-facts-of-art. Accessed 2 Jan. 2020.

Dobrin, Sidney I., J. A. Rice, and Michael Vastola, eds. *Beyond Postprocess.* Utah State UP, 2011.

Dobrin, Sidney I., *Ecology, Writing Theory, and New Media: Writing Ecology.* Routledge, 2012.

Douglass, Frederick. "What Does July Fourth Mean to the Negro?" *Mass Humanities,* 5 July 1852, masshumanities.org/files/programs/douglass/speech_complete.pdf. Accessed 13 Jan. 2021.

Dow, Bonnie. "Feminism, Miss America, and Media Mythology." *Rhetoric & Public Affairs,* vol. 6, no. 1, 2003, pp. 127–49.

DuBois, W. E. B. *The Souls of Black Folks.* 1903. Millenium, 2014.

Dyson, Michael Eric. "Foreword." *White Fragility: Why It's So Hard for White People to Talk about Racism,* by Robin DiAngelo, Beacon, 2018, pp. ix-xii.

—. *Long Time Coming: Reckoning with Race in America.* St. Martin's, 2020.

Edbauer, Jenny. "Unframing Models of Public Distribution: From Rhetorical Situation to Rhetorical Ecology." *Rhetoric Society Quarterly,* vol. 35, no. 4, 2005, pp. 5–24, bit.ly/unframing. Accessed 8 June 2020.

Ede, Lisa and Andrea Lunsford. "Audience Addressed/Audience Invoked: The Role of Audience in Composition Theory and Pedagogy." *College Composition and Communication,* vol. 35, no. 2, 1984, pp. 155–71, doi. org/10.2307/358093. Accessed 24 May 2020.

"Editorial Cartoons on Trayvon Martin Case, July 2013." *The Free Press,* 71 July 2013 and 2 Sept. 2014, bit.ly/tmeditorialcartoons. Accessed 24 Jan. 2021.

Edwards, Jonathan. "Sen. Josh Hawley Says Liberals' Attacks on Manhood Are Driving Men to Pornography and Video Games." *Washington Post,* 2 Nov. 2021, www.washingtonpost.com/nation/2021/11/02/josh-hawley-pornography-video-games/. Accessed 8 Nov. 2021.

Eliade, Mircea. "Myth in the Nineteenth and Twentieth Centuries." *Encyclopedia of Ideas.* sites.google.com/site/encyclopediaofideas/literature-and-the-arts/myth-in-the-nineteenth-and-twentieth-centuries. Accessed 9 Oct. 2020.

"Emmett Till | David Jackson 1955." *Time 100 Photos,* 100photos.time.com/photos/emmett-till-david-jackson. Accessed 2 Nov. 2020.

Emmett Till Legacy Foundation. 2020, emmetttilllegacyfoundation.com. Accessed 29 Jan. 2021.

Emig, Janet. *The Composing Processes of Twelfth Graders,* NCTE, 1971.

Enfield, Nick J. "The Theory of Cultural Logic: How Individuals Combine Social Intelligence with Semiotics to Create and Maintain Cultural Meaning." *Cultural Dynamics,* vol. 12, no. 1, 1 Mar. 2000, pp. 35–64.

Enoch, Jessica. *Refiguring Rhetorical Education: Women Teaching African American, Native American, and Chicano/a Students, 1865–1911.* Southern Illinois UP, 2008.

Erasmus, Desiderius. *On Copia of Words and Ideas.* 1512. Translated by Donald B King and H. David Rex, Marquette UP, 1963.

Facebook, "Data Policy." 11 Jan. 2021, www.facebook.com/policy.php. Accessed 13 Feb. 2021.

Fanon, Frantz. *Black Skin, White Masks.* Translated by Charles Lam Markmann, Grove, 1967.

"Fatal Violence against the Transgender and Gender Non-Conforming Community in 2021." *Human Rights Campaign,* 2021, www.hrc.org/resources/fatal-violence-against-the-transgender-and-gender-non-conforming-community-in-2021. Accessed 9 Nov. 2021.

Fitzgerald, Jill. "Research on Revision in Writing." *Review of Educational Research,* vol. 57, no. 4, 1987, pp. 481–506.

Flower, Linda. "Talking across Differences: Intercultural Rhetoric and the Search for Situated Knowledge." *College Composition and Communication,* vol. 55, no. 1, 2003, pp. 38–68.

Flynn, Elizabeth, Patricia Sotirin, and Ann Brady, eds. *Feminist Rhetorical Resilience.* UP of Colorado, 2012.

Fontaine, Sheryl I., and Susan M. Hunter. *Collaborative Writing in Composition Studies.* Wadsworth, 2005.

Foreman, Tom. "New Timeline Shows Just How Close Rioters Got to Pence and His Family." *CNN,* 15 Jan. 2021, www.cnn.com/videos/politics/2021/01/15/mike-pence-close-call-capitol-riot-foreman-vpx.cnn. Accessed 9 Feb. 2021.

Freud, Sigmund. *The Standard Edition of the Complete Psychological Works of Sigmund Freud.* Translated and edited by James Strachey, 24 vols., Hogarth, 1953–1974.

Frey, Renea. "Rhetorics of Reflection: Revisiting Listening Rhetoric through Mindfulness, Empathy, and Non-Violent Communication." *JAEPL: The Journal of the Assembly for Expanded Perspectives on Learning,* vol. 23, article 10, 2018, trace.tennessee.edu/cgi/viewcontent.cgi?article=1330&context=jaepl. Accessed 4 Oct. 2021.

Fuss, Diana. *Identification Papers.* Routledge, 1995.

"Galileo Galilei." *Stanford Encyclopedia of Philosophy.* Stanford University, 17 May 2017, plato.stanford.edu/entries/galileo/. Accessed 17 May 2020.

Garrett, Mary M., and Xiaosui Xiao. "The Rhetorical Situation Revisited." *Rhetoric Society Quarterly,* vol. 23, no. 2, 1993, pp. 30–40.

Gates, Henry Louis. *The Signifying Monkey and the Language of Signifyin(g).* Oxford UP, 1988.

Gee, James. "Literacy, Discourse, and Linguistics: Introduction." *Journal of Education,* vol. 171, no. 1, 1989, pp. 5–17.

Geisler, Cheryl. "How Ought We to Understand the Concept of Rhetorical Agency? Report from the ARS." *Rhetoric Society Quarterly,* vol. 34, no. 3, 2004, pp. 9–17.

Gilyard, Keith, and Adam Banks. *On African American Rhetoric.* Routledge, 2018.

Giovanni, Nikki. *Racism 101.* Quill. 1995.

Glenn, Cheryl, et al, eds. *Rhetorical Education in America*. U of Alabama P, 2004.

Glenn, Cheryl. *Rhetorical Feminism and This Thing Called Hope*. SIUP, 2018.

—. *Unspoken: A Rhetoric of Silence*. Southern Illinois UP, 2004.

Glenn, Cheryl, and Krista Ratcliffe, eds. *Silence and Listening as Rhetorical Arts*. Southern Illinois UP, 2011.

"The Global Rise of Fascism in the 21st-Century." *Madras Courier*, 10 Sept. 2021, madrascourier.com/opinion/the-global-rise-of-fascism-in-the-21st-century/. Accessed 30 Oct. 2021.

Grady, Constance. "The Waves of Feminism, and Why People Keep Fighting over Them, Explained." *Vox*, 20 July 2018, www.vox.com/2018/3/20/16955588/feminism-waves-explained-first-second-third-fourth. Accessed 5 Oct. 2021.

Grandin, Greg. *The End of Myth: From the Frontier to the Border Wall in the Mind of America*. New York, Macmillan, 2019.

Grayson, Mara Lee. *Teaching Racial Literacy: Reflective Practices for Critical Writing*. Rowman and Littlefield, 2018.

Gries, Laurie. "Agential Matters: Tumbleweed, Women-Pens, Citizens-Hope and Rhetorical Agency." Dobrin, pp. 67–91.

Gross, Daniel. *Being-Moved: Rhetoric as the Art of Listening*. U of California P, 2020.

Habermann, Maggie, and Annie Karni. "Pence Said to Have Told Trump He Lacks Power to Change Election Results." *New York Times*, 5 Jan. 2021, www.nytimes.com/2021/01/05/us/politics/pence-trump-election-results.html. Accessed 7 Feb. 2021.

Hannah-Jones, Nikole. "What Abigail Fisher's Affirmative Action Case Was Really About." *ProPublica*. 23 June 2016, www.propublica.org/article/a-colorblind-constitution-what-abigail-fishers-affirmative-action-case-is-r. Accessed 17 May 2020.

Harrington, Rebecca, et al. "241 People Have Been Charged in the Capitol Insurrection So Far. This Searchable Table Shows Them All." *Insider*, 8 Feb. 2021, www.insider.com/all-the-us-capitol-pro-trump-riot-arrests-charges-names-2021-1. Accessed 9 Feb. 2021.

Heath, M. "The Substructure of Stasis-Theory from Hermagoras to Hermogenes." *Classical Quarterly*, vol. 44, no. 1, pp. 114–29. core.ac.uk/download/pdf/190509533.pdf. Accessed 6 Jan. 2021.

Heidegger, Martin. *What Is Called Thinking*. 1954, Translated by Fred D. Wick and J. Glenn Gray, Harper, 1968.

Heller, Meredith. *Queering Drag: Redefining the Discourse of Gender-Bending*. Indiana UP, 2020.

Hesford, Wendy, and Eileen Schell. "Introduction: Configurations of Transnationality: Locating Feminist Rhetorics." *College English*, vol. 70, no. 5, 2008, pp. 461–70.

Hill, Carolyn Erikson. "Changing Times in Composition Classes: *Kairos*, Resonance, and the Pythagorean Connection." *Rhetoric and Kairos: Essays in History, Theory, and Praxis,* edited by Philip Sipiora and James S. Baumlin, State U of New York P, 2002, pp. 211–25.

Hill Collins, Patricia, and Sirma Bilge. *Intersectionality.* Polity, 2016.

Hinshaw, Wendy Wolters. "Making Ourselves Vulnerable: A Feminist Pedagogy of Listening." Glenn and Ratcliffe, pp. 264–77.

Hinton, Anthony Ray. *The Sun Does Shine: How I Found Life, Freedom, and Justice.* St. Martin's, 2019.

Holmes, Ashley J. *Public Pedagogy in Composition Studies.* Studies in Writing and Rhetoric Series, 2016.

Horner, Winifred Bryan. *Composition and Literature: Bridging the Gap.* U of Chicago P, 1983.

Howard, Rebecca Moore. "Review: Reflexivity and Agency in Rhetoric and Pedagogy." *College English,* vol. 56, no. 3, 1994, pp. 348–55.

Human Rights Watch. 2021, www.hrw.org/about/about-us. Accessed 6 Nov. 2021.

"In Defense of Rhetoric: No Longer Just for Liars." Uploaded by Clemson English, 27 June 2011, www.youtube.com/watch?v=BYMUCz9bHAs.

Indigo Girls. "Galileo." *Rites of Passage,* Epic, 1992.

Ingle, Sean. "Simone Biles Pulls Out of Olympics All-Around Gymnastics Final to Focus on Mental Health." *The Guardian,* 28 July 2021, www.theguardian.com/sport/2021/jul/28/simone-biles-withdraws-from-tokyo-olympics-all-around-gymnastics-final. 12 Nov. 2021.

Inoue, Asao. *Antiracist Writing Assessment Ecologies: Teaching and Assessing Writing for a Socially Just Future.* Parlor P and The WAC Clearinghouse, 2015.

—. "Foreword." Condon and Young, pp. xi-xx.

Jackson, Matthew. "The Enthymemic Hegemony of Whiteness: The Enthymeme as Antiracist Rhetorical Strategy." *JAC,* vol.26, nos. 3–4, 2006, pp. 601–41, www.jaconlinejournal.com/archives/vol26.3–4/jackson-enthymematic.pdf. Accessed 7 Oct. 2017.

Jaffe, Alex. "13 Black DC Heroes Before Black Lightning." *DC Universe,* 6 June 2020, www.dcuniverse.com/news/13-black-dc-heroes-black-lightning/. Accessed 13 Jan. 2021.

Jameson, Frederic. *Postmodernism, or the Cultural Logic of Late Capitalism.* Duke UP, 1991.

Jamieson, Kathleen Hall. "Generic Constraints and the Rhetorical Situation." *Philosophy and Rhetoric,* vol. 6, no. 3, 1973, pp. 162–70.

Jay, Gregory, and Sandra Elaine Jones. "Whiteness Studies and the Multicultural Classroom." *Meleus,* vol. 30, no. 5, 2005, pp. 99–121, doi.org/10.1093/MELUS%2F30.2.99. Accessed 20 May 2020.

Jensen, Derrick, "Linda Hogan." *Listening to the Land: Conversations about Nature, Culture, and Eros.* Chelsea Green, 2002.

Jensen, Kyle, and Krista Ratcliffe. "Mythic Historiography: Refiguring Kenneth Burke's Deceitful Woman Trope." *Rhetoric Society Quarterly*, vol. 48, no. 1, 2018, pp. 88–107.

Jensen, Kyle. *Reimagining Process: Online Writing Activities and the Future of Writing Studies*. Southern Illinois UP, 2015.

Johnson, Gene. "2 Washington State Republicans Support Impeaching Trump." *AP*, 13 Jan. 2021, bit.ly/supportimpeaching. Accessed 21 Jan. 2021.

Jonas, Eva, et al. "Confirmation Bias in Sequential Information Search after Preliminary Decisions: An Expansion of Dissonance Theoretical Research on Selective Exposure to Information." *Journal of Personality and Social Psychology*, vol. 80. no. 4, 2001, pp. 557–71.

Jordan, Chris. "Press Release." *Running the Numbers: An American Self Portrait.*" 2009, www.kopeikingallery.com/exhibitions/running-the-numbers-an-american-self-portrait/press_release. Accessed 29 Jan. 2021.

—. "Whale." *Running the Numbers II: Portraits of Global Mass Culture*. 2011, www.chrisjordan.com/gallery/rtn2/#whale. Accessed 29 Jan. 2021.

Jordan, Jay. "Revaluing Silence and Listening with Second-language Users." Glenn and Ratcliffe, pp. 278–92.

Kennedy, George. "A Hoot in the Dark: The Evolution of General Rhetoric." *Philosophy and Rhetoric*, vol. 25, no 1, 1992, pp. 1–21.

Kennedy, Tammie. "Enthymematical, Epistemic, and Emotional Silence(s) in the Rhetoric of Whiteness." *JAC*, vol. 27, nos. 1–2, 2007, pp. 253–75.

Kent, Thomas ed. *Post-Process Theory: Beyond the Writing Process Paradigm*. Southern Illinois UP, 1999.

Killingsworth, M. Jimmie. *Appeals in Modern Rhetoric: An Ordinary-Language Approach*. Southern Illinois UP, 2005.

Kimmerer, Robin Wall. *Braiding Sweetgrass: Indigenous Wisdom, Scientific Knowledge, and the Teachings of Plants*. Penguin, 2013.

Kinneavy, James L., and Catherine R. Eskin. "*Kairos* in Aristotle's *Rhetoric*." *Written Communication*, vol. 11, no. 1, 1994, pp. 131–42.

Kinneavy, James L. "*Kairos*: A Neglected Concept in Classical Rhetoric." *Rhetoric and Praxis: The Contribution of Classical Rhetoric to Practical Reasoning*, edited by Jean Dietz Moss, Catholic U of America P, 1986, pp. 79–105.

Kirchhoff, Michael David. "Research Unit on Material Culture, Cognition, and Nature." *Techné*, vol. 3, no. 3, Fall 2009, scholar.lib.vt.edu/ejournals/SPT/v13n3/pdf/kirchhoff.pdf. Accessed 10 Oct. 2020.

Kohrs Campbell, Karlyn. "The Ontological Foundations of Rhetorical Theory." *Philosophy and Rhetoric*, vol. 3, no. 2, 1970, pp. 97–108, debate.uvm.edu/asnider/campreadings/Resources/campbell_ontologyinrhet.pdf. Accessed 8 Feb. 2021.

Kopelson, Karen. "Rhetoric on the Edge of Cunning; Or, The Performance of Neutrality (Re)Considered as a Composition Pedagogy for Listener

Resistance. *College Composition and Communication*, vol. 55, no. 1, 2003, pp. 115–46.

Landreau, John C. "Queer Listening as a Framework for Performing Men and Masculinities." *Queering Masculinities: A Critical Reader in Education*, edited by John C. Landreau and Nelson M. Rodriguez, Springer, 2012, pp. 155–68.

Langer, Suzanne K. *Philosophy in a New Key: A Study in the Symbolism of Reason, Rite, and Art*. Harvard UP, 1942.

Lauer, Janice. "Historical Review: Issues in Rhetorical Invention." *Invention in Rhetoric and Composition*, Parlor P and The WAC Clearinghouse, 2004, pp. 11–44, wac.colostate.edu/docs/books/lauer_invention/history.pdf. Accessed 17 May 2020.

Leatherby, Lauren, et al. "How a Presidential Rally Turned into a Capitol Rampage." *New York Times*, 13 Jan. 2021, www.nytimes.com/interactive/2021/01/12/us/capitol-mob-timeline.html. Accessed 4 Feb. 2021.

Leff, Michael. "Tradition and Agency in Humanistic Rhetoric." *Philosophy and Rhetoric*, vol. 36, no. 2, 2003, pp. 135–47.

Leipold, Sina, and Georg Winkel. "Discursive Agency: (Re-)Conceptualizing Actors and Practices in the Analysis of Discursive Policymaking." *Policy Studies Journal*, 21 July 2016, onlinelibrary.wiley.com/doi/abs/10.1111/psj.12172. Accessed 21 Oct. 2020.

Lemay, Bronwyn Clare. *Personal Narrative, Revised: Writing Love and Agency in the High School Classroom*. Teacher's College P, 2016.

Leong, Phillip. "Simone Biles' Stand Brings Discussion of Mental Health and Sports to the Forefront." *Pittsburgh Post-Gazette*, 10 Aug. 2021. www.post-gazette.com/news/health/2021/08/10/Simone-Biles-Olympics-twisties-mental-health-sports-psychology-west-virginia-jaason-butts-kpex/stories/202108040100. Accessed 12 Nov. 2021.

Lester, Neal. "Dr. Neal Lester Interview on Critical Race Studies." *YouTube*, By Alexis Moulton, 22 Sept. 2021, www.youtube.com/watch?v=p2XBW-8Kg0g. Accessed 8 Oct. 2021.

Lévi-Strauss, Claude. *The Savage Mind*. 1962. Translated by George Weidenfield and Nicholson Ltd, U Chicago P, 1966.

—. *Wild Thought*. 1962. Translated by Jeffrey Mehlman and John Leavitt, U Chicago P, 2021.

Lindquist, Julie. "Class Affects, Classroom Affectations Working through the Paradoxes of Strategic Empathy." *College English*, vol. 67, no. 2, 2004, pp. 187–209.

Liptak, Adam. "Supreme Court Upholds Affirmative Action Program at University of Texas." *New York Times*. 24 June 2016, www.nytimes.com/2016/06/24/us/politics/supreme-court-affirmative-action-university-of-texas.html. Accessed 17 May 2020.

Logan, Shirley Wilson. *Liberating Language: Sites of Rhetorical Education in Nineteenth-Century Black America.* Southern Illinois UP, 2008.

Lowery, Annie. "Don't Blame Econ 101 for the Plight of Essential Workers. *The Atlantic,* 13 May 2020, www.theatlantic.com/ideas/archive/2020/05/why-are-americas-most-essential-workers-so-poorly-treated/611575/. Accessed 7 June 2020.

Mabule, D. R. "What is this? Is It Code Switching, Code Mixing or Language Alternating? *Journal of Educational and Social Research,* vol. 5, no. 1, 2017, pp. 339–50, bit.ly/codeswitchingcodemixing. Accessed 22 Oct. 2021.

MacArthur, Charles A. "Evaluation and Revision." *Best Practices in Writing Instruction,* 3rd ed., edited by Steve Graham, Charles A. MacArthur, and Michael Herbert, Guilford Publications, 2019, pp. 287–308.

Martin, Peter J., and Alex Dennis, eds. *Human Agents and Social Structures.* 1st ed., Manchester UP, 2010. *JSTOR,* www.jstor.org/stable/j.ctvnb7pp3. Accessed 12 Jan. 2021.

Martin, Savannah. "Bidding *"bon voyage"* to *la pensée sauvage*: Why the 'Savage Minds' Name Change Couldn't Come Soon Enough." *Anthrodendum,* 11 Nov. 2017, savageminds.org/2017/11/11/bidding-bon-voyage-to-la-pensee-sauvage-why-the-savage-minds-name-change-couldnt-come-soon-enough-2/. Accessed 30 Oct. 2021.

May, Stephen, and Christine E. Sleeter, eds. *Critical Multiculturalism: Theory and Praxis.* Routledge, 2010.

McCluney, Courtney L., et al. "The Costs of Code-Shifting." *Harvard Business Review,* 15 Nov. 2019, hbr.org/2019/11/the-costs-of-codeswitching. Accessed 22 Oct. 2021.

McKee, Heidi A., and James E. Porter. *The Ethics of Internet Research: A Rhetorical, Case-Based Process.* Peter Lang, 2009.

McNay, Lois. "Chapter 2: Agency." *Oxford Handbook of Feminist Theory,* edited by Lisa Disch and Mary Hawkesworth, Oxford, 2016, pp. 39–60.

Metzinger, Thomas. "The Myth of Cognitive Agency: Subpersonal Thinking as a Cyclically Recurring Loss of Mental Autonomy." *Frontiers in Psychology,* 19 Dec. 2013, doi.org/10.3389/fpsyg.2013.00931. Accessed 21 Oct. 2020.

Middleton, Joyce Irene. "Rhetorical Listening: When the Eye Defers to the Ear for Civic Discourse." *English Journal,* vol. 101, no. 1, 2011, pp. 105–07, www.jstor.org/stable/23047861. Accessed 28 Jan. 2021.

Miller, Carolyn. "Genre as Social Action." *Quarterly Journal of Speech,* vol. 70, no. 2, 1984, pp. 151–67.

Mohsen, Hussein. "Race and Genetics: Somber History, Troubled Present." *Yale Journal of Biological Medicine,* vol. 93, no. 1, 27 Mar. 2020, pp. 215–19, www.ncbi.nlm.nih.gov/pmc/articles/PMC7087058 /. Accessed 9 Jan. 2021.

Moneyball. Dir. by Bennett Miller, performances by Brad Pitt, Jonah Hill, Sony Pictures, 2011.

Morris, Charles E. "The Archival Turn in Rhetorical Studies; Or, the Archive's Rhetorical (Re)turn." *Rhetoric and Public Affairs,* vol. 9, no. 1, 2006, pp. 113–15, muse.jhu.edu/article/198652. Accessed 19 Jan. 2021.

Morrison, Toni. *Beloved.* 1987, Vintage, 2004.

—. "Melville and the Language of Denial." *The Nation,* 7 Jan. 2014, www.the-nation.com/article/melville-and-language-denial. 31 Accessed Oct. 7, 2020.

—. "Nobel Lecture." *The Nobel Prize,* 7 Dec. 1993, www.nobelprize.org/prizes/literature/1993/morrison/lecture/. Accessed 1 June 2020.

Moseley, Alexander. "Just War Theory." *Internet Encyclopedia of Philosophy,* iep.utm.edu/justwar/. Accessed 21 Sept. 2021.

Mountford, Roxanne. *The Gendered Pulpit: Preaching in American Protestant Spaces.* Southern Illinois UP, 2005.

—. "Our Philosophy." *College of Arts and Sciences First Year Composition The University of Oklahoma,* www.ou.edu/cas/fyc/about/philosophy. Accessed 8 Jan. 2021.

Murphy, James J., and Cleve Weise, eds. *Quintilian on the Teaching of Speaking and Writing: Translations from Books One, Two & Ten of the Institutio Oratoria.* 2nd ed., Southern Illinois UP, 2016.

Noor, Iqra. "Confirmation Bias." *Simply Psychology,* 10 June 2020, www.simplypsychology.org/confirmation-bias.html. Accessed 7 Jan. 2021.

"A Note on the Nonbinary 'They': It's Now in the Dictionary." *Merriam-Webster Dictionary.* www.merriam-webster.com/words-at-play/nonbinary-they-isin-the-dictionary. Accessed 11 Oct. 2021.

Nunley, Vorris. *Keepin' It Hushed: The Barbershop and African American Hush Harbor Rhetoric.* Wayne State UP, 2011.

Ochs, Ellinor, and Bambi Schieffelin. "Language Socialization: An Historical Overview." *Encyclopedia of Language and Education,* edited by P. Duff and S. May Language, 3rd ed., Springer, Cham, 2017, pp. 1–14.

Oleksiak, Timothy. "A Fullness of Feeling: Rhetorical Listening and Emotional Receptivity." *Peitho,* vo. 23, no. 1, Fall 2020, cfshrc.org/article/a-fullness-of-feeling-queer-rhetorical-listening-and-emotional-receptivity/. Accessed Jan. 2021.

Oleksiak, Timothy, and Raechel Tiffe. "Queering the Ear: Listening Queerly to Anger and Decorum." *Queer Praxis: Questions for LGBTQ Worldmaking,* edited by Dustin Bradley Goltz and Jason Zingsheim, Peter Lang, 2015, pp. 187–93.

Oleksiak, Timothy, ed. "Queering Rhetorical Listening: An Introduction to a Cluster Conversation." *Peitho,* vo. 23, no. 1, Fall 2020, cfshrc.org/article/queering-rhetorical-listening-an-introduction-to-a-cluster-conversation/. Accessed 6 Jan. 2021.

Olson, Christa J. *Constitutive Visions: Indigeneity and Commonplaces of National Identity in Republican Ecuador.* Pennsylvania State UP, 2014.

Ore, Ersula. *Lynching: Violence, Rhetoric, and American Identity.* UP of Mississippi, 2019.

Pantiledes, Kate. "Kairos." *Writing Commons,* writingcommons.org/article/kairos/. Accessed 8 Nov. 2020.

Papillon, Terry L. "Rhetoric, Art, and Myth: Isocrates and Busiris." *The Orator in Action and Theory in Greece and Rome: Essay in Honor of George A Kennedy,* edited by Cecil C. Wooten, Brill, 2001, pp. 73–93.

Patterson, Pat, and Leland G. Spencer. "Towards Trans Rhetorical Agency: A Critical Analysis of Trans Topics in Rhetoric and Composition and Communication Scholarship." *Peitho,* vol. 22, no. 4, 2020, cfshrc.org/article/toward-trans-rhetorical-agency-a-critical-analysis-of-trans-topics-in-rhetoric-composition-and-communication-scholarship/. Accessed 26 Sept. 2021.

Peeples, Timothy, Paula Rosinski, and Michael Strickland. "*Chronos* and *Kairos,* Strategies and Tactics: The Case of Constructing Elon University's Professional Writing and Rhetoric Concentration." *Composition Studies,* vol. 35, no. 1, 2007, pp. 57–76.

Pimentel, Octavio, Charise Pimentel, and John Dean. "The Myth of the Colorblind Classroom." Condon and Young, pp. 109–22.

Powell, Malea. "Blood and Scholarship: One Mixed-Blood's Story." *Race, Rhetoric and Composition,* edited by Keith Gilyard, Boynton/Cook, 1999, pp. 1–16.

—. "Stories Take Place: Performances in One Act." *College Composition and Communication,* vol. 64, no. 2, 2012, pp. 383–406.

"Pro-Trump Protesters in Capitol building Chanting 'Stop the steal." *DailyMail.com,* www.dailymail.co.uk/video/news/video-2327454/Video-Pro-Trump-protesters-Capitol-building-chanting-stop-steal.html. Accessed 8 Feb. 2021.

Pruitt, Sarah. "5 Myths About George Washington, Debunked." *History.com,* 6 Feb. 2020, www.history.com/news/top-george-washington-myths-cherry-tree-wooden-teeth. Accessed 14 Jan. 2021.

Queen Latifah. "*U.N.I.T.Y.*" *Black Reign,* Motown, 1993.

@R_Denhollander. "Every Word of This." *Twitter,* 27 July 2021, 5:18 p.m., twitter.com/R_Denhollander/status/1420119112580206596.

Rankine, Claudia. "I Wanted to Know What White Men Thought about Privilege. So I Asked." *New York Times Magazine,* 17 July 2019, www.nytimes.com/2019/07/17/magazine/white-men-privilege.html. Accessed 17 May 2020.

Rapp, Christof. "Aristotle's Rhetoric: 6. The Enthymeme." *Stanford Encyclopedia of Philosophy,* May 2002, plato.stanford.edu/entries/aristotle-rhetoric/#enthymeme. Accessed 28 Sept. 2017.

Ratcliffe, Krista. *Rhetorical Listening: Identification, Gender, Whiteness.* Southern Illinois UP, 2005.

Ratner, Carl. "Agency and Culture." *Journal for The Theory of Social Behavior,* vol. 30, 2000, pp. 413–34, lchc.ucsd.edu/mca/Paper/00_01/agency.htm. Accessed 25 Oct. 2020.

Reddish, David. "Billy Porter on Bringing Queer Realness to 'Cinderella': 'Magic Has No Gender.'" *queerty.com,* 3 Sept. 2021, www.queerty.com/ billy-porter-brining-queer-realness-cinderella-magic-no-gender-20210903. Accessed 17 Nov. 2021.

Renegar, Valerie, and Stacey K. Sowards. "Contradiction as Agency: Self-Determination, Transcendence, and Counter-Imagination in Third Wave Feminism." *Hypatia,* vol. 24, no. 2, 2009, pp. 1–20.

Reynolds, Milton. "Shifting Frames: Pedagogical Interventions in Colorblind Performing Practice." *Seeing Race Again: Countering Colorblindness across the Disciplines,* edited by Kimberlé Williams Crenshaw, et al., U of California P, 2019, 352–76.

Reynolds, Nedra. "Interrupting Our Way to Agency: Feminist Cultural Studies and Composition." *Feminism and Composition Studies: In Other Words,* edited by Susan Jarratt and Lynn Worsham, MLA, 1997, pp. 58–73.

Rhodes, Jacqueline. *Radical Feminism, Writing, and Critical Agency.* State U of New York P, 2005.

Rich, Adrienne. "Split at the Root: Notes on Jewish Identity." *Blood, Bread, and Poetry.* Norton, 1986, pp. 100–23.

Rickert, Thomas. *Ambient Rhetoric: The Attunements of Rhetorical Being.* U of Pittsburgh P, 2013.

Roberts-Miller, Patricia. "Fighting without Hatred: Hannah Arendt's Agonistic Rhetoric." *JAC,* vol. 22, no. 3, 2002, pp. 585–601.

Rose, Joel. "Even If It's 'Bonkers,' Poll Finds Many Believe QAnon and Other Conspiracy Theories." *Morning Edition,* NPR, 30 Dec. 2020, www.npr. org/2020/12/30/951095644/even-if-its-bonkers-poll-finds-many-believe-qanon-and-other-conspiracy-theories. Accessed 7 Jan. 2021.

Rosenberg, Matthew, and Ainara Tiefenthaler. "Decoding the Far-Right Symbols at the Capitol Riot." *New York Times,* 13 Jan. 2021, www.nytimes. com/2021/01/13/video/extremist-signs-symbols-capitol-riot.html. Accessed 24 Jan. 2021.

Royster, Jacqueline Jones, and Gesa Kirsch. *Feminist Rhetorical Practices: New Horizons for Rhetoric, Composition, and Literacy Studies.* Southern Illinois UP, 2012.

Royster, Jacqueline Jones. "To Call A Thing by Its True Name: The Rhetoric of Ida B. Wells." *Reclaiming Rhetoric: Women in the Rhetorical Tradition,* edited by Andrea Lunsford, U of Pittsburgh P, 1995, pp. 167–84.

Russ, Joanna. "What Can a Heroine Do? Or Why Women Can't Write." *To Write Like a Woman: Essays in Feminism and Science Fiction,* Indiana UP, 1995.

Rutz, David. "Senate Republicans will be 'very united' against convicting Trump after he left office: Graham." *Fox News*, 4 Feb. 2021, www.foxnews. com/politics/lindsey-graham-republicans-very-united-against-trump-impeachment-conviction. Accessed 8 Feb. 2021.

Sanchez, Raul. "In Terms of Writing as Such." Dobrin, Routledge, pp. 24–33.

Schlosser, Markus. "Agency." *The Stanford Encyclopedia of Philosophy*. Winter 2019, plato.stanford.edu/archives/win2019/entries/agency/. Accessed 22 Oct. 2020.

Schmitz, Rachel M., and Emily Kazyak. "Masculinities in Cyberspace: An Analysis of Portrayals of Manhood in Men's Rights Activist Websites." *Social Sciences*, vol. 5, no. 18, 2016, www.mdpi.com/2076–0760/5/2/18. Accessed 12 Feb. 2021.

Scruggs, Afi-Odelia E. "Colorblindness: The New Racism?" *Teaching Tolerance: A Project of the Southern Poverty Law Center*, vol. 26, nos. Fall, 2009, www.tolerance.org/magazine/fall-2009/colorblindness-the-new-racism. Accessed 2 Oct. 2017.

Shabad, Rebecca. "'We Have Been Failed': Simone Biles Breaks Down in Tears Recounting Nassar's Sexual Abuse. *nbcnews.com*, 18 Sept. 2021. www. nbcnews.com/politics/congress/we-have-been-failed-simone-biles-breaks-down-tears-recounting-n1279255. Accessed 12 Nov. 2021.

Shapiro, Rich. "Stun Guns, 'Stinger Whips'" and a Crossbow: What Police Found on the Capitol Protesters." *NBC News*, 13 Jan. 2021, www.nbcnews. com/news/us-news/stun-guns-stinger-whips-crossbow-what-police-found-capitol-protesters-n1254127. Accessed 24 Jan. 2021.

Sheneman, Drew. "Editorial Cartoon." *Tribune Content Agency*. 12 July 2016, tribunecontentagency.com/article/sheneman-drew-editorial-cartoon-20160712edshe-btif/. Accessed 5 Oct. 2017.

Sheridan, David, Tony Michel, and Jim Ridolfo. "*Kairos* and New Media: Toward a Theory and Practice of Visual Activism." *Enculturation: A Journal of Rhetoric, Writing, and Culture*, vol. 6, no 2, 2009, enculturation.net/6.2/sheridan-michel-ridolfo. Accessed 9 June 2020.

Sherman, Sean. "The Thanksgiving Tale We Tell Is a Harmful Lie. As a Native American, I've Found a Better Way to Celebrate the Holiday. *Time*, 19 Nov. 2018, time.com/5457183/thanksgiving-native-american-holiday/. Accessed 18 Nov. 2020.

Shugart, Helene A. "Counterhegemonic Acts: Appropriation as a Feminist Rhetorical Strategy." *Quarterly Journal of Speech*, vol. 83, no. 2, 1997, pp. 210–29.

"The Significance of 'The Doll Tests.'" *NAACP Legal Defense and Educational Fund*, 2020, www.naacpldf.org/ldf-celebrates-60th-anniversary-brown-v-board-education/significance-doll-test/. Accessed 2 June 2020.

Smith Lillian. *Killers of the Dream*. 1949. Norton, 1994.

Smith, Robin. "Aristotle's Logic." *Stanford Encyclopedia of Philosophy*, 18 Mar. 2000, plato.stanford.edu/entries/aristotle-logic/. Accessed 28 Sept. 2017.

Sommers, Nancy. "Revision Strategies of Student Writers and Experienced Adult Writers." *College Composition and Communication*, vol. 31, no. 4, 1980, pp. 378–88, community.macmillan.com/docs/DOC-1291. Accessed 19 May 2020.

Sotomayor, Sonia. "Texas Now Has Abortion 'Bounty Hunters': Read Sonia Sotomayor's Scathing Legal Dissent." *The Guardian*, 2 Sept. 2021, www.theguardian.com/commentisfree/2021/sep/02/sonia-sotomayor-dissent-texas-abortion-ban-law-supreme-court. Accessed 12 Nov. 2021.

Southward, Belinda A. Stillion. *How to Belong: Women's Agency in a Transnational World*. Pennsylvania State UP, 2018.

Spaggiari, Bianca. "How the Female Body Evolved in Art." *Mutual Art*, 18 June 2020, medium.com/mutualart/how-the-female-body-evolved-in-art-20ecc3f179c9. Accessed 30 Oct. 2021.

"Stasis Theory." *Purdue Owl*. owl.purdue.edu/owl/general_writing/the_writing_process/stasis_theory/index.html/. Accessed 2 Oct. 2020.

Stenberg, Shari. "Cultivating Listening: Performing from a Restored Logos." Glenn and Ratcliffe, pp. 250–63.

Stephenson, Hunter. "(Re)Claiming the Ground: Image Events, *Kairos*, and Discourse." *Enculturation: A Journal of Rhetoric, Writing, and Culture*, vol. 6, no. 2, 2009, enculturation.net/6.2/stephenson. Accessed 10 June 2020.

Stevenson, Brian. *Just Mercy: A Story of Justice and Redemption*. One World, 2015.

Subotnik, Daniel. "What's Wrong with Critical Race Theory: Reopening the Case for Middle Class Values." *Digital Commons @ Touro Law Center*, 1 Jan. 1998, pp. 681–756, digitalcommons.tourolaw.edu/cgi/viewcontent.cgi?article=1186&context=scholarlyworks. Accessed 29 Sept. 2017.

Svokos, Alexandra. "Former Olympians React to Simone Biles Having the Decision to Withdraw." *abcnews.com*, 30 July 2021, abcnews.go.com/Sports/olympians-react-simone-biles-decision-withdraw/story?id=79121854. Accessed 12 Nov. 2021.

Swales, John. "The Concept of Discourse Community." *Genre Analysis: English in Academic and Research Settings*. Cambridge UP, 1990, pp. 21–32, mjreiff.com/uploads/3/4/2/1/34215272/swales.pdf. Accessed 26 Nov. 2020.

Takayoshi, Pamela. "Foreword." Banks, et al., pp. xi–xv.

"Teaching Tolerance." *Southern Poverty Law Center*, 2020, www.tolerance.org. Accessed 18 May 2020.

Tell, Dave. *Remembering Emmett Till*. U of Chicago P, 2019.

"Texas Senate Bill 8." *Legiscan*, 19 May 2021, legiscan.com/TX/text/SB8/id/2395961. Accessed 12 Nov. 2021.

Thompson, A.C., and Ford Fischer. "Members of Several Well-Known Hate Groups Identified at Capitol Riot." *Frontline*, 9 Jan. 2021, www.pbs.org/

wgbh/frontline/article/several-well-known-hate-groups-identified-at-capitol-riot/. Accessed 8 Feb. 2021.

Thompson, Ayanna. *RaceB4Race.* www.ayannathompson.com/raceb4race. Accessed 11 Oct. 2021.

Thompson, Matt. "Five Reasons Why People Code-Switch." *Code Switch: Race. In Your Face,* NPR, 13 Apr. 2013, www.npr.org/sections/codeswitch/2013/04/13/177126294/five-reasons-why-people-code-switch Accessed 9 Jan. 2021.

Thompson, Rowan. "Feminist Thought and Transcending the Gender Binary." *The Classic Journal,* vol. 4, no. 1, 2019, theclassicjournal.uga.edu/index.php/2019/05/24/feminist-thought-and-transcending-the-gender-binary-a-discussion/. Accessed 26 Sept. 2021.

Tongson, Karen. "The Countermelodies That Changed Us: A Lifetime of Loving the Indigo Girls." *Turning the Tables,* NPR, 21 May 2020, www.npr.org/2020/05/21/858267498/the-countermelodies-that-changed-us-a-lifetime-of-loving-indigo-girls. Accessed 8 Oct. 2021.

Tonn, Jenna. "Gender." *Encyclopedia of the History of Science,* lps.library.cmu.edu/ETHOS/article/id/20/. Accessed 8 Oct. 2021.

Townsend, Camilla. "The True Story of Pocahontas." *Smithsonian Magazine,* 23 Mar. 2017, www.smithsonianmag.com/history/true-story-pocahontas-180962649/. Accessed 2 June 2020.

Trauger, A. "Social Agency and Networked Spatial Relationships in Sustainable Agriculture." *Area,* vol. 41, no. 2, 2009, pp. 117–28, rgs-ibg.onlinelibrary.wiley.com/doi/pdf/10.1111/j.1475–4762.2008.00866.x. Accessed 26 Nov 2020.

Treitler, Vilna Bashi. "Social Agency and White Supremacy in Immigration Studies." *Sociology of Race and Ethnicity,* vol. 1, no. 1, 2015, pp. 153–65.

Trouble with the Curve. Dir. by Robert Lorenz, performances by Clint Eastwood, Amy Adams, and Justin Timberlake, Warner Brothers, 2012.

"Understanding Drag." National Center for Transgender Equality, 2021, transequality.org/issues/resources/understanding-drag. Accessed 12 Feb. 2021.

United American Indians of New England. "National Day of Mourning." *United American Indians of New England,* 2020, www.uaine.org. Accessed 18 Nov. 2020.

Vallejo, Justin. "Trump 'Save America Rally' Speech Transcript from 6 January: The Words That Got the President Impeached." *Independent,* 13 Jan. 2021, www.independent.co.uk/news/world/americas/us-election-2020/trump-speech-6-January-transcript-impeachment-b1786924.html. Accessed 9 Feb. 2021.

van Dijk, Teun A. *Discourse as Structure and Process: Discourse Studies: A Multidisciplinary Introduction.* Sage P, 1997.

Vatz, Richard. "The Myth of the Rhetorical Situation. *Philosophy and Rhetoric,* vol. 3, no. 3 1973, pp. 154–61, www.joycerain.com/uploads/2/3/2/0/232

07256/vatz_the_myth_of_the_rhetorical_situation.pdf. Accessed 10 June 2020.

Vieregge, Quentin D., Kyle D. Stedman, Taylor Joy Mitchell, and Joseph M. Moxley. *Agency in the Age of Peer Production.* NCTE, 2012.

Villadsen, Lisa. "Speaking on Behalf of Others: Rhetorical Agency and Epideictic Function in Official Apologies." *Rhetoric Society Quarterly,* vol. 38, no. 1, 2008, pp. 25–45.

Villanueva, Victor. *Bootstraps: From an American Academic of Color.* NCTE, 1993.

Vitanza, Victor. *Negation, Subjectivity, and the History of Rhetoric.* SUNY, 1996.

Walker, Alice. "In Search of Our Mothers' Gardens." *In Search of Our Mothers' Gardens: Womanist Prose,* Harvest, 1983, pp. 229–43.

Walker, Jeffrey. "The Body of Persuasion: A Theory of the Enthymeme." *College English,* vol. 56, no. 1, 1996, pp. 46–55.

—. *The Genuine Teachers of This Art: Rhetorical Education.* U of South Carolina P, 2011.

Welton, Katherine. "Nancy Hartsock's Standpoint Theory," *Women & Politics,* vol. 18, no. 3, pp. 7–24.

Wells, Ida B. *Southern Horrors and Other Writings: The Anti-Lynching Campaign of Ida B. Wells, 1892–1900,* edited by Jacqueline Jones Royster, 2nd ed, Bedford, 2016.

West, Cornel. "Lukács: A Reassessment." *Minnesota Review,* vol. 19, 1982, p. 86–102, *Project MUSE* muse.jhu.edu/article/428337. Accessed 8 Feb. 2021.

—. *Race Matters.* Beacon P, 1993.

West, Jenna. "LeBron James on US Capitol Siege: 'We Live in Two Americas.'" *Sports Illustrated,* 8 Jan. 2021, www.si.com/nba/2021/01/08/lebron-james-us-capitol-siege-response-two-americas. Accessed 21 Jan. 2021.

"Why the Word 'Woman' Is Tying People in Knots." *The Economist,* 2 Oct. 2021, www.economist.com/leaders/2021/10/02/why-the-word-woman-is-tying-people-in-knots. Accessed 22 Oct. 2021.

"What Does Thanksgiving Mean to Native Americans?" *Native Hope,* blog. nativehope.org/what-does-thanksgiving-mean-to-native-americans. Accessed 17 Nov. 2020.

Williams, Bronwyn. "Agency in, and Beyond, the Literacy Classroom." *Literacy Practices and Perceptions of Agency: Composing Identities,* Routledge, 2017, pp. 181–90.

Williams, Matt. "What Is the Heliocentric Model of the Universe?" *Phys. org.* 5 Jan. 2016, phys.org/news/2016–01-heliocentric-universe.html. Accessed 7 Oct. 2021.

Williams, Monica. "Colorblind Ideology Is a Form of Racism." *Psychology Today,* 27 Dec. 2011, www.psychologytoday.com/blog/culturally-speaking/201112/colorblind-ideology-is-form-racism. Accessed 3 Oct. 2017.

Williams, Patricia J. *Seeing a Color-Blind Future: The Paradox of Race.* Farrar, Straus, and Giroux, 2016.

Wilson, Reid. "At least 6 GOP legislators took place in Trump-inspired protests." *The Hill.com,* 7 Jan. 2021, thehill.com/homenews/state-watch/533160-at-least-6-gop-legislators-took-part-in-trump-inspired-protests. Accessed 8 Feb. 2021.

Wise, Tim. *Colorblind: The Rise of Post-Racial Politics and the Retreat from Racial Equity.* City Lights Books, 2010.

Wisse, Jakob. *Ethos and Pathos from Aristotle to Cicero,* Hakkert, 1989, bit.ly/wisse-ethos-pathos. Accessed 31 Oct. 2020.

Woll, Jordan. "The Mattaponi Oral Tradition." *The Pocahontas Project,* 12 Mar. 2013, nupocahontasproject.wordpress.com/2013/03/12/the-mattaponi-oral-tradition/. Accessed 31 Oct. 2021.

"Women's Rights." *Human Rights Watch,* 2021, www.hrw.org/topic/womens-rights. Accessed 6 Nov. 2021.

Woolf, Virginia. *A Room of One's Own.* 1929. Harcourt, 2001.

Wright, Mark H. "Burkean and Freudian Theories of Identification." *Communication Quarterly,* vol. 42, no. 3, 1994, pp. 301–10.

Wu, Hui. "The Feminist Rhetoric of Post-Mao Chinese Writers: A Perspective from the Rhetorical Situation." *Alternative Rhetorics,* edited by Laura Gray-Rosendale and Sibylle Gruber, SUNY P, 2001, pp. 219–34.

Yancey, Kathleen Blake, ed. "Introduction." *A Rhetoric of Reflection,* edited by Kathleen Blake Yancey, Utah State UP, 2016, pp. 3–22.

Index

About the Authors

Krista Ratcliffe is Foundation Professor and Chair in the Department of English at Arizona State University. She earned her doctorate from The Ohio State University (1988) and has been a professor and chair of English at Marquette University and Purdue University. Her research focuses on intersections of rhetoric, feminist theory, and critical race studies. Her books include: *Anglo-American Challenges to the Rhetorical Traditions: Virginia Woolf, Mary Daly, and Adrienne Rich* (1996); *Who's Having This Baby?* (2002); *Rhetorical Listening: Identification, Gender, Whiteness* (2006), which won the 2006 JAC Gary Olson Award, the 2007 CCCC Outstanding Book Award, and the 2007 Rhetoric Society of America Book Award; *Performing Feminist Administration in Rhetoric and Composition Studies* (2010) co-edited with Rebecca Rickly; *Silence and Listening as Rhetorical Arts* (2011) co-edited with Cheryl Glenn; and *Rhetorics of Whiteness: Postracial Hauntings in Popular Culture, Social Media, and Education* (2017) co-edited with Tammy Kennedy and Joyce Middleton, which won a 2018 CCCC Outstanding Edited Book Award. Her work has also appeared in edited collections and academic journals, such as *CCC, JAC, Rhetoric Review, College English*, and *Rhetoric Society Quarterly*. Her national service has included serving as president of the Rhetoric Society of America (RSA) and the Coalition of Feminist Scholars in the History of Rhetoric and Composition (CFSHRC) and. She is also a Fellow of the Rhetoric Society of America.

Kyle Jensen is Professor of English and Director of Writing Programs at Arizona State University. He is the author or co-editor of five previous books, including *Reimagining Process: Online Writing Archives and the Future of Writing Studies* (2015), *The War of Words by Kenneth Burke* (2018), and *Kenneth Burke's Weed Garden: Refiguring the Grounds of Modern Rhetoric* (2022). His work has also appeared in edited collections and academic journals, including *Rhetoric Society Quarterly, Quarterly Journal of Speech, JAC*, and *Rhetoric Review*.

Printed in the USA
CPSIA information can be obtained
at www.ICGtesting.com
CBHW032038240724
11963CB00004B/14